THINK LIKE AN ARCHITECT

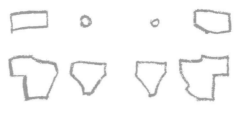

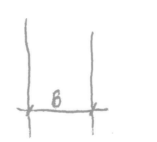

**ROGER FULLINGTON
SERIES IN ARCHITECTURE**

Production of this book
was made possible in
part by support from
Roger Fullington and
a challenge grant from
the National Endowment
for the Humanities.

HAL BOX | THINK LIKE AN ARCHITECT

 UNIVERSITY OF TEXAS PRESS, AUSTIN

Library of Congress
  Cataloging-in-Publication Data
Box, Hal.
  Think like an architect / Hal Box. — 1st ed.
    p. cm. — (Roger Fullington series in
  architecture)
  Includes bibliographical references and
  index.
  ISBN 978-0-292-71635-3 (cloth : alk. paper)
  ISBN 978-0-292-71636-0 (alk. paper)
  1. Architecture. I. Title.
  NA2550.B69   2007
  720—dc22   2006038758

DESIGN AND TYPOGRAPHY BY TERESA W. WINGFIELD

FRONTISPIECE: San Nicolás
Tolentino, Nonoalco,
Hidalgo, Mexico, sixteenth
century.

TO MY LOVE, EDEN

CONTENTS

Preface   ix

Acknowledgments   xi

PART ONE   **The Place**

ONE   Aspirations   3

TWO   Dreaming and Seeing   11

THREE   Finding the Best Buildings   21

FOUR   Exploring Ideas in Architecture   29

FIVE   Has Architecture Left the Building?   49

PART TWO   **The Ground Floor**

SIX   Making Architecture with an Architect   57

SEVEN   Becoming an Architect   69

EIGHT   Thinking Like an Architect: The Design Process   81

NINE   Visualizing with Drawings and Models, Pencils and Computers   97

TEN   The Critique   105

ELEVEN   Building Architecture: An Example   109

TWELVE   Adding Meaning   123

THIRTEEN   Making Design Decisions   133

FOURTEEN   Style, Taste, and Design Theory   151

PART THREE   **The Upper Levels**

FIFTEEN   Making Connections   161

SIXTEEN   Finding Possibilities   177

Reading List   187

Seeing List   193

Photo Credits   199

Index   201

PREFACE

If you want to make architecture rather than just a building, you have three choices: hire an architect, become an architect, or learn to think like an architect. This book is about all three; it addresses laypeople as well as students, aficionados, builders, developers, building committees, educators, and architects—and also those who want to become architects. It concerns how successfully one makes investments and how gracefully people can live their lives.

My purpose is to communicate ways to give the necessary care to designing buildings that's needed to enhance the quality of life for the people who live with them as well as the environment around them. Through the years, I've discussed relevant questions about architecture again and

again. In response, I've written, for this book, a group of letters to friends, colleagues, and you readers about the process of making architecture. The letters describe aspirations for architecture and their fulfillment. They give a history of how architecture became what it is today. They present ways of understanding and creating architecture, and methods of arriving at the multitude of decisions required to create good design.

This exploration can be extended infinitely from the Reading List and the Seeing List provided. Both offer ways to explore the intellectual, technical, and artistic aspects of architecture broadly, in depth, and in actual experience—the real joy of architecture.

ACKNOWLEDGMENTS

My experience in writing this book has been a delight because of the many friends who helped me. For this I give heartfelt thanks to those who came to San Miguel to lead me through this work: to Bill Wittliff for his early encouragement and coaching while sitting on a bench in the Jardín; to John Trimble for his encouragement, his kind efforts on the Roof Terrace in teaching me to write, and his dedicated e-mails of multitudes of refinements; to Betty Sue Flowers for offering her wisdom in the Portico on how to clarify and put my random thoughts together; to John McLeod for marking out the non-sense in my first draft while we were at the beach. Many thanks to my friends in Austin who gave their time and knowledge to keep me on the right track: to Anthony Alofsin for guidance and assessment of my view of history; to Michael Benedikt for years of enlarging my brain and for encouraging me in the final stages; to Eden Box, my wife of thirty years and in-house editor who would tell me when it was rotten or good; and a special thanks to Joanne and James Pratt for their careful reading and wise advice on all manner of detail and philosophy as well as for the past fifty years of working together.

And for help in the final crafting of the book at the School of Architecture, thanks to Sarah Hill, whose skillful help with the illustrations and permissions let me finish, and to Raquel Elizondo, who was always on hand to help, and to Elizabeth Schaub, of Visual Resources Collection, Charlotte

Pickett, photographer, and Nancy Sparrow of the Alexander Architectural Archive. I'm also grateful to those who gave me permission to use their photographs: Blake Alexander, Larry Doll, Sinclair Black, Lawrence Speck, Bill Cox, Greg Hursley, Baltazar Korab, the archives of Pratt, Box and Henderson, and especially the Visual Resource Center of the School of Architecture, University of Texas at Austin.

Many thanks to the dedicated people I worked with at the University of Texas Press, including Theresa May, who encouraged me to submit a proposal; Jim Burr, who sought to teach me how to put a book together; the readers who critiqued my early manuscript; Lawrence Kenney, who edited and helped me clarify; and Teresa Wingfield, who designed the book as you see it.

PART ONE | THE PLACE

CHAPTER ONE | ASPIRATIONS

That far land we dream about,
Where every man is his own Architect.
ROBERT BROWNING
(1812–1889)

Dear Martin:

When you told us in your drawing class that we had to visit a building to appreciate it, I didn't realize that it is the actual *experiencing* of architecture that reveals, personally, in real time, the essence of the art. I learned that even beyond design, construction, intellectual content, and real estate value, your actual experience of the architecture is what affects your senses. And most important, your way of life—for better or worse. True, your quality of life is largely determined by how the art of architecture and city planning have made the physical *place* you inhabit. The benefits of gracefulness created by design can be priceless. I can't relay to you the experience of a work of architecture in this letter, but I will describe examples of how I experienced the architecture of two special places.

Exploring central Mexico with a client in search of a site for a health spa, my wife and I were invited to see a house that might interest us because of its setting and its newly reduced price. At the end of a long day, we reluctantly turned off the main street and drove down a tree-lined drive paved with mosaic stones through an antique gate. It opened to reveal an extraordinary progression of architectural space made of carefully crafted indoor and outdoor spaces that melded the building in to, and out of, the landscape. Skillfully executed in the manner of the great Mexican modernist Luis Barragán, it was so suc-cessful that when one of the key architects of the last century, Charles Moore, walked through the house with an appraising eye, he looked back at the ethereal mass of landscape integrated with structured spaces and said, "Frank Lloyd Wright, eat your heart out."

Only from the garden could you see the white stucco walls with large planes of glass dappled with light from mature flowering trees. Because the house was set in a tropical garden of green, with a sequence of fountains, ponds, and streams, it was hard to tell what was outside and what was inside. The transitions between

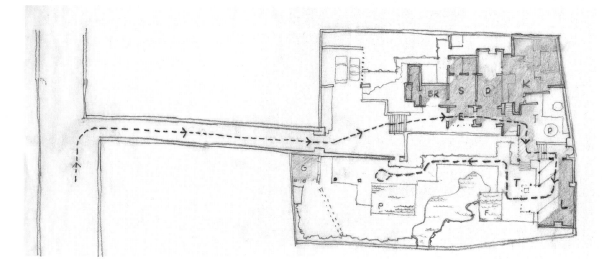

spaces were so subtle and the openings so large that it seemed the house didn't exist; the house denied being photographed. It was all transparency with a few walls modulating the space. The purity of style in Modernism was finessed with European antiques of various provenances in a manner that seemed just right. The architecture, garden, and interiors were by the noted Mexican interior designer Arturo Pani. It was the most beautiful house we had ever seen. It was not large but engaged us more deeply than the great historical houses— a magical place in the world that more than fulfilled every aspiration imaginable to us.

On impulse, my real estate executive

Portion of the architectural accretion built over four hundred years. El Señor de Sacromonte, Amecameca, Mexico, 1524 onward.

wife made a half-price offer to buy the house. The seller laughed at the offer, and we went away simply enjoying the deep feeling of having experienced a place of wonder. A month later, though, our offer was accepted, and a new life in a foreign country where we didn't speak the language had just begun.

Compounding the experience of this timeless Mesoamerican Spanish-Mexican culture, we drove our new Mexican car over the Paso de Cortez between the two great volcanoes in search of the sixteenth-century churches of the Spanish friars. In the village of Amecameca, where Cortez had said a mass for his small army as they moved toward the Aztecs, we sought the pilgrimage chapel of Sacromonte by spiraling up a small hill overlooking the village. This sacred place had been a cave for meditation by Fray Martín de Valencia, who arrived in 1524 as one of the first friars in the New World. As the cave became important, the village built a portico to define the entrance, and over the next three centuries the cave was expanded by sacred spaces of advancing size, chronologically growing through several styles into a hexagonal dome terminating in an unusual nineteenth-century forecourt portico. We were fascinated with this unique assemblage of time and stone.

We bought a beer and a taco from a vendor in front of the church. The cold beer and warm blue corn taco filled with sautéed squash blossoms gave me a sensation that anchored me to this place. I identified with the architecture around me with such curiosity that within a few months I had formed a team of Earthwatch volunteers to document the church with measured drawings and photographs—the first of many such places in all parts of Mexico that we documented over the next twelve summers.

I had found a new way to appreciate architecture—from earthen caves to Modernism—in a continuum of ageless labors producing architecture that raised questions about what we architects are doing today.

Does all architecture have to be by architects? The nonarchitect friars of New Spain and the native Mesoamerican stonecarvers created a dramatically effective piece of work that borrowed from the buildings they knew and the materials and technology available to them at that particular place. The buildings of the nearby village were handsome indigenous buildings of distinctive forms and textures that had certainly been built by nonarchitects—put together out of the earth with adobe bricks formed by the same hands that patted out their tortillas. The vitality and dignity of those walls were timeless.

Realizing that the buildings in this village and most buildings in modern cities are built by nonarchitects, I became acutely aware of the plain fact that professional architects build only about 5 percent of what is built.

I had been aware of the fact of that 5 percent, but this scene, which I found so beautiful, caused me to realize that I had spent most of my career educating young men and women to be professional architects, signing hundreds of diplomas, and had not reached the men and women who would actually be designing 95 percent of the buildings. They were over in the

schools of business and of engineering, or they were in all walks of life, people who simply built the facilities they needed. The reality of the other 95 percent was beginning to sink in.

To improve the built environment, the nonarchitects who are building now will have to know more about the making of architecture and actively aspire to it. In the past, before architecture schools and professional licensing, master builders received their training through apprenticeships in the crafts of building; they gained further learning from the examples of craftsmen before them, some of which were the great buildings of the age, made by builders who traveled across Europe to learn from the masters. Their building crafts were in stone, brick, and wood—earlier they had used mud and reeds, and later they used iron, glass, and early forms of concrete. Today, the designer's vocabulary has a multitude of materials with which to work, including inexpensive, imitative, ersatz materials. Because of this, the task of the nonarchitect builder of today is more complex: new materials, a demand for

Town of Amecameca and mountain seen from under the sheltering portico. El Señor de Sacromonte, Amecameca, Mexico.

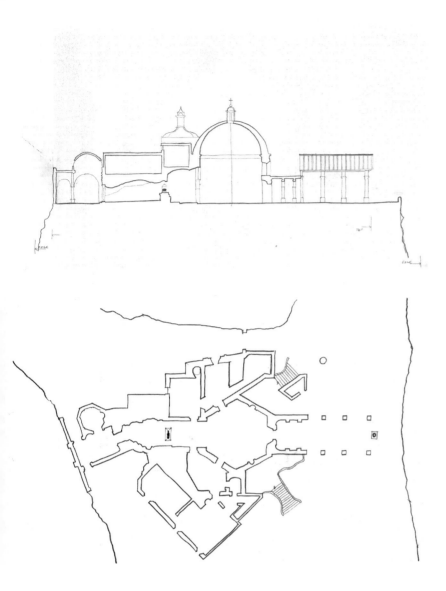

TOP: Section through cave, crypt, sanctuary, and portico. El Señor de Sacromonte, Amecameca, Mexico.

Plan, El Señor de Sacromonte, Amecameca, Mexico.

speed and economy, and the lack of a good vernacular from which to work. So the difference between today's builders and builders of the past is that in the past there were better models that were studied with more care and focus on the quality of the architecture. I believe that the commercial and residential nonarchitect builder, with an aspiration toward architecture and attention to detail, will be rewarded with an improved product for a better position in the market—an excellent motivation. This book can be a beginning of that process.

The need to build shelter is primal; building it as architecture endures as a quest for beauty that engages us personally at our core. As I said in the preface, to make architecture rather than just a building, you have three choices: hire an architect, become an architect, or learn to think like an architect as an enthusiastic, informed participant in the design of the places we think of as architecture.

When I told my physics professor father, who at the moment was laying brick, that I had decided to become an architect, he looked up from his work and said, "Do you know the Greek orders, their columns: Doric, Ionic, Corinthian?" I said no and walked away to find the encyclopedia. At age fifteen, I had never even seen architecture or met an architect. I just liked to draw and make things. I never looked back, and architecture became my passion.

I was hardly alone. A recent survey of fifteen-year-old American boys revealed that fully 25 percent of them wanted to be architects when they grew up. People of all ages tell me that they had once wanted to be an architect but decided otherwise for various reasons.

In a television interview, James Lipton asked Michael Caine, who had just won an Oscar for Best Actor, what he would have done had he not gone into acting. Caine replied, "I would like to have been an architect."

How do we account for this interest in architecture? Experiencing architecture gives us thrills—it stirs our emotions as only works of art can. We love to build things. We like to draw too. Lots of people delight in planning projects and visualizing ways to build them. We love to dream, to fantasize about designing and making things. We love to acquire things, to be artists, to put together complex organizations. There's a curiosity about architecture—a desire to experience architecture, to anticipate it in an exotic setting, to understand it as a work of art, to keep it in our memory as a story, or to feel the thrill of making it ourselves. It's a way of creating something from nothing, of bringing order to things in a satisfying way. It's a way of helping people improve the way they live. It's an art that rewards you and the community.

Should you want to, you can be a professional architect. The profession is indeed a thrilling one. You could be an active enthusiast—someone with a passion for beautiful architecture but no interest in designing it yourself. Or perhaps you could be an architecture scholar—someone who takes to architecture the way Civil War buffs take to that history—and maybe even extend that interest into doctoral studies.

The education of architects for the profession involved half of my career. It was a cause that I believed would make for better architecture and better cities. Yet, as I became an emeritus professor and at the same time moved to a 450-year-old mountain village in Mexico, I had a new look at the making of architecture.

My village, a solid mass of architecture-without-architects, gained its special architectural character from its many eighteenth-century religious and public buildings. The indigenous architecture built in local traditions supported a delightful lifestyle in a visually satisfying whole.

This was a different world. It became clear that I had been educating only a small fraction of the people who design buildings, because the fact is that nonarchitects, holding no professional degree or license, build almost all the buildings in the United States and probably everywhere else. The magnitude of this fact is rarely acknowledged, but nonarchitects are clearly the major force in the making of buildings and cities.

Street space formed by walls of residences and shops at the street edge in San Miguel de Allende, Mexico, 2000.

Houses set on a plane of grass with a street running through it. Residential street in United States.

Some nonarchitects excel at making architecture, while others seek the benefits of a better product to sell. They produce valuable products and come from many professions, particularly engineering. Those who aspire to make architecture rather than just building have the positive quality of the amateur. I use the word *amateur* in its original sense. The French word *amare*, meaning "to love," is a root for the word *amateur*. The amateur, "one who loves an activity," will be a focus of this book because to do architecture well you have to love it. *Amateur* is an enthusiastically positive term; it is not used pejoratively here. As I see it, the loving spirit of the amateur is essential to good architecture, irrespective of professional degrees or licensure.

Giving importance to this role of the amateur, Daniel Boorstin, the eminent historian, spoke eloquently on "the amateur spirit." He said, "The rewards and refresh-

ments of thought and the arts come from the courage to try something, all sorts of things, for the first time. An enamored amateur need not be a genius to stay out of ruts he has never been trained in. . . . In the long run, the ruts wear away, and adventuring amateurs reward us by a wonderful vagrancy into the unexpected."

Helping nonarchitects learn about architecture obviously deserves our attention. In this book I hope to bring knowledge and confidence to discerning nonarchitects and to encourage them to take care to enhance the environment. Having worked with architects most of my life, I intend some of my thoughts to be for them as well.

I hope to address these topics from a point of view that comes from a life as a practicing architect and dean of an architecture school, and with a background that begins as one of those fifteen-year-old boys who wanted to be an architect.

CHAPTER TWO | DREAMING AND SEEING

Dear Gregory:

When you ask, "How do we experience architecture in our imagination and in reality?" you point to a fundamental of the discipline. Of course, it is our senses that are at work, yet before we can appreciate what we see, a fuller experience can be gained from information about the building, its setting, and the designer's aspirations for the building.

Dreaming happens. You dreamed as a child digging in a sandpile or making a fort on the playroom floor out of seat cushions, pillows, and sheets. You were making spaces and forms that you could see, feel, and maybe hear. You may imagine a dream house as you look through books and magazines. Your dreaming imagination is at work as you contemplate any building project. Dreaming is essential. Dreaming about seeing a place puts you in the action. Dreaming of being the architect of something seems to express a deep personal desire to make something happen.

Dreaming, in a disciplined sense, is visualization—the key to design and building. Between the dream and the building there are needs for skill and knowledge, but first and always you must focus on the dream. The dream is the most important part of your effort. Have you ever watched children draw? They will often draw a house or a church in simple form with all the appropriate iconography in place. Children have great imaginations; they make spaces out of cardboard boxes to enclose themselves and their friends. I watched in awe as a nine-year-old girl drew large, detailed plans of her dream house with chalk all over her concrete driveway. With great enthusiasm she described all the rooms of the dream house, drawing furniture, stairways, a second floor, and an attic, using considerable powers of visualization and uninhibited drawing skill to express her dream as a drawing.

Seeing takes work. Vision produces over 80 percent of the information coming to us from our five senses—even more when we are experiencing architecture. Yet it's not automatic; seeing is a skill that requires educated vision and perhaps new glasses. I mention that at the beginning of this chapter because poor vision is common; I myself first saw clearly only after college. Confirming that you see clearly and distinctly will enhance your perception and enjoyment.

"Training your eye," for a designer, is

like fitness training for an athlete—it determines your level of performance. Find architecture that is known to be exceptional or that you personally connect with. Enjoy it by experiencing its spaces and finding its delights, find its surprises. It may be a real thriller; or it may be just good. Then, study what you are experiencing by digging deeper: study plans and sections of the building if published. Read about the building's purposes and how they were fulfilled.

For example, in my preparation for experiencing my first Gothic cathedral, I examined the history of Rheims Cathedral in several sources. (Now you can Google it.) My reading reminded me that the kings of France had been crowned there, that it suffered heavy damage in the Great War, and that it had recently been restored for the glory of France. I also looked at cross-section drawings of the nave to refresh my mind about how the great weight of the structure could span the nave and be taken to the ground with only stone upon stone. The plan was the familiar form, yet it demonstrated the complexity of the structure and the intricacy of the minor spaces.

I began my actual *seeing* when I saw the great mass of medieval stonework gleaming in the morning sun on the distant horizon like a ship. Approaching it, I followed the movement toward the great mass of stone that was growing closer and larger by standing up in our Volkswagen bus and looking out the sunroof. Arriving at the site, we saw the façade rising out of a strong, brightly lit ground plane with people and color moving through it on a Sun-

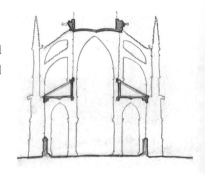

Section cut through the nave of the cathedral at Rheims shows the rib vaulting of the nave and side aisles.

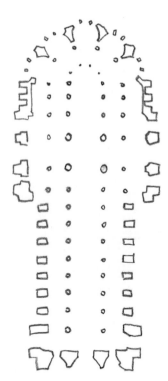

Plan of Notre Dame Cathedral of Rheims, France, shows the base of its skeletal structure, ca. 400–1300.

LEFT: A Gothic structural triumph of sculpture and enclosure presents itself at Rheims.

CENTER: Significant urban scale presented by Notre Dame Cathedral of Rheims.

RIGHT: Spatial progression of walking through the rib-structured nave of the cathedral at Rheims.

day morning. I insisted we have coffee and a croissant within the aura of the façade so I could analyze it before we went in. Moving into the sacred space through the great portal amid a miraculous cacophony of bells, I walked slowly down the left aisle while the choir's recessional moved in the opposite direction up the center nave, singing a hymn based on Dvorak's *New World*. Just as I reached the transept and looked up to the glorious bright circle of stained glass and stone tracery, the huge chancel organ burst forth with Widor's *Toccata*. It was so overwhelming that my knees buckled, and I was brought to tears by the beauty. It was far better than the dream— I was almost literally "transported." That's experiencing architecture. That's the way of seeing.

How do you learn to see places and sense spaces? Let me suggest ten ways to explore and understand a building.

FIRST, as you begin to experience a build-

ing, try to learn *why it was built and what its function in the community was and is now*, so you can understand it socially before you begin your physical understanding. Note, too, how it relates to its neighbors— the buildings and activities around it.

SECOND, *raise your normal view* and look up as you walk around. Much of the architect's effort is above eye level. See how the light hits the surfaces. Notice the shape of the shadows. Notice the number of layers in the façade, starting with the layers of mass closest to you and receding to the window glass. Focus, in turn, on color, form, texture, proportion, rhythm, silhouette, mass. Look only for form for a bit, then look only for proportion, then the other elements of design—each in its own time.

THIRD, *sense the space* by the size and shape of the spaces, how they sound as you speak, and how the light slides in and bounces around. Sense the space formed

FAR LEFT: Light, shade, and shadow express form, making ornament at the Quadrangle, Dallas, Texas, 1964.

Layers start at the glass and progress forward through each plane and molding edge of the window of Casa Canal, San Miguel de Allende, Mexico, ca. 1850.

by the building outside, and, as you go inside, see also how the spaces relate to each other and transition from one to another. Architecture being the art of space, it cannot be fully communicated in pictures, drawings, or words but must be sensed to be fully appreciated. You can't hold architecture like a book in your lap. You need to experience it full size. But when you can't travel to the building and must rely on pictures and words, take time to let your imagination make it real to you.

FAR LEFT: A post and lintel structure has columns in compression and beams in bending. Marsh House, by author, Austin, Texas, 1978.

TOP RIGHT: Spaces of Casa Pani progress along the straight line of an enfilade.

Follow gravity as it pulls the weight of the wall above, around the arch, and down the wall and column to the foundation in the earth. Lindos, Greece, 1983.

Frank Lloyd Wright's cantilever is made possible by the tensile materials of the twentieth century at Fallingwater, Bear Run, Pennsylvania, 1934.

Tension structure of Santiago Calatrava spans the Guadalquivir River in Seville, Spain, 1992.

FOURTH, *train your eye to understand the structure* of the building you are seeing. How is gravity pulling down on the building? How is the structure itself keeping the materials in place?

FIFTH, *determine how the materials are working.* Are they in compression (pressing down) or tension (pulling apart like cables)? Heavy and massive? Light and airy? Are the materials hard or soft? Rough or smooth? Opaque or transparent? Solid or void? Reflective or dull? Man-made or natural? Warm or cold? Are they local or exotic? What colors are they? What texture? What ideas do they conjure up for you? Are they permanent or transient? Fragile or strong? Common or extraordinary?

SIXTH, *determine how the building was constructed.* Is it steel frame or concrete frame? Stone masonry laid by hand or precast concrete panels installed by machine? Wood framing with thin masonry veneer or thick, load-bearing masonry? Metal or glass panels? Exposed structure with curtain walls or a solid mass? Was the building just well built or was it, in fact, exactingly crafted—that is, did individual craftsmen lavish their special art on the building?

SEVENTH, *examine the historical prece-*

dents of the architecture you are seeing. This fascinating question, the subject of entire libraries, is the basis of an important academic discipline in itself. You will find that history is the source, whether you are going to look only at this century, as is the wont of Modernists, or at the eight thousand years of humans' efforts at creating habitat. Historic architecture was eliminated from the academic design studio after World War II, but, as you will find, architectural history gives design its direction and meaning—gives us the cultural antecedents of the building's form, the materials and techniques, as well as the decorative arts. A whole world of architectural history and anthropology is ours to learn from, even though many designers have avoided it.

Francesco Borromini's Baroque church St. Ivo is in a long line of precedents. Rome, 1642.

Rhythms of an arcade dominate the composition in the Stockholm City Hall, Ragnar Ostberg, 1911.

Lines of alignment help compose and organize objects, solids, and voids. Taj Mahal, Agra, India, 1630–1653.

Intervention of the Modernist, Stadthaus, Richard Meyer & Partners. Ulm, Germany, 1993.

EIGHTH, *analyze the composition, the proportions, the rhythms* of what you're seeing. What relates to what? What lines up? What vectors of force do you see in the composition? Is it a classical composition having a well-defined bottom, middle, and top? What are the colors and textures doing to each other? What are the qualities of light and shadow? What spaces have been formed? How do they feel to you as you move through them? Do they give delight?

NINTH, *observe the appropriateness of the building* in terms of its setting. Does it complement that which is around it, be it natural landscape or urban form? It had to take the place of something. Is it as good as what was there before? Has it improved the beauty or meaning of the setting?

TENTH, *analyze what makes this building special*. Beyond seeing and understanding the architecture, visit some construction sites and see how architecture is built. You will see that it's a rather primitive operation, not like a manufacturing plant turning out repetitive products with machines. Each building is unique. The joys of construction are many. One is the thrill of seeing the space you have imagined that's just been created by the structure and how the sun hits it. Another is the interaction with the many workmen and craftsmen actually doing the construction. Fine workmanship may offer the most satisfaction for you, the client, and the craftsman. I once asked an elderly carpenter laying a hardwood floor to help me make the transition between two rooms really special and gave him a rather complex integrating pattern of inlays within a rectangle to visually connect the two rooms. He took my drawing home to work on it, and when I saw the design installed I was as thrilled with his execution as he was. It was a handsome addition to the building. Some months later I received a letter from his wife saying that he had died but that he was pleased that he had built one beautiful thing in his life.

Each construction site seems to have its own culture. On some jobs there will be a close-knit team that works together from beginning to end. Others will have a number of subcontractors who aren't connected except insofar as they are parts of the job and who arrive in trucks and then depart for lunch and for the evening—each group a specialist. The sound of the job is a mix of rock 'n' roll for the carpenters, country and western for the masons, and ranchero music for the tile setters. There are no hammering sounds anymore; nail guns work on compressed air and sound like *chuk*. If it is wood-frame construction, the smell of freshly cut wood gives a special aura to the place.

By tradition, when the frame of the building is "topped out," workers place a fir tree on the roof.

On a construction site in Mexico, there will be no sound of hammering and sawing because wood is too expensive to use. The buildings there are of masonry—brick, stone, concrete, rubble—or some version of adobe. The sound is the *chink, chink, chink* of hand chiseling on masonry or carving on stone. The smell of the job is the smell of food cooking for *almuerzo*, which is cooked and eaten communally around a charcoal fire that heats each person's meal. The men often play cards, and lunchtime is a precise one-hour recess. The workers are usually the extended family of the *maestro*, or job superintendent, as was the case on a recent job of mine where the maestro's father drove the truck, his grandparents were the night watchmen, his brother was a mason, and his ten-year-old son sold Cokes and candies on nonschool days. Cousins and uncles were also spread out in the job. The architect, who is usually the contractor, visits the job daily and personally brings the weekly payroll to the job site.

When a building is "topped out" in Mexico, a handmade cross decorated with ribbons and flowers is taken by the work crew in procession to be blessed in the church of Santa Anna, patron saint of

masons, and returned to the building in solemn fashion, where it's placed in a prominent spot on top of the ongoing product of their labors. After that, the families of the workers arrive and a lengthy party ensues. At my first such party as architect-owner, the crew dug a roasting pit in one corner of the living room, slaughtered a pig in another corner, and barbequed the pig all afternoon while enjoying the beer and music.

Get permission to go on a construction site and take some time to see how things go together, how various construction trades work, how the craftsmen work their materials; see how all the trades coordinate the construction of a one-of-a-kind building.

My favorite professor, Martin Kermacy, once asked us, "How can you design a great building if you've never seen one?" Examine the Reading List I've appended to this book. It's not an academic list, but rather one that I think is useful to anyone who wants to participate in the making of architecture. I have also been bold enough to list the architecture that I think is most important both to see and experience in real life. You'll find those buildings in my Seeing List.

Go see the great architecture, and on the way see also the minor architecture you admire. For architecture you are unable to visit, go to the library, bookstore, or the Web, where there is a tremendous amount of information. Find well-known examples and study them in plan, section, and photographs. As part of such study, it's useful to draw sketches, even to trace a drawing, to help you understand the building. This also helps you learn to draw. Filling your memory with images and ideas of great architecture gives you something to work from, and like learning a piece of music or a poem, you get to participate in the art. Fourteen-year-old Alex Pratt responded to a great building with these lines in her diary: "If you ever want to witness what looks like a piece of Heaven, or at least something holy-looking, go to the Pantheon on a sunny day . . . there is a vastness and greatness which you must grasp . . . you must then realize what stone is like. It is cold, hard and it makes things very dark. This adds to the grandeur of a building . . . [and to] a building's sense of timelessness. Stone makes everything seem so old.

It gives a building an aura wood can never do."

The question is, How do you inform your dreams, give them rich backgrounds, lead them along, and elaborate on them? One answer is to build a memory bank of architecture through a lot of seeing. The architect Charles Moore, formerly dean of architecture at Yale, department chair at Berkeley and UCLA, and then professor at the University of Texas, described his approach to architectural education as "taking students to see places and listen to people." Seeing and understanding through travel, reading, drawing, theorizing, contemplation, and conversation make the key—but the most important learning comes from *seeing*.

The surest test of the civilization of a people . . . is to be found in their architecture, which presents so noble a field for the display of the grand and the beautiful, and . . . is so intimately connected with the essential comforts of life.

WILLIAM H. PRESCOTT
(1796–1859)

Dear Mr. Kenneth:

I agree that what we call architecture is rare and that excellent architecture is even rarer. On our tours we had to search for the few buildings to admire. A lot of the architecture we admire exists because it had a long, productive life, making it also an excellent investment. Some of the great architecture is in ruins but remains valued because of its history. To experience architecture requires effort, but because the high points of a civilization are often expressed in its architecture, the search for a region's best buildings is rewarding on many levels, sensual and intellectual.

In search of the best buildings, I began the requisite architectural tour of Western civilization, traveling and camping in a Volkswagen bus over two six-month periods in 1964 and 1967. I had been removed from architecture while in the Navy and had had a few years as a practicing architect. I wanted to experience the new modern buildings we had studied in school and while abroad, look around at the old buildings we had read about in our architectural history courses. I remember the shock of discovering that the modern buildings appeared to be architecturally impoverished compared to the buildings of earlier epochs. Basically, I decided they lacked *content*. After months of exploring Denmark, France, Italy, Spain, Switzerland, Germany, and Austria, I felt that I had been deceived.

The historic architecture excelled in all categories, as I saw it. I felt compelled to question Modernism; it was simply not equal to what was there before. Not even close. Nothing compared with the Gothic architecture I was experiencing. The Baroque, Renaissance, and Neoclassical architecture that made up the historic cities shone boldly as works of art, while most modern buildings looked starkly inadequate—often cheap and out of place. This all took a while for me to assimilate, but it was clear that the historic buildings had greatness and that many of these buildings had been designed and built by extraordinarily skilled and inspired builders who did not fit our current model of an architect.

Clearly, some of the best buildings are by architects without professional degrees or licenses. Designers of the best buildings learned from other buildings and as apprentices; most were never named in

history until the Renaissance. Professions, as we know them, didn't come into being until the mid-nineteenth century—well after what I think are the best buildings had been built.

Some say that the essence of wonderful architecture comes to life in the passion of the architect—amateur or professional. The "passion to build," shared with a king, emperor, or pope or, now, a corporate, institutional, or individual client, is the force that creates great architecture. Or maybe not. Sometimes the passion is only for building at the least cost and sometimes the professional or amateur, however enthusiastic, proves inadequate to the task. But the building happens anyway, no matter what its objective or the skill level of the maker, and the world either rejoices or bows its head in shame—or worse, seems to be indifferent.

Roman Temple of Jupiter in Baalbek, Lebanon, ca. 15 BC.

The Renaissance architect Filippo Brunelleschi built the dome of Santa Maria del Fiore in Florence, Italy, 1417–1434.

Today, laws restrict our use of the title *architect,* although the great buildings of history were designed and built by genius talents without a license. The title *architect* has been used to connote dignity in many cultures. There have been court architects, priest architects, and gentleman architects. These impassioned builders were not licensed or certified by academic degrees. Some Roman and Greek architects had the authorship of their work on record. The medieval architects who designed and built the great Gothic cathedrals were rarely known by name. Others were paid for their construction skills rather than their design skills, so they fit the positive aspects of "amateur," which I'll call them just for the purposes of this chapter, even though they built some of history's greatest architecture. Beginning again in the fifteenth century, with Filippo Brunelleschi and his accomplishment in building the extraordinary dome of Florence's landmark cathedral (the Duomo), the individual architects were named. Mimar Koca Sinan, a six-

teenth-century architect of Turkish mosques, was also given recognition as an individual architect.

Nonarchitect building projects today sometimes enjoy the care of an amateur architect and succeed beautifully. Of course, many burst forth thoughtlessly aloof to the idea of architecture, blindly built solely for immediate needs by a default amateur architect (here I'm using the word in its negative sense). Thoughtlessness is the worst sin. If the thoughtless builder became an informed, sensitive amateur, everyone would benefit.

While most buildings are built without the involvement of professional architects, most never aspire to be architecture—that is, artful. Some buildings, perhaps most, are conceived as merchandise for sale as real-estate development or as thoughtless functional buildings pretending to be invisible, "just happening," because they are needed immediately for business or housing or government. A very few building projects involve architects, and unfortunately not even all of those, or even most, are visual assets to the community. In a different business and cultural setting, however, there are buildings, like those in pre-industrial, Third World areas using traditional forms, that can be so sensible, strong, and right that they are a visual delight—and they exist without the benefit of any architect's involvement and only through a common knowledge of building (of course when that knowledge was simpler).

The word *amateur,* now corrupted by common usage to mean "unprofessional" or, worse still, a "dabbler," once conveyed the same meaning as the Spanish word *aficionado*, meaning "someone who has a fervent interest in and appreciation of something." The spirit of the enthusiast engages here as well. You'll notice that my definition is broad enough to allow even professional architects to qualify as people willing to take risks to satisfy their desire to create something bigger than life, and perhaps take a larger risk of personally investing in it or even living in it. I'm pleased to be an amateur flutist and a professional architect who performs with amateur and professional musicians. You may be an amateur architect and, for instance, a professional lawyer working on a building.

Being an amateur architect who builds carries gratifications such as being in love with what you are doing as well as being able to work with technology and construction, where, in the process, you fulfill yourself. Effective amateurs improve homes, public buildings, neighborhoods, and cities by educating themselves, by being involved in the design process, and by being responsible citizens helping make good design decisions in their community. Being a corporate or politically appointed client for a public building is an opportunity to play a critical role by learning, through reading and travel, how to make intelligent and sensitive design decisions. There are too many accountants, engineers, government officials, and executives, on building committees, for example, who have not developed the architectural literacy to make such important decisions. They tend to use, as their sole guide, cost and expedi-

ency—important values, yes, but easily forgotten by the building's occupants or passersby, whose quality of life will be either enhanced or diminished by the building for decades or centuries.

Envisioning a new house for the family or working on a committee with professional architects planning a school or new corporate headquarters requires an informed, passionate, actively involved client, an aficionado. The old truism "Architecture is no better than its client" pays homage to the client's critical importance. When that client is an informed amateur, able to communicate and collaborate with constancy and tenacity, the prospects for good architecture soar.

I think the amateur is important to enhancing the discipline of architecture as well as being a creative leading edge, a critical spokesman, a patron who is more concerned about the art of architecture than some academics and professional architects. You may feel unqualified to serve in any of these roles, most especially that of a creative leading edge. But I plan to show you that even that role is realistic and critically needed.

Even though every building can be created as architecture, some buildings, by their place in the world, have a responsibility to be architecture. Public buildings, high-visibility buildings, symbolic buildings—all have a broad influence generated by the quality of their design. Don't you think that when more buildings seek to be architecture, a more beautiful city evolves, our quality of life improves, and values of all sorts soar beyond the ordinary?

While thrills for the amateur may come from doing something to the best of his or her abilities, the quality of the end result will require enough self-criticism to refine and nurture initial conceptions of proportion, scale, composition, and other elements of the design. This requires that you lavish a great deal of time on making thoughtful design decisions. There will, in fact, be thousands of them. For many of us, refining the design becomes one of the main delights. And it offers the opportunity for artistic growth for both amateurs and professionals.

I hope I have established the importance of the amateur. I want to offer a test to see if you might be a dedicated amateur. Try these questions:

1. Do you travel to see the great buildings and cities of the world and enjoy discovering wonder-filled exotic places where people seem to live in a work of art?

2. Do you keep a clip file of magazine photos showing beautiful rooms you like and would enjoy incorporating someday in a place of your own design?

3. Do you think about ways to make your city and neighborhood more beautiful?

4. Do you like to make things?

5. When you look at a piece of land, do you sometimes imagine building something on it and imagine what it would be like to be there?

6. Do you get giddy just thinking about what you could see from the rooms or how your building would fit into the landscape or the streetscape?

7. When you put pencil to paper to describe an architectural idea, do you get excited about getting it down so that you can understand it and explore it?

8. Have you found yourself engaged in building projects that are so important to you that they overwhelm you and give you goosebumps?

9. Does your collection of books on architecture, cities, landscape, and interiors outnumber your other books?

10. Do you think about what you might have done, or might do, as an architect?

If these thoughts stir you, particularly the first five questions, you are definitely an aficionado, an amateur. I want to give your role of amateur both dignity and respect, helping fan an enthusiasm into a passion that has the power to make better architecture as well as better cities and neighborhoods. Now, if you responded positively to the last five questions as well, you might consider becoming an architect and read that chapter carefully.

Truly grand projects, those magnificent works done for a king, priest, pope, bishop, or emperor or for a landlord, industrialist, or philanthropist, were each made by an experienced master builder, an Archi (chief) -tecton (builder), or Architecton, the basis for our word *architect*. The chief, or master, builder trained for his work just as an amateur would—by working with more experienced master builders and by traveling, drawing, reading, and gaining knowledge

Master builders designed
and built Gothic cathedrals
by learning from other masters and their examples.
St. Maclou, Rouen, France,
1435–1521.

and skill. Until the mid-nineteenth century, the "schools" of architecture were the nearest buildings under construction or the architecture within traveling distance of the aspiring (amateur) builder-architect.

The traditional professional, a specialist having skill and experience in a particular activity, differed from the amateur only in that he was paid for his work. Architects, doctors, and lawyers did not come into being as professionals certified by the state and practicing a profession until the nineteenth century. I find it curious that by that time most of the great buildings of the world had already been built, and due to other circumstances the general quality of architecture had begun to decline. Forces such as the industrial revolution had brought new technology; increasingly, rapid growth and expansion had caused a

great volume of building, and new architectural theories emerged. Capitalism looked at capital and returns rather than at beauty and art. And Modernism offered the new professionals what seemed an exciting path to a brave new world.

Today, only those who are certified by the state can use the title architect. In the United States, the American Institute of Architects (AIA) created a tradition whereby it was deemed unethical for an architect to build the architecture he or she designed, reasoning that it created a conflict of interest in representing the client. That stricture, making it unethical to build what one designed, eliminated the "builder" component of the word *architect* as chief builder. Other countries, meanwhile, continued the older tradition. Fortunately, in the late 1970s, the AIA revised its ethics to again allow architects to build their own work, provided they sign a thorough non-conflict-of-interest clause. Unfortunately, the tradition of design-but-not-build had already been established. With this change the U.S. architect can again be a master builder, and the AIA now provides contract documents for such work, although in many building types the technology has become so complex that the design process requires the help of a team of professionals.

Even without building anything, the amateur can get some of the greatest pleasures of the art by experiencing wonderful architecture—by seeing and by being in a space and moving through it. Experiencing architecture is one of the major reasons people travel. They want to see the wonders of the world that various cultures have created. It's also a way of "seeing" the past.

By experiencing architecture, I mean using all the senses. Start with looking, of course, but don't forget listening, moving, touching, sometimes even smelling, and if there is food, sitting down and enjoying both flavors and ambience. Enhancing the enjoyment of the senses, the experience can be greatly improved by knowing the building intellectually, by learning its history and social purpose; and of course, as an architect would, by studying it in plan and section to understand its anatomy.

When I was teaching architecture, I insisted that my students walk slowly along the main axis of the nineteenth-century Texas state capitol building with their eyes looking up into the great vertical dome; I wanted them to watch as the concentric rings of balconies moved to reveal the Lone Star at the top of the dome, and then see it eclipsed as their motion continued. I also insisted that students visit Louis I. Kahn's Kimbell Museum for as many hours and as often as they could. A Greek colleague of mine was told by his Athenian teachers to spend three hours a week at the Acropolis. When I experience a place several times, a kind of cumulative effect happens, just as in listening to music or looking at paintings—the senses acquire a familiarity, an appreciation, a memory of the experience, a knowing of the art. I like to spend time to get to know them. During my family's six-month architectural tour, we camped for a

A special place to learn architecture is in Louis I. Kahn's Kimbell Museum in Fort Worth, Texas, 1973.

week in Florence on a hill overlooking Brunelleschi's dome. One morning, my twelve-year-old son, Rick, and I walked up the hill to San Miniato al Monte and sat for a long time on a low wall, looking intensely at its magnificent marble façade. I showed him how to analyze the façade's composition and how to explore its complex interior spaces, an experience that may have contributed to his eventually becoming an architect.

Amateurs who love and demand good architecture are sorely needed. We need people who so love good architecture that they will demand it in all buildings, especially the public buildings that give form to our cities. We need amateur architects who themselves, with help, can create good buildings. We want to remember that most of the world's buildings are still built by amateurs—both the loving, thoughtful amateurs and the thoughtless ones. Hope-

fully, the thoughtless amateur will become aesthetically responsible. The best professionals will continue to be "amateurs." I would like to encourage the thoughtful amateur and help him or her excel and succeed through their love of architecture.

San Miniato al Monte offers basic lessons in composition. Florence, Italy, ca. 1000–1288.

We all see more of architecture than of any other art. Every street is a gallery of architects' work.

C. E. MONTAGUE

(1867–1928)

Dear James,

You're right. Architecture is not a static art. It is always changing. And each designer has his or her individual approach, formed by experience and education. You and I began architecture school at the time of two significant changes. One was the fresh new ideas and objectives that surfaced at the end of World War II, when people were ready for a new start and well-traveled veterans returned to college. The other was the revolutionary ideals of Modernism that were replacing the traditional training of architects—the design styles taught by the influential Ecole des Beaux-Arts.

This exciting period in architecture and architectural education would create a new kind of architect and architecture. Everything was new. Our professors had been educated in the Beaux Arts, so they too were new to Modernism. Both professors and students could now happily avoid teaching and learning the tedious old theories, designs, and skills of the various styles and invent something new. I had started college at age fourteen and was as impressionable as one could get in this milieu. But my apprenticeship with O'Neil Ford, the early definer of Southwest Regionalism and explorer of Modernism, helped me find my own path near his. This experience gave me a Modernist education but with a strong feeling for place—leaving me more a Regionalist than a Modernist. Observing the profession of architecture from a career spanning some fifty years, I see its changes as a continuous stream of development but moving at glacial speed compared to the technology around us.

What is architecture all about today? How did most of it get to be so, well, unappealing? What happened to the kind of architecture we value in the historic buildings we so revere? Where are the ornament, symbolism, mythology, romance, human scale, and proportions that we still enjoy? Why are so many public and commercial buildings as well as millions of individual houses so, excuse the expression, ugly? Is it really enough for a building to be only functional, economical, or Green? Fortunately, here and there we can still find wonderful new architecture that seems just right. So, what is architecture and what is not?

There are so many definitions of *archi-*

tecture—and so many opinions about architecture held by people who love it—that I suggest starting with the common definition from *Merriam-Webster's Collegiate Dictionary*, Eleventh Edition:

1. The art or science of building; *Specif.* : the art or practice of designing and building structures and esp. habitable ones; 2 a : formation or construction as or as the result of conscious act <The — of the garden>; b : a unifying cohesive form or structure <the novel lacks — >; 3 : architectural product or work; 4 : a method or style of building.

My favorite definition of *architecture* is in Nikolaus Pevsner's introduction to his *An Outline of European Architecture* (1943):

A bicycle shed is a building; Lincoln Cathedral is a piece of architecture.
Nearly everything that encloses space on a scale sufficient for a human being to move in is a building; the term architecture applies only to buildings designed with a view to aesthetic appeal. Now aesthetic sensations may be caused by a building in three different ways. First, they may be produced by the treatment of walls, proportions of windows, the relation of wall-space to window-space, of one storey to another, of ornamentation such as the tracery of a fourteenth-century window, or the leaf and fruit garlands of a Wren porch. Secondly, the treatment of the exterior of a building as a whole is aesthetically significant, its contrast of block against

block, the effect of a pitched or flat roof or a dome, the rhythm of projections and recessions. Thirdly, there is the effect on our senses of the treatment of the interior, the sequence of rooms, the widening out of a nave at the crossing, the stately movement of a Baroque staircase. The first of these three ways is two-dimensional; it is the painter's way. The second is the three-dimensional, and as it treats the building as volume, as a plastic unit, it is the sculptor's way. The third is the three-dimensional too, but it concerns space; it is the architect's own way more than the others.

What distinguishes architecture from painting and sculpture is its spatial quality. In this, and only in this, no other artist can emulate the architect. Thus the history of architecture is primarily a history of man shaping space, and the historian must keep spatial problems always in the foreground. This is why no book on architecture, however popular its presentation may be, can be successful without ground plans. But architecture, though primarily spatial, is not exclusively spatial. In every building, besides enclosing space, the architect models volume and plans surface, i.e., designs an exterior and sets out individual walls. That means that the good architect requires the sculptor's and the painter's modes of vision in addition to his own spatial imagination. Thus architecture is the most comprehensive of all visual arts and has a right to claim superiority over the others.

To those definitions let me add some historical perspective to the current scene to help you appreciate where we are in the evolving art of architecture. A dramatic change of design direction consumed architects at the beginning of the twentieth century. The new concepts, which were in full force by the time I entered architecture school in 1946, meant that all of the traditional studies of classical proportions, ornament, and different styles had been abandoned. We were told that we must create our designs with absolutely no preconceptions, to start with a clean piece of paper—innovate. Theoretically it was a clean slate, yet on that slate would be only Modernism in an ideology rarely questioned by architects for almost a hundred years now. But this design freedom proved to be a tall order for the nongenius 99.99999 percent of us designing the world's buildings.

Using only *new* ideas obviously left architects without a tradition to work from and left nonarchitects without a useful guide. *Innovation* became the only design direction respected or condoned by our teachers, and only innovation was newsworthy in the architectural press. To not innovate was to be *derivative*; everything had to be new, starting from near zero with each project. This conceptual blinder continues to distort most of today's architecture, subordinating all other aesthetic values to the quest for innovation, "the New."

Modernism had begun two generations before mine in progressive circles in Western Europe. By the end of World War II it had replaced the monolithic doctrines of the Ecole des Beaux-Arts on which much

The Neoclassic Battle Hall Architecture and Planning Library by Cass Gilbert was built in the same decade as the Bauhaus by Walter Gropius. Austin, University of Texas, 1917.

Antonio Gaudí's Casa Mila presented Modernismo in contrast to Modernism, in Barcelona, Spain, 1910.

of academic architectural education had been founded. The great new freedom proved a relief to everyone, students as well as teachers, for architecture felt like a stimulating and open new world to explore. Reinforcing the movement were plenty of new books and magazines full of the new ideas. There were only a few rules to follow, the chief one being "Form follows function." The previous discipline was thrown out along with the plaster casts of ornament and moldings that students had previously drawn to learn how light defines surfaces. The classical sourcebooks, such as Giacomo da Vignola's, had been put on the top shelf to gather dust, their place taken by books on the "modern masters." Ideas and images were changing so fast that some journals and magazines were carrying the message more than books. The art of architecture had undergone an intellectual makeover. Do we wonder why we see so much inept detailing trying to imitate the classical?

Enormous diversity in design was possible; many divergent philosophies and idiomatic expressions typified the excitement, and confusion, as the new era began. The major forces, each of which could have provided the direction for the new era, were, in my mind, these seven legendary figures: Antonio Gaudí (1852–1926), Frank Lloyd Wright (1867–1959), Eliel Saarinen (1873–1950), Gunnar Asplund (1885–1940), Ludwig Mies van der Rohe (1886–1969), Charles-Edouard Jeanneret, Le Corbusier (1887–1965), and Alvar Aalto (1898–1976). One could make a case for following the lead of each of these genius architects, and one could even visualize how architecture

Gunnar Asplund's Woodland Chapel shows classic precedents of form and proportion to establish the desired character. Ornamental column capitals were stripped away as in many early examples of Modernism. Stockholm, 1918.

The human scale of Alvar Aalto's brick forms in the Saynatsalo Town Hall has provided a memorable architectural image for decades. Saynatsalo, Finland, 1949.

The simplicity of the planes in the composition of Mies van der Rohe's "Barcelona Pavilion," characterized as one of the two dominant icons of Modernism. Barcelona, Spain, 1929, demolished 1930, shown here as rebuilt in 1959.

The sculpture on stilts of Le Corbusier's Villa Savoy was the other dominant icon of Modernism, often emulated. Poissy, France, 1928.

might have proceeded had that architect's influence been dominant.

The groundswell of Modernism covered up the spectacular earlier work of other promising modern movements: the Modernismo of Barcelona, the Secessionist of Vienna, the Art Nouveau and, later, Art Deco of Paris, and all the others. Modern-

The Bauhaus school sought to abandon the influences of history. Dessau, Germany, 1919.

ism, by definition, is a self-conscious break with the past and a search for new forms of expression—an aesthetic introduced as "the International Style," which was the controversial name given to Modernism by Henry Russell Hitchcock and Philip Johnson.

In the midst of these great architects was Walter Gropius (1883–1969), founder of an influential school that proposed a new kind of design education, one that turned its back on history. The Bauhaus in Germany (1919–1933) began as a design school for industrial production and later included architecture in the new aesthetic of Modernism developing from the de Stijl group of Dutch artists and Russian Constuctivism. Gropius then came to Harvard in 1937 to aid Joseph Hudnut in begetting a new model of architectural education in the United States—a doctrine which other schools either paid close attention to or emulated directly. Gropius urged his students, "Don't look back," and architecture was turned upside down through the education of young architects who looked to the new heroes of Modernism rather than to the world before. Harvard's Graduate Center, designed by Gropius at that time, now seems out of place as a building that didn't look back.

Actually, there was a lot more going on in the beginnings of Modernism before the dominance of the Bauhaus-Harvard philosophies. I urge you to enjoy some of the documentation of the era found in my Reading List. Here, though, I hope to explain the various influences and directions in Modernism as well as how they affected the education of architects, who have, for the past seventy years, led both other architects and nonarchitects to design what makes up most of what you see in American cities.

With Modernism in total command of architectural education by the mid-1940s, it was exciting for us to think that we were washing away the past and replacing it with something we would invent on our own clean piece of paper. It was an ideology impenetrable by any other intellectual or artistic force, so strong that it was considered a *moral imperative* rather than a style. Because it was happening all over the country, schools quickly climbed on the bandwagon; one school claimed in 1948 that it was the first regional school to embrace Modernism. But they were wrong, because by 1946, my first year at the University of Texas, the students and faculty had not only embraced Modernism, they had married her.

At this point I need to introduce another concept, that of Regionalism—a different direction from International Style. Regionalism challenged the lack of human dimension in Modernism. While keeping up-to-date with technology, Regionalism demanded some adjustment of the International Style to fit the regional, more localized cultural and environmental characteristics that Modernists, in their zeal, meant to ignore. Regionalism can be romantic or nostalgic because it doesn't dogmatically exclude those warm, human emotions. As its very name implies, it emphasizes *place*—the particulars of a geographic or cultural region. Its determinants are the particulars of climate, especially extremes of hot or cold, sunny or cloudy, wet or dry, as well as particular traditions: social traditions and lifestyles, construction traditions, dwelling types, patterns of urban life, and, of course, available local materials and crafts that are both practical and visually appropriate for the region. For example, the traditional Swiss chalet works well in the snow and cold of its region, but would seem alien on a tropical coast. A New Mexico adobe pueblo, meanwhile, would seem out of place—in fact, would melt away—in a South American rain forest. When designing university facilities in several parts of the United States, I knew there would be differences because of the regional determinants—all would be considered modern, but they would at the same time be regional. A university building in Oregon was quite different from one in New Mexico. However, many of today's architects were taught to consider invalid any concerns for context, harmony, and regionalism. While one could find the rare exception, a sharp-edged, shiny-white International Style building would be inappropriate in an urban context defined by regional characteristics.

Thanks to the good sense of Regionalism, there was not a total acceptance of International Style Modernism in some schools. Most faculties had been educated in a strong Beaux-Arts tradition, although the younger faculty had experienced that tradition on the wane. There were directions of Art Modern, Art Deco, Classicism, Eclecticism, and various revivals, as well as Regionalism, still active in design studios and on construction sites. The most important architectural critic of the time, Lewis Mumford, recognized that Modernism and Regionalism were not necessarily opposed. To illustrate the dilemma, let me use the experience at the University of Texas. Being far removed from the epicenters of Modernism on the East Coast and Europe, the school felt free to consider some of the other, less dominant directions of the Modernist movement. At this time, the faculty and students, while aware of the International Style, were enthusiastic about the work of Wright, Aalto, and Eliel Saarinen as well as the regional architectural expressions being developed on the West Coast by William Wurster and Pietro Belluschi and by two local Regionalist architects, David Williams (1890–1962) and O'Neil Ford (1905–1985). These were the forces that activated the design studios of the time.

With a strong interest in Regionalism, an acknowledgment of Modernism, and a respect for Wright, the Texas school went in search of a new dean in 1950. They chose an influential California architect, Harwell Hamilton Harris (1903–1990),

Harwell Hamilton Harris made wood and brick valid in the white stucco and steel aesthetic of Modernism, Eisenberg House, Dallas, Texas, 1961.

Seeking a regional expression of the Southwest, O'Neil Ford expresses natural materials and simple construction in buildings of the Trinity University Campus, San Antonio, Texas, 1949–1989.

who was extraordinarily sensitive to all three design directions in his own highly admired work. Harris represented a fusion of the three values.

To explore design under the influences of the International Style, Wright, and Regionalism, Harris, together with a new professor, Colin Rowe (1920–1999), gathered a bright, energetic, young international faculty that would eventually call themselves the Texas Rangers, canonized by Alex Caragonne in his book by that name. They had a deep respect for regional design issues and traditional aesthetics. Though they questioned the tenets of Modernism, they were, like everyone else at the time, overwhelmed by the momentum of Modernism in Europe and on the East Coast. In fact, that is where the Texas Rangers moved after a few years, all to create design curricula at architecture schools of importance—Cornell, Syracuse, Cooper Union. An opportunity for fusion of the three design directions pursued in the fifties was lost to the zeitgeist of the Interna-

tional Style. The architect's ability to create and extend the designs of the preceding era had disappeared, while the conceit that Modernism could solve the ills of the modern city drove design and political decisions of the era.

The focus moved to two modern masters, Le Corbusier and Mies van der Rohe. Le Corbusier had been a strong force in initiating Modernism. His early ideas virtually dominated the minds of architects in

Harwell Hamilton Harris and the "Texas Rangers" joining the faculty of the University of Texas School of Architecture in Austin, 1953.

The "Marseilles Block" of Le Corbusier became a social, structural, and compositional model for buildings of medium height. Marseilles, France, 1946–1952.

the fifties and sixties. He created extraordinary buildings that we consider heroic models: Villa Savoy and the Marseilles Unite d'Habitation, and later, toward the end of his career, he remained a true visionary in his designs for the Ronchamps Chapel and La Tourette Convent. These buildings, together with many of his well-published theories, had a huge impact on both practicing architects and academics.

Parallel to Corbu, as he was called, there formed a group of devout followers of Mies

van der Rohe, who invented architecture of such elegance and apparent simplicity that it seemed made to order for modern high-rise buildings in the new technology of steel, concrete, and glass. The influence of Mies generated the most popular commercial "style," mainly because it could be emulated at such low cost. Some architects scoff at the idea that this was a style, but it was. During this time Sigfried Gideon, secretary general of the influential Congrés Internationaux d'Architecture Moderne, defined architecture for my generation of students in his seminal work *Space, Time, and Architecture* (Harvard University Press, 1940). Along with other manifestos, it introduced us to a new age and effectively brainwashed us about the past, filling our cleansed crania with a singular idea: the glory of Modernism. Fifty years later, a fellow student and I made a pilgrimage to the ultimate shrine of our early education, the great icon of Modernism, Mies van der Rohe's Barcelona Pavilion, 1929 (reconstructed 1985). We found it hollow, soulless—far from the elegant design state-

The fluid shapes of Le Corbusier's Notre-Dame-du-Haut of Ronchamps, uncontrolled by the usual grid, presaged dynamic sculptural forms for Modernism and created another icon of the era. Ronchamp, France, 1955.

ment that its singular photographs had conveyed to the world. One could now look back at it and consider it only a stylish new idea—a fashion surrounded by mystic rhetoric. The design "truth" it claimed to represent was artifice; it was in reality another "style." More than a fallen idol, it was, at this viewing, depressingly comic.

Having been involved as an architect and educator for half of the last century, I thought Modernism was exciting, but if you will examine the beginning of this chapter in light of today, you can say that my generation of architects and those to follow were more than excited—we were thoroughly brainwashed. *How else could we have so ignored the earlier architecture?*

Looking for the New, we students of Modernism did not learn the basics of classical proportion and composition as the originators of Modernism had learned in their own education. The architect's main guide, the architecture of the past, had been denigrated, and the skills involved in its creation, in large part, lost. Had these skills not been lost and had we continued to validate historical examples, the amateur and the nongenius professional would today have better guides from which to build.

Such guides were available to the sixteenth-century Spanish friars who brought European architecture to the Americas. The friars knew their art from woodcut prints of architectural elements as well as from their memory of authenticity. The plan books of the nineteenth century reached a high degree of success in creating buildings that we admire today in the

United States. Had the tradition developed logically and organically through the years, the derivatives of the traditions would be more successful than what we have now.

The search for the New was ushered in by radical manifestos. Below, with apologies to all historians, I take a simplified look at the credos of five architects whose ideas helped form the modern movement in architecture.

Adolf Loos (1870–1933) espoused more

The Seagrams Building of Mies van der Rohe was the exemplar for the modern office building. New York, 1954.

ideas than he built buildings. He believed that reason should determine the way we build, he opposed the decorative Art Nouveau movement, and, in "Ornament and Crime" and other essays, he described the suppression of decoration as necessary for regulating passion, wherein comes his famous quote, "Ornament is a crime." Actually, he himself used color as dramatic ornament.

Frank Lloyd Wright, the most famous American architect, built many innovative buildings in his ninety-one years. He felt that his organic architecture was the only valid way to build and ridiculed all others, as when he accepted the high honor of the AIA Gold Medal only to say, "It's about time." Some called him "the greatest living nineteenth-century architect," but his Usonian House was the important model for middle-class housing in the postwar period, and his Broadacre City influenced the city planning ideal of sprawling suburbs in the United States. (See the Reading List.)

Le Corbusier introduced the influential functionalist architectural concept, "A house is a machine for living." His extremist proposal to raze Paris and replace it with modern skyscrapers influenced the building of the United States. His Swiss background as a painter led us all into sharp-edged, white, prismatic forms and simplified cubist compositions leading into dynamic sculptural form decades later. (See the Reading List.)

Mies van der Rohe, an architect much admired as a master of abstraction, simplification, and elegant detail, taught us that

"Less is more." That dictum spawned such reactions as "Less is less," "Less is more profitable," and "More is not Enough."

Walter Gropius championed what he called the New Architecture. Sidelining the classicist Joseph Hudnut, Gropius created a new curriculum for architectural education based on his watchword, "Don't look back." He banned color from class projects for fifteen years. His polemical teaching had much more influence than his buildings.

This exciting revolution pressed a "restart button" that had architects—and in fact, all designers—rethinking the form of everything from cities to coffeepots for the next four or five generations. The manifestos are relearned by each generation from teachers who still subscribe to the Modernist manifestos, either because nothing better has come along or, more likely, because of their own brainwashing. Perhaps the more important truth is that Modernism provided a needed cleansing of the tired interpretations of building styles. As I mentioned earlier, many architects, students, and teachers of this era looked upon these new theories and models as moral imperatives, using words like *honesty*, *integrity*, and *truth*. The aesthetic had been intellectualized beyond visual sensitivity to become in many cases strident and raw.

The reaction to relieve this stridency came from architects of the generation that followed the original "modern masters": Louis I. Kahn (1902–1974), in the concrete, sculptural expressions of space, structure, and functional elements of the Kimbell Museum and Salk Center; Jørn

Jørn Utzon's bold design for the Sydney Opera House became one of the world's great landmarks. Sidney, Australia, 1957–1993.

Utzon (1918–), in the magic of the Sydney Opera House; Charles Moore (1925–1993), in the quiet repose of his buildings at Sea Ranch; Robert Venturi (1925–), in his questioning of Modernist form and resurrection of the decorative arts; and I. M. Pei (1917–), in his mastery of technology and form in his many urban building types of the period. This generation continued to refine and enhance the ideals of Modernism, yet found it easier to follow the safe, narrow Modernist views in training the next generation.

Following a period that included several really good modern buildings and thousands of not-so-good buildings, there came some big steps forward. The inventive California architect Frank Gehry (1929–) made a masterpiece of sculpture and architecture in his Guggenheim Museum in Bilbao, Spain, and followed that with the Disney Concert Hall in Los Angeles. These buildings had nothing to do with Regionalism, International Style,

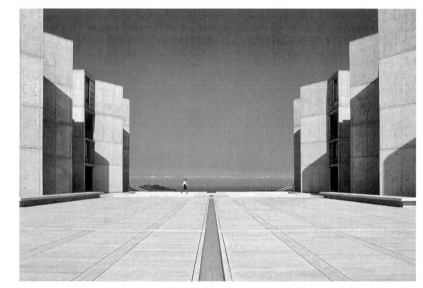

Louis I. Kahn graced the sea with pure sculpture made of complex functions in the Salk Institute. La Jolla, California, 1959–1966.

Postmodernism, or Deconstruction, Minimalism, or any other -ism. They represent a personal design evolution in which digital software and innovative technology were employed by an individual genius who had been exposed to all the influences above but produced something extraordinary and fundamentally new and beautiful. Architecture critics have named this new paradigm the Bilbao Effect. In a similar jump ahead, the Spanish architect/engineer Santiago Calatrava (1951–) accomplished extraordinary sculptural expression at the scale of architecture in

BELOW: Charles W. Moore, in his Sea Ranch work, found form generated by indigenous buildings to provide a model for a generation of small buildings in the United States. Sea Ranch, California, 1964.

RIGHT: I. M. Pei, the master of many building types, enhanced a mountain landscape in the manner of a Greek monastery in the Atmospheric Research Center outside of Boulder, Colorado in 1965.

his dramatic structural approach to form in bridges and buildings. The singular sculptural nature of these designs gives them qualities that might be inserted into a natural or urban landscape without compromising the local identity of Regionalism. These examples suggest that in the era of globalization, local identity may gain greater value.

At the same time, examples of Regionalism evolved at a sophisticated level by such architects as James Cutler (Seattle), Fay Jones (Arkansas), Hugh Newell Jacobson (East Coast), David Lake and Ted Flato (San Antonio), and Rick Joy (Tucson). These architects work in the realm of Modernism but, in addition, are exploring the path of Regionalism with new ideas and refinements.

A parallel design universe that thrives in Mexico and Spain as Modernism, and still exudes Regionalism, is the extraordinary architecture of Ricardo Legorreta and Rafeal Moneo, to mention two of the leading figures. This work satisfies both ideologies and adds the dimension of Minimalism, making for an architecture that seems to work in many different contexts.

These new ideas and evolutions are the joy of architecture and are producing wonderful results. Unfortunately, in most current design thinking, Modernism still demands that we erase previous ideas. It's a kind of "Architectural Alzheimer's Effect." Older architecture became what educators called "history," that is, it was not appropriate for current use in design, only for architectonic and cultural background. Most important and regrettably, many "modern" ideas failed to fulfill their early promises: buildings will be better without ornament—e.g., new materials will last longer than traditional materials, life will be simpler and better, cities will be more convenient to use, etc. And, worse, because of the purge of the old ideas and old design skills, craftsmanship either faded away or

LEFT: Frank Gehry's Guggenheim Museum in the Spanish city of Bilbao grandly accomplished its task of bringing notoriety and visitors to the city, while presenting an architectural landmark to the world and the history of architecture. Bilbao, Spain, 1997.

RIGHT: The virtuosity of the architect and engineer Santiago Calatrava brought structural technology and artistic finesse to bridges and buildings with the use of tensile forces. Quadracci Pavilion of the Milwaukee Art Museum, Milwaukee, Wisconsin, begun 1995.

LEFT: The architects David Lake and Ted Flato have teamed up to explore, exploit, and finesse the vernacular design idioms of Texas and the latest materials and technology of the Modernist. Lake Austin Residence and Boathouse, 1980.

RIGHT: Fay Jones, a follower of Frank Lloyd Wright, produced in a forest of the Ozark Mountains the ephemeral glass and wood structure Thorncrown Chapel, which has a magic rarely found in man-made objects. Eureka Springs, Arkansas, 1980.

was lost through neglect. I would hold that to derive from tradition is far better than having a cold start from zero. Most of Modernism is as derivative of itself as is Neoclassicism. How could it not be derivative of itself after a hundred years?

The outstanding popular advantage of Modernism was, and is, this: it can be cheap. Cheap proved instantly popular simply because one could use the building construction budget for all sorts of things other than buildings. Profits could soar. The shorter life of cheaper buildings would offer more opportunities to build the New. The cheapness of the Modernist idioms created a boon to developers, bankers, and the construction industry, at least in the short term.

If I sound reactionary here, please know

that I relish the New—certainly in the genius buildings and also in my own efforts. Relating to these ideas personally, I found that I was not a traditionalist at all because I, too, was a maverick. I'm unable to reduce my current thinking to a theory, but I'll share some thoughts of how I personally relate to these issues.

Clearly, I have moved on to a very different view of architecture, a viewpoint different from the intellectual and moral notions of Modernism as well as stylistic extensions into Postmodernism, Deconstruction, Minimalism, and such. Of one of the recent design fads, AIA Gold Medalist Fay Jones said, "I think I'll sit this one out." I agreed. The terms *anachronistic* and *romantic* that once held such negative connotations for us in the era of Sigfried Gideon

have become terms I'm comfortable with, for I've learned to associate them with architecture that has afforded me many delights.

My quest for new old ideas led my wife, Eden, and me to move to a storied eighteenth-century town of central Mexico, San Miguel de Allende. Here they still build in the ways of the eighteenth century or earlier, with artful imagination made cohesive by the complete absence of Modernism. Their architectural protection laws, placed on the center of the city in 1927, have allowed the historic center of San Miguel de Allende to have nothing to do with the architecture or city planning concepts of the twentieth century. The town skipped the nineteenth and twentieth centuries and continues as a charming, romantic, picturesque, scenically beautiful, historically textured, timeless town of nearly seventy thousand. Almost every view in the historic center is a light-filled delight of color and texture, unexpected forms and silhouettes, personal façade decorations, and engaging ground plans, all combined in a heterogeneous mixture that allows one to shop for daily needs without a car and walk only on stone rather than asphalt or concrete. The buildings are no more than two stories and are without side yards or backyards, thus allowing high density. The minimal parking allows it to be a

The architect Ricardo Legorreta, enhancing the simple native forms and saturated colors of Mexico, created the expansive spaces of the Museo de Arte Contemporáneo (MARCO) in Monterrey, Mexico, in 1991.

The architect Rick Joy's Tucson Mountain House fits the land—the slope of the horizon, the verticals of the saguaro cactus, and the building materials that thrive in the desert. West Tucson, Arizona.

Looking from the *zaguán* of this "eighteenth-century house" one would not know that it was handmade by artisans in 1997 using traditional tools and materials of the eighteenth century; no power tools were used. Casa Quebrada, San Miguel de Allende, Mexico. By the author, 1997.

RIGHT: A block away from Casa Quebrada is Casita Blanco, also by the author, which used the same tools, materials, and artisans, together with the idioms of Modernism. San Miguel de Allende, Mexico, 2003.

pedestrian town. Crowded with cars, yes, but still pedestrian. This isn't a place of great beauty like Florence. More populist, it's content to be charming, a place of delightful everyday architecture and intensely human urban form. In addition, its climate and compactness as a historic city allow it to be less energy-dependent. San Miguel de Allende and thousands of towns like it challenge us to rethink our assumptions about appropriate architecture for the future. We shouldn't need to move to a historic town to enjoy a more humane lifestyle and rediscover charm. While the historic areas are becoming

more and more precious because of high demand and limited availability, their example could usefully inspire new towns and the rebuilding of old.

The quest for an appropriate architecture begs to be a major public issue because it affects our quality of life. Fortunately, some key architectural thinkers today are groping with new forms in thrilling ways. Also encouraging is that the students of today are more questioning, and because they are very bright—and perhaps also more immune to the brainwashing of the two previous generations—design may evolve in fruitful ways.

CHAPTER FIVE | HAS ARCHITECTURE LEFT THE BUILDING?

Form follows function.
LOUIS SULLIVAN
(1856–1924)

Form follows finance.
STEVE ROSS
(1957–)

Dear Richard:

You say that "architecture has left the building," and your letter talks about how fulfilling architectural dreams in a meaningful way involves the deepest aspects of society, far beyond the qualities of the individual building. I agree. And you as a fellow architect and, further, as a developer have much at stake in the effectiveness of your investment as well as in the public's reaction to it over time. So if architecture has left the building, how will we get it back?

Thinking beyond the functional needs of the building and beyond the current manner of architectural expression involves serious questions. Bright minds continue to search for answers at drawing boards and computers and in articles, books, seminars, and public forums, far beyond bricks and mortar. It is a lively discussion to join. Buckminster Fuller epitomized such great thinkers and excited audiences everywhere.

In one such forum years ago at which my partner and I were asked to give a talk, we discovered that we would follow Mr. Fuller—about the most humbling experience that could happen to young architects. And this was not only because of his greatness in conceptual thinking and his invention of the geodesic dome, but also because he was known for talking nonstop for three or four hours. To everyone's surprise, that morning he finished within his allotted hour. After the long applause for his brilliance subsided, my partner and I took the stage to present a live multimedia presentation, *Space Is an Illusion*, using two narrators and two projectors to elaborate on concepts of space in nature, in architecture, and in urban life. The audience of three hundred public school art teachers at their 1967 state convention in Dallas was attentive and appreciative. But after we finished, Fuller came over to the two of us and said, "You boys are like crustaceans crawling around on the bottom of the air ocean. You've got to think beyond this. Meet me at my hotel tomorrow at eight for breakfast." That evening we heard one of his legendary four-hour lectures at the Dallas Museum of Fine Arts, during which, in the middle of his talk about energy for movement and lightweight structures for shelter, he asked, "Who is the director of this museum?" When Director Jerry Bywaters stood up, Fuller said, "Sir, how much does your

museum weigh?" No one could answer, but another broad topic had been launched. Our breakfast was yet another thrilling four-hour lecture, this time for just us two, covering the universe and Fuller's manner of addressing the challenges. Agog, we put him on the plane at noon and began to do our best to "think beyond."

Thinking beyond your own project can give you rewarding insights. Think about how your project might affect the quality of life in your community, how it relates to its urban setting, its environment, the traditions of the place, other architecture, its neighbors, its time, its overall sustainability. Even if your own architectural project is as simple as a boathouse, you might enjoy contemplating its features more if you think about what Palladio, Corbu, or Kahn might have done with your project. So before you start to design, step back and consider some of the issues involved in architecture today.

Thinking beyond in the twentieth century resulted in some great architecture: Kahn's Kimbell Museum, Gehry's Bilbao Guggenheim Museum, Utzon's Sydney Opera House, Le Corbusier's Ronchamps Chapel, and Wright's Fallingwater. These, and more, will be known as individual works of major significance as histories are written.

Yet, as you look around, you'll see that most of our urban environment is unattractive and not at all exemplary of the high level of civilization we otherwise enjoy. Our suburban and rural settings are polluted by the thoughtlessness of indiscriminate buildings in the vast areas between the well-designed architecture. To understand the magnitude of the challenges, consider that the total number of buildings we've built is the *gross physical product* of our era, and consider the good architecture to be our *net*. Clearly, our net-to-gross ratio is infinitesimal. Surely we can do better. Please understand, my concern is the scarcity of *good* architecture, not the scarcity of great architecture. Great architecture has always been scarce.

We live in the most advanced civilization in history. Why, then, is most of what we see being built so unsatisfying and inadequate, visually and socially? Developed nations like ours have the technology, the wealth, and the governmental and business mechanisms to build great places to live, work, and play. Why can't our everyday streets and buildings be beautiful? A big reason, beyond cost, is that beauty is out of fashion—we seem to no longer seek it. Why? Only recently did conversations in

Graceful, charming, comfortable, and harmonious, this seating area could be called *anastilo*, without style, and more or less without time. Casita Blanco, by the author, 2003.

architecture schools get beyond function and reason to even mention the concept of beauty. Architects have seemed embarrassed to use the word *beauty*. What's wrong with beauty? It's certainly something amateurs understand. We love beauty in people, we love it in nature, so why not in buildings and cities? Similarly, the words *graceful, charming, comfort,* and *harmony* are rarely heard. Instead, one will hear *social purpose, intervention, function, workable, style,* and *sustainability,* along with many esoteric concepts and just plain jargon. Eventually the intellectualization becomes expressed in concrete.

It would help the amateur and the non-great architect (yes, there are many of us) if we knew how to achieve those time-honored attributes. We need to know how to make beauty, charm, grace, and comfort for our lives with appropriate architecture—to improve the thousands of buildings that lie in the large distances between the rare great buildings.

What's happening? The public streets are scenes used by designers to "make a statement," "make it new," "innovate," and "intervene." These objectives, encouraged in schools of architecture, are inherently different from a harmonious streetscape—cacophonous to the minds of some, glorious in-your-face moral interventions in the eyes of others. To consider this propensity to stand out, I suggest the analogy of the music school. Music students are taught to stand up like a soloist when they play, even though, once out of school, most will sit in the orchestra rather than stand up as soloists. Shouldn't architects, while being taught to be soloists, also learn how to sit down and be part of the orchestra? Let's face it, of the thousands of architecture students in schools today, will we get one great soloist architect per year, or even per decade? Maybe not, so why not focus on the nongreat and the nonarchitect and insist that they learn to sit down and be part of the ensemble, the orchestra?

Ensemble or not, the buildings produced in our economy are cheap buildings with short lives. We are in a culture concerned mainly with business. Private enterprise, which builds most of our buildings, naturally must make a good return on its investment or it's not an investment worth making. The market tends to create many disposable, throwaway buildings. Cities are choked with obsolete buildings that are underutilized, left behind by new buildings seeking to replace them with a more competitive design and a better market position. Are investors expecting too much, too soon? Compared to today, pre–World War II building investments had lower returns, in the short term, from more-expensive, better-built buildings, having put more resources into quality design and construction. This raises questions like: Can building budgets include quality-of-life issues and still be profitable enough to merit investment? Does "beauty"—or, if you like, "high visual quality"—subtract from or add to profitable returns? If good architecture isn't valued in the marketplace, is the marketplace the absolute arbiter for the quality of our lives? The dilemma is that we want both a good market and good architecture.

Most of the architectural profession serves a clientele that builds large commercial buildings, high-rise buildings, and institutional buildings, but very few residences. The profession is rarely asked to participate in the design of ordinary buildings, commercial strips, big-box retail, or any kind of housing, regardless of price. Even multimillion-dollar residences built for the speculative market are usually built without the aid of an architect—or with the aid of a licensed architect only to "draw it up" for building permit purposes. What are our aspirations?

Why is the use of the profession so limited in these buildings? One reason is that the cost of professional architectural services is one item that can be omitted from the building costs; construction drawings can be made somewhere in the building industry where architecture isn't an objective. Another reason is the profession's isolation from the rest of the building industry. Design services can be offered through the building contractor at a financial advantage. Our tradition of professional service doesn't like the idea of packaging services with the contractor, citing the obvious conflict of interest in managing the construction. Yet what we give up in so doing is the opportunity to put a higher value on architectural services when we join a team with contractors to produce a well-designed and well-constructed product. Many countries place the design and construction tasks in the same organization. Both building contractors and architects could benefit from this manner of doing business.

Though it's often not realized, the cost

of design is almost insignificant compared to the cost of construction, furnishings, debt service, taxes, operating budgets, building maintenance, and utility costs over the years. If beauty is so cheap, why do most building developers abandon it to save an infinitesimal amount of cost by not engaging architects? Is it arrogance or ignorance? We notice that highly success-ful developers like Gerald Hines of Hous-ton are wise enough to hire the world's best architects to design large speculative buildings that receive a market advantage by being of good design. Such developers benefit the community as well as their own profit line.

The barriers to good design go beyond cost and are seemingly infinite: the regula-tory challenges, the financial challenges, the societal challenges, the engineering challenges, the sustainability challenges, and the multitude of other design chal-lenges. The game is to win one challenge at a time.

Amateurs (remember, amateurs are those who love) can encourage investment in good building and good community with public and private dollars as well as by investing their attention as individuals. Proposed new public buildings deserve massive input from concerned citizens. New public buildings are an expression of the community, so the selection of the architect requires its input and oversight. Excellence in design is a matter of pride, a matter of aesthetic responsibility, that shares importance with our social and political responsibilities. To assist the objective of aesthetic responsibility, the reintroduction of art programs in the ele-mentary and secondary schools could help, and—more radical still—we could include exposure to the art of architecture in public schools if we think that is an important part of our lives.

The architecture where people live, work, or just hang out comprises an art form in which I like to walk around: the architecture of the city, a college campus, a sixteenth-century village, and any place that has been made wonderful by design. My thinking beyond doesn't reach as far as Buckminster Fuller's; he was probably thinking beyond Mars.

Communal open spaces offer a place to walk, meet friends, and have events. West Mall, University of Texas at Austin.

PART TWO | THE GROUND FLOOR

The bitterness of poor quality is remembered long after the sweetness of the cheapest price is forgotten.
ANON.

Dear Thomas,

Of the three choices you have in making architecture—hire an architect, become an architect, or learn to think like an architect—the most assured choice is working with an architect. As chairman of the building committee you described, you have, I'm sure, many questions. How do you choose an architect? What does it cost? What services are provided? How do you work with an architect? What do you gain?

Choosing an architect is in many ways the same as choosing other professionals, such as your doctor, lawyer, or accountant. You have seen or heard that their work is of the quality you seek, that they have a good reputation, or that there is an individual in the firm that you would trust with your project.

In other ways, though, the selection of an architect is quite different. This relationship is personal and often intense. You will share your dreams and hopes for the building that will ultimately emerge; you will share how you live and want to live (if this is a house for yourself), or how to achieve your particular goals in an institutional or commercial building. You are also looking for a personality that would work well with yours.

The professional and artistic quality you seek has the capability to bring to your project the *commodity, firmness,* and *delight* of the Vitruvian triad—that is, functional workability, structural and mechanical soundness, and delight of the senses. Plus, you want it completed it on schedule and within your budget. The choice of architect will come with investigating, assessing, and reaching a consensus on the decision with your partner, committee members, or board members.

You want an architect who is a good listener and pays attention to the details of your needs and desires. But because you want the architect to make architecture, not just build at your direction like some draftsman, he or she must have the design latitude that is essential to the project's architectural success. The client and architect work together.

To illustrate, let me share a story. Once when working on a house with an experienced and architecturally astute client, I designed what seemed like a wonderful abstraction of geometric form in an ideal landscape. It was so perfect that I worried about my being overbearing in forcing functions into this idealized architectural form, so I asked for a meeting with the cli-

ent. I had an agenda of seven proposals, each listing one or more ways in which I was prepared to give ground and let the building function a bit better even though it would compromise the architecture. But the client smilingly dismissed each of my seven proposals, proclaiming, "Client, 7; Architect, 0!", allowing it to be a much better building—based, in this instance, on subordinating Vitruvian commodity to delight. The client was smart enough to see that he was sacrificing only a minor functionality but gaining a major delight. This was yet another proof of the axiom, "The architecture is only as good as the client."

Another reason the selection of an architect requires care is that your relationship may last for years. You will probably spend more time with your architect than you will ever spend with your doctor, lawyer, or accountant. As an architect, I have worked with some clients as long as fifteen years through many projects.

From the architect's perspective, I tried to become known to clients with whom I wanted to work, knowing likewise that those prospective clients were looking for architects with whom they would like to work. Toward that end, in the early days, my partner and I would go to a concert and, at intermission, race down four floors from cheap balcony seats to say hello to prospective clients in the main lobby. We saw the clients we sought regularly, and it eventually worked.

Most selection decisions involve interviews, which are often competitive and intense because the client is seeking someone to trust with spending sometimes millions of dollars and the architect is trying no less seriously to get the commission. Both parties seek a good fit through being open about needs, qualifications, and budgets.

Before starting the selection process, you will have formed a general idea of what you want to build, its purpose, and where you want to build it. You will be well advised to keep an open mind rather than be too specific because, as you progress, you will be getting new information about the sort of building you are doing and the nature of its construction. The architect will have the education and, usually, broad experience upon which to base artistic and professional opinions. At the same time, your role as client comes from a different set of experiences and is equally critical to the quality and effectiveness of the building. Both roles will set the "chemistry" of the relationship, and you will become partners in the realization of the project. The construction contractor, the third major member of the team, usually comes later.

Forming your general ideas into specific requirements is the predesign process of *programming*—perhaps the most important set of decisions you will make. In a complex building, programming can be done either by the architect or by a separate professional. Either one will help you decide what kind of space is actually needed, how the parts relate to each other, and what the mission of the facility should be, and will thereby define the project before beginning the design. In a complex institutional or business facility, the program often benefits from the services of a professional programmer working with your staff and leadership to assess your needs and intentions.

In the case of an income-producing project, programming will work with a business pro-forma. The architect will work through the program in more detail and elaborate on the specifics. The objective is to make major decisions before construction begins rather than after.

An individual designing a house or an entrepreneur planning a commercial project is far different from a board of directors of an institution seeking to build a museum or hospital with public funds. Yet in all cases there will be a personal relationship between architect and client. As projects get more complex, the makeup of the architect's organization and his or her team of consultants must be defined, as well as the complexities of the client's building committee and staff, and perhaps adjusted for an effective working arrangement.

The actual selection process takes several forms. The simplest is to select three to five architects with the best information you can find and begin talking with them about your project. Ask those architects who still interest you to take you on a tour of their projects and introduce you to their clients. Look for how they actually solved a particular client's building program, how successful the client thinks it was, and how comfortable you yourself feel with the final product. Find out how well it fit the budget and the time schedule. Ask yourself if you would be enthusiastic about going through this long process with this particular architect. Talk about fee arrangements. Make sure that you have looked at enough architects to feel that you can make a good decision. Then get started.

In a large public project, about the same thing happens as with a board of directors but with a more inclusive search, more transparency, and more attention to the public responsibility. The first step is to appoint a selection committee whose task will be to interview and recommend to the board a first, second, and third choice. The selection committee might include major donors, political representatives, building professionals, and knowledgeable architects who will not be considered for the job, or a hired architectural consultant who can recommend candidates and comment on those being considered. The consultant might be a respected retired architect or a local architecture professor who is knowledgeable about the particular kind of project.

If you are selecting an architect when public funds are involved, you must send out a Request for Qualifications (RFQ) to the profession at large in an appropriate publication so that all interested and qualified architects will have a chance to be considered. The committee or its consultant will recommend a broad list of architects to be contacted and sent an RFQ. Because the most respected architects get many RFQ's and their response can cost thousands of dollars, the most desired architects may have to be courted by the committee to encourage their response; personal contacts may be necessary in order to get them sufficiently interested in the project to submit an RFQ. The architects who respond to the RFQ and appear qualified are then reviewed. The review, best done by the entire committee, may involve a hundred portfolios on an important project. Each

member ranks a firm, and the group decides how to arrive at a list of ten or twelve for further discussion. Firms are eliminated one by one in this discussion, and a group of three to five is decided upon for further review. Those three or five are often invited to come to the committee and the site and present themselves along with their objectives in the project, their ideas about the project, and their team of consultants. It is unwise to ask the architects for other than verbal ideas at this time because they will not know enough about your project to present a well-informed sketch or a mode—that would be premature, before they have an understanding of the project, the site, and your intentions. A further committee deliberation may lead to two or three architects whose offices as well as some of their most recent projects and clients should be visited. A detailed review of exactly who in their office will be working on the project, the fee arrangements, the actual consulting firms and their qualifications, time schedules, and details of communication can then be discussed before making a final decision and signing an agreement.

The simplest way is for an individual entrepreneur to decide on an architect and simply get to work. And that's the way most of my own projects began.

The most complex way involves a design competition, which is open to all architects and which follows specific AIA procedures. The competition is conducted under the auspices of a professional advisor, who will (1) lay out the procedures for the competition, including the design program, (2) select the jury who will evaluate the designs submitted, (3) address questions, and (4) receive final proposals. The jury, not the client, determines the winning design, though the jury might include a representative of the client. The architect of the chosen design is awarded a cash prize or the commission to do the project or both. Some competitions are open to all and some to invited architects only. An expensive process, the design competition is more popular in Europe than in the United States. The risk is that the winning architect may not be the best one to serve the client; the advantage is that young, as well as established, architects may present concepts exceeding all expectations.

When my partner and I entered our first international design competition in 1957, it was one of the first postwar design competitions circulated in the United States. The Enrico Fermi Memorial Plaza in Chicago was to be judged by a jury of significant figures of the twentieth century: Ludwig Mies van der Rohe, Gordon Bunshaft, Jose Luis Sert, Pier Luigi Nervi, and Lancelot White. We entered the competition because we were eager to know what these great men thought of what we might do. Joining with Joanne Pratt as sculptor, we managed to win the second prize and Recognition of the Jury, among 355 entries from 25 countries—with publication to follow in important journals. It was a thrilling win and also a huge encouragement to think that we might be going places. Soon we entered another competition, this one to design a neighborhood, the Better Living for Middle Income Families Design Competition, sponsored by Matico, Inc., in 1959; the chairman of the jury was the distinguished architect and dean of MIT, Pietro Belluschi. We won the Grand Prize of $10,000, considerable recognition, and commissions to plan neighborhoods in Virginia and Kentucky. When, a decade later, we felt that the Downtown St. Louis Urban Design Competition was right up our alley, we spent months working on designing the progression from the Gateway Arch at the Mississippi River through downtown to Union Station and the Carl Miles Sculpture Garden. All three of us partners went to St. Louis for several days to study the place. The competition, which, alas, we didn't win, cost us each at least a month's salary, proof that such competitions can be expensive for all parties.

Another consideration in complex

International Design Competition for the design of an urban plaza commemorating Enrico Fermi, Nobel Laureate, who developed the first nuclear reactor. Chicago, Illinois, Second Place Entry of James Pratt, Joanne Pratt, and Hal Box, 1957.

building projects is that they involve a team of specialists, sometimes in-house within the architect's office, but more often independent consultants working within a specialty with many different architects. The consultants may include specialists in urban design, traffic, site design, foundation, structure, energy and water conservation, plumbing, lighting, acoustics, food service, elevators, building code, fire protection, security, interior design, landscape, heating, ventilating, and air conditioning (HVAC), as well as building-type specialists for hospitals, sports facilities, and airports. It should be clear in your agreement when and if these services will be needed and who will pay for them.

What will your architect's services cost? The extent of the service, the building type, and the fees of individual firms will be the key determinants. The simplest fee basis is a *cost plus a multiple of direct expense* agreement whereby the principals of the firm and its employees are billed to the client at cost plus a multiplier—2.0 to 3.0 times being typical. This kind of agreement can be for a few hours of consultation or an ongoing open-ended agreement that is billed monthly. I've had some such arrangements last for years through many projects without negotiating a new contract for each service.

A fee based on a percentage of construction cost is the traditional basis for full service, beginning with the initial predesign phase through the final construction phase, with monthly statements upon the completion of each phase of work. Percentage fees are definite; the only change would be if the scope of the work changed

and the architect were required to repeat phases that had already been completed. The fees vary. For institutional work, the typical fee is 6 percent of the construction cost up to 10 percent for technical projects like hospitals or the intricacies of remodeling. Fees for commercial work are much less and vary with the building type. Fees for full services on a residence will be at least 12 percent of construction cost, and some of the better architects will require an 18 percent fee. Lump-sum contracts for the architect's services are sometimes used when the project is well defined. The most common form of contract is the most recent edition of the appropriate contract in the American Institute of Architects' series of contracts.

The owner usually has the responsibility of providing the technical information on the site: a legal description of the site with boundary stakes in the ground; a topographic site plan showing the location of trees and other features, including utility entry points; and a subsurface soils and foundation survey.

The work progresses in phases. The Predesign Phase may include the programming mentioned above as well as visiting similar building types around the country to inform client and architect. When designing a hotel, I was privileged to explore with my client some of the best hotels and restaurants in the United States. When selecting a museum architect, our committee traveled around the country to learn about museums, their architects, and the opinions of clients. In some situations architects travel abroad with their clients, both of them seeking knowledge and inspiration from the great architecture. The architect you select should be well traveled and be able to tell you of the important precedents that can inform the design of your project. Once a good understanding of the program and intentions has been reached, the formal phases of the work proceed, after Predesign and Programming, in this order: Schematic Design, Design Development, Construction Documentation, Bidding and Negotiating of Construction Contracts, and Construction Administration.

In the Schematic Design Phase, the architect outlines the parameters of the project while working with consultants on structure, mechanical, landscape, interiors, and with other specialists. He or she brings the functional elements into an efficient arrangement and begins to determine the character of the spaces and the relationship to the site. The basic organizational and architectural decisions will be made in this phase. Sometimes it will take many trials; sometimes it will happen on the first try. The process should not be rushed because both architect and client need to be satisfied before proceeding, and to achieve this, the architect may want to make several other trial designs to ensure that the best one is developed. At this stage the architect can usually work as fast as the client can make decisions. The schematic design determines how big the building will be, what its arrangement of functions will be, and how it will relate to the site; it will give an idea of what its spaces and character will be and a preliminary estimate of cost based on square footage and type of construction. It is only a schematic design,

but it should be a design that will ensure a wonderful design in the next phase. Schematic Design comprises 15 percent or sometimes more of the design team's work and compensation. When the client decides that the architect's schematic design is what is to be built, and preliminary cost estimates are made and approved, the design can proceed to the next phase for further development.

The Design Development Phase is exactly what it says: it's the development of the design in all its detail, in every room and every exterior surface. Design decisions will have been made on all spaces— their materials, lighting, heating and air conditioning, sound, energy consumption, and other building systems. The consultants are all reinvolved in the design team to confirm and adjust the many systems involved in the building. This phase of the work is mainly internal to the architect's design team because this is where they hammer out the intricacies of the building systems. Design studies of all parts of the building will be made, examined, and tied together into a whole. The client will want to check the progress; the architect will want to get detailed questions answered by the client. There may be preliminary viewing of the design as it is taking place. At the end of this phase, about 35 percent of the design team's work has been completed. When the client approves the Design Development documents and the preliminary estimate of cost, signing off on both, the project can proceed into the next phase: preparation of detailed designs, drawings, and specifications for use in estimating, bidding, and construction.

The Construction Documents Phase describes the design in terms that can be understood by the contractors and subcontractors who will be building the building. These drawings and specifications define precise forms and proportions, materials and methods of construction, individual pieces of mechanical, electrical, and plumbing equipment and their systems. These documents form the basis for the contract between the owner-client and the general contractor. At this point, about 80 percent of the architect's work is completed.

In the Bidding and Negotiating Phase the most appropriate general contractor is selected, and costs and conditions are agreed upon in legal documents: the plans, specifications, general conditions, and contract between owner and contractor being the four elements of the contract to be agreed upon. The general contractor may be selected by putting the project out for competitive bids either to a selected group of contractors or to all contractors, as would be the case in a public project. The lowest qualified bidder is carefully considered along with other low bidders. (A small spread between the high bid and the low bid indicates the contractors' thoroughness in preparation of the bids that have been assimilated from many suppliers and subcontractors. It also measures the clarity of the architect's documents that are bid upon.) In a public job, the contract will go to the low bidder unless there is good cause for change. Before an award is made, the owners will want to investigate the contractor, satisfying themselves that they are

willing to go forward by talking to previous owners and architects for whom the contractor has worked and by examining the contractor's financial condition. Actual construction costs can be determined only by the contractor agreeing to build the building for a specific cost; architects, engineers, and estimators obviously cannot guarantee a price. The construction cost will vary according to what is happening in the economy, the variable cost in labor and material, and the local competition in building activity at the time of bidding.

Another arrangement for selecting a contractor is to make the selection early in the project, based on the merits of the contractor. The advantage here is that you can get his or her expert opinions and cost esti-

Brick, concrete, and wood construction in progress. Marsh House, by author, 1978.

mates during the design phases, then negotiate a price when the documents are completed.

The contracts for construction can be a lump-sum "turnkey" price for the work described in the documents, where the contractor takes the risk and changes are handled by change order. Or the agreement can be the actual cost plus a fee, preferably fixed rather than a percentage, so that the fee doesn't escalate with the construction cost. I have had good experience with both types of selection and both types of contracts because of the care taken in qualifying the contractors who might be interested in doing the job. All communities have some contractors that are better than others, and to get those contractors sometimes requires lobbying them and fitting into their work schedule. Taking a low bid from a marginal contractor and expecting that you can simply require that the work be done right and in accord with the plans can lead to big frustrations and expense. Low bidders can be what we call "change-order artists," who make up for their low bid with change orders.

In making decisions on cost, know that the most expensive thing you can buy is something you don't want.

The construction phase is messy, changeable, dangerous, complex, and exciting. Anything can happen, beginning with the excavations and foundations, where one might unexpectedly find hard rock, soft soil, historic artifacts, or water, any of which will often require revisions and consume time. And all the way through the job one can expect the unexpected and can also

respond in a way that improves the design of the building rather than detracts from it. This is why it's good to have the architect on hand during construction. Example: I once worked with a contractor who told me that he would do anything to save the client money, irrespective of my design. I agreed, with the proviso that he let me work on the problem before making the change. He agreed, and an excellent working relationship lasted through five large building projects, because when he presented me with an opportunity to save money, I improved it from a design point of view and usually saved more than he had expected. This is the way architect and contractor can have a beneficial relationship rather than an adversarial one, for both their own interests and the owner's. The client-owner will also be involved in those decisions and always when there is a change in cost requiring a change order.

Taking shape on the ground and in the sky, the spaces of the building and its views will come into a much clearer reality than on plans or models. It will be exciting. Rare is the project that will go straight through without changes. Changes offer an opportunity to make small adjustments that make it better. When such adjustments appear to be beneficial, ask the contractor to give you a proposal for the cost of such a change. The contractor's saying "It's too much" is not really an answer because the contractor doesn't know how much you think would be "too much" for this particular improvement. Get the numbers and then make a decision. There will be thousands of these decisions to be handled by you or your representative, so my advice is to enjoy them.

To enjoy the construction process more, you can ease the financial stress by having personal or corporate contingency funds in addition to the contingencies that might be in the contract. In that way, you can take advantage of opportunities that arise or resolve problems that are encountered. Five percent of the construction cost is appropriate for that extra contingency.

There is much to admire on a construction job. Compliments encourage the good workmanship you seek. Building architecture in a personal way means making many visits to the site. When finish work is being done, whether in wood, stone, tile, or glass, watching the individual craftsmen can ensure the quality of finish. When a new craftsman comes on the job, watch his work for a day or two, and if it isn't good enough, dismiss him. On only three occasions have I had to have a workman replaced, but the big one was when I removed an inept superintendent of construction on a five-building school complex. His replacement arrived the next morning—red-faced, late, and hungover. I asked his name, and he said, "John Smith." What was your last job? He said, "I just got out of the army." Had I made a big mistake? I couldn't visit the job until two days later, but when I did, I saw a new small building that had nothing to do with the plans. I yelled, "What's that?" He said, "That's my office." It was complete with phones, electricity, and air conditioning, all built in two days, and it even included a place for me. I was both impressed and confused, but it turned out beautifully. John Smith was the best superintendent I ever knew—a true miracle worker. He had been an Army Corps of Engineers master sergeant and ran the construction in that manner, treating me as his commanding officer. He went on to become a general contractor of large commercial projects around the United States. When he unexpectedly appeared at my university office ten years later in a handsome suit, he had become a vice president and member of the board of one of the nation's largest corporations! So much for first impressions.

Change orders will be requested by the owner, architect, or contractor, priced by the contractor for cost and time delay, then reviewed by the architect and presented to the owner for approval. Contractors will need to make a monthly or weekly draw on the construction account in order to meet their payroll and their subcontractors' charges. Your important hold on this operation is that you stipulate, and AIA contracts *do* stipulate, that the owner retains 10 percent of each payment until the satisfactory completion of the project. It's important to have a signed release from all the subcontractors before final payment.

Ensure that the general contractor also retains 10 percent from all of the subcontractors. This 10 percent will be their motivation for finishing the job satisfactorily. The retainage helps you get your project to final completion with good craftsmanship and on time.

Completion requires that all of the conditions of the contract be met. This one-of-a-kind project, with lots of variables, using many building crafts, is nothing like Dell making you a perfect computer within hours of your order.

There are shortcuts to this process, such as going to a design-build company and telling them what you want and how much you want to spend. This kind of service has extreme variations in quality of design and construction. Most popular are the quick and cheap alternatives that have nothing to do with architecture. In the case of a residence, a home builder might modify a standard plan and call it "custom." This is, in fact, the way most buildings happen. However, a design-build process can be in the time-honored manner of building in which the architect builds what he or she has designed and produces extraordinary results for the client. This kind of professional service is standard in other countries. Recent AIA contracts have been refined to make clear distinctions in roles that eliminate conflicts of interest between the architect-builder and the client-owner, making this an attractive and efficient method of making architecture.

The many specific details to be completed, or redone, before the project is complete are noted in a "punch list," the device that owners, architects, and contractors use to complete all the details of the project before final payment is made and the retainer is paid to the contractor and subcontractors. Making punch lists and crossing off the completed items marks the final stage of the project—painters are touching up; electricians are checking out lighting; in fact, almost every trade will be coming in to finish its work. When the contract is complete, the general contractor turns the project over to the owner. With the construction crews off of the site, the landscape and interior furnishings and equipment installation can begin.

The landscape and interior designers have been working during the construction, usually under separate contracts, and have been involved with the architect in the design process from the beginning. The client will have been working closely with these specialists as the building finally comes together and is ready to function. At this point, the furnishings become more important than the building. Then it's all integrated when each space is comfortable for each user. Installation of electronic equipment, art, special facilities, and such may take weeks—with even more decisions to be made by the client-owner.

After the building is completed and shaped into its best form, you should have architectural photographs made of both exteriors and interiors. There are two reasons: first, the client and the architect can offer them for publication if desired; and second, the architect needs a record of the work because it will change over time through remodeling and will no longer represent his or her work. The architecture will simply become real estate on the market, to be remodeled in unexpected ways, and the only record may be in photographs.

One last suggestion: have a grand opening event to celebrate everyone's accomplishment and enjoy your new building!

CHAPTER SEVEN | BECOMING AN ARCHITECT

This generation should prepare broadly—
for more than one career, perhaps as many
as four.
HENRY CISNEROS
(1947–)

Dear Amelia,

"What's it like to be an architect?" you
ask.

Your entry into architecture school is
part of your dream and you have chosen a
great school. For others who are about to
build, becoming an architect is the second
and most dramatic choice in their effort to
make architecture rather than just a
building.

The sheer joy of being an architect
comes from the way you feel in your head
and gut when you are being creative, when
you solve a complex problem with clarity,
making something happen that's better
than you thought it could be. Or when you
feel yourself applying hard-earned knowledge from study, travel, and experience to
the creative process and you approach the

edge of beauty. Or when you arrive at your construction site early in the morning and feel goosebumps.

The dream of becoming an architect seems to be deep-seated. Mine was realized with an early decision. Most people don't let themselves even consider becoming an architect because they imagine such a career to be unrealistic for them. They tell me, "I'm bad at math" or "I can't draw" or "It would take too long" or "I wouldn't make enough money." I'd answer with the following, in order: "There's actually little math involved"; "You can be taught how to draw"; "The formal schooling is five to seven years"; "The financial rewards vary significantly—some architects drive Porsches, some drive pickups. I've driven both."

Others think about the long education and never do it. Still others start architecture school in their thirties or forties. Philip Johnson, one of the legendary architects of the twentieth century, was a successful museum curator before setting off for architecture school in his midthirties. Andrea Paladio, perhaps the most copied architect in history, was a stonemason until, at age forty-two, he called himself an architect. Filippo Brunelleschi, who led architecture into the Renaissance, had been a goldsmith.

Some of the best students I can remember started in their late thirties. Some who make a career change want to be professionals; others want an education in architecture to pursue careers in historic preservation, urban design, sustainable development, or environmental issues— or perhaps even doctoral studies in architectural history and theory. Many schools have degree programs in these specialties without the long training required to become a practicing architect. For example, you will find that some universities now offer undergraduate and graduate degrees in Architectural Studies in which limited amounts of technology, drawing, and design are required. These programs focus on architectural history and theory, specialized issues, and two or three years of design study. Because these students are smart and come from varying backgrounds, they help create an exciting intellectual milieu in the school. In the field, they create a better architecture by preserving good architecture of the past and helping to design more humane cities while working in roles as consultants or as community leaders and in public office. Being passionate and educated, they can be extremely effective.

To explore a career change or choice, consider enrolling in such programs as the Career Discovery Program at Harvard, or the Summer Academy at the University of Texas, or others listed at www.aia.org. If you are making a career change, look for the program that best fits your needs in a city where you would like to live for a while.

The probability of success in architecture school is not easy to measure because architecture requires so many aptitudes and talents. And after exploring the field, many students decide to seek another career instead. For instance, among famous actors there is Jimmy Stewart, who graduated from the architecture school at Princeton, James Mason, who studied architecture at Cambridge, and John Denver, who studied architecture at Texas Tech.

Architecture, being the domain of the generalist, doesn't have a special entrance exam like the LSAT or GMAT, which supposedly gauges an applicant's likely success in law or business school. Only one deficiency completely inhibits a person from understanding architecture: poor spatial perception. The three-dimensional aspects of architecture are the heart of the matter, and if abstract space cannot be perceived, architecture cannot be conceived. Math is used mainly to understand physical principles and for its elegant lessons in logic. You don't have to be good at drawing because architecture school will teach you how to draw adequately if not beautifully. I've learned how to draw four times—first in architecture school, then again when starting a practice, then again when starting my one-man office after heading a large firm where others drew for me, and the last time, when my design students felt so insecure in their drawing skills that they insisted I learn to draw again so I could teach them! However, drawing improves seeing, and drawing in the form of sketching is the key to visualization. The more facile one is in such sketching, the better.

Parents ask me how their aspiring high school student might best prepare for architecture school. I suggest a good general education; a start in a second language so as to explore other cultures, enough high school math and physics to handle introductory college courses, experiences in freehand drawing, and, most important, extensive travel. It helps to visit with several architects you know or can be introduced to, to see what their lives are like, what they do in their offices, and, if possible, to follow them around for a day or so to learn what their world is like. If you are really lucky, you may find a mentor who will guide you in school and beyond.

Almost everyone enjoys architecture school even though it's known to be a strenuous course of study. The two most important ingredients for success in school seem to be high intelligence and enthusiasm for the crushing thrill of the work involved. Fortunately, it's fun; if it's not fun for you, don't do it.

Students practically live in the studios—drawing, building models, and learning from each other while making lasting friendships. It's seductive and consuming. Those who don't feel jazzed by it feel distinctly out of place and drop out quickly. My first impression of architecture

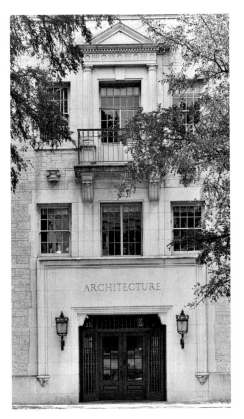

North portal of the School of Architecture, University of Texas at Austin. Paul Cret, 1936.

school was shock upon seeing the lobby of the architecture building filled with huge watercolor drawings of beautiful buildings by the year's top students. I had no idea that architects did that, and I was sure that I couldn't do anything like that. But when I visited the school soon after graduation, I saw my thesis in the same lobby.

In choosing an architecture school, look at the student work, the backgrounds of the faculty, the studio and support facilities, the library, the administration, the curriculum of the particular degree you want, and the city, since you'll be living there for a while. Explore *CollegeBoard.com* for information. It seems that every school, even the less prominent ones, have a few really good students. Because a school is only as good as its students, one gauge of a school is "How good is the weakest student, and how fantastic is the best student?"

There are now 114 architecture schools in the United States. But back in 1971, Dallas/Fort Worth was the largest urban area in the United States without a school of architecture. That soon changed. In an unexpected telephone call I received one evening, Dean Charles Green of the University of Texas at Arlington asked, "Would you consider coming out here and starting an architecture school?" I asked him to say that again because I thought he must think he's talking to someone else. After he assured me that I'd heard him correctly, I asked, "Why me?" He said, "We've read your comments in the news about the need for a school. You have a good reputation as an architect, and we think you can make an architecture school here." I told him I'd

never thought of being an academic—I didn't even have a graduate degree. He asked me to think about it. But at the time, I was three years deep into the most exciting project of my life, so I called back after a week to say that I appreciated the opportunity but I couldn't do it. A few weeks after that, my clients unexpectedly sold the big project and I was up in the air. When Dean Green called again with the same question, I said that I would come out and talk about it.

Thus I entered academe as a tenured professor and dean of what would become a new architecture school. I was on an exciting but steep learning curve, writing course descriptions, the curricula for architecture and four other environmental design degrees, hiring the faculty and staff, remodeling buildings for space, and starting a library. Five years later, with a great deal of help from local architects and engineers, we had produced an accredited school of architecture and our first graduates.

Having completed that mission, I was then asked to be dean of architecture at my alma mater, the University of Texas at Austin, in 1976 and assigned the charge of rebuilding the school. I made a full commitment there and enjoyed the next twenty-two years amid an extraordinary group of colleagues, students, and ideas.

Degree programs in architecture started at universities in the United States in the late nineteenth century: MIT in 1866, Harvard in 1895, the University of Texas in 1909. Some architecture schools started within a college of Engineering, some in a college of Fine Arts, and some in graduate schools; most programs evolved eventually into independent schools within their universities, many also offering education in the related disciplines of city planning, landscape architecture, interior design, other design specializations, and construction.

Degree programs are structured in several ways. If you also have a degree in another area, you typically start in a graduate program that could be completed in about three years. If you're just starting college, the odds are you will do a four-year undergraduate degree followed by a two-year graduate degree. But you may get a baccalaureate degree in another area first and then go to a graduate architecture program. Or another choice is the long-standing five-year undergraduate professional degree that could be followed by a graduate degree. Course work includes Design, Drawing, Architectural History and Theory, Structures, Environmental Controls, Construction, and Professional Practice, plus a thorough liberal arts experience. Around 60 percent of the students are men and 40 percent are women—up from just 3 percent women in the 1940s. A college freshman anxious to get into architec-

Design studio in the School of Architecture, University of Texas at Austin.

ture can plunge right into architecture school with enthusiasm, but many freshmen take a little longer to decide, so they start out in liberal arts and benefit from a broader education and more campus life before committing to a professional program.

Students from all disciplines can succeed in architecture school. Musicians and literature majors stand out as some of the biggest stars that I remember. Science and engineering majors, though seemingly well prepared for architecture, often require an adjustment to a teaching method that is far more subjective than their familiar objective processes. Students with a mechanical drawing background or digital expertise can often draw faster than they can design well.

The teaching method for design and drawing differs from most disciplines. We use a one-on-one discussion of the student's work, similar to teaching in a music or art school. One who has difficulty with the process of criticism may experience limited progress in the study of design. It's the special and personal way we teach and learn, which is of course rare in the large universities of today. Small classes and daily personal contact with the professor in the studio and on field trips create a healthy learning environment. On one such field trip to see the work of a famous architect, a student asked, "Can you teach me to think like that?"

Life revolves around the design studio, where about fifteen students each have their own workspace, usually with computers. Because studio classes last fifteen hours a week all semester, studio life becomes the ecosystem of the school. Students live in the studios literally day and night when a project nears completion. I would sometimes go by the school to find my entire class working in the studio at midnight, high on the intensity and endurance of the "charrette," smelling of pizza, and having a good time.

The phenomenon of the charrette comes from the tradition of the Ecole des Beaux-Arts in Paris, the most important architecture school of the early twentieth century, where students lived and did their work in little apartments all over Paris. As the story goes, a horse-drawn cart—in French *charrette*—was used to go around to the students' residences and pick up their drawings. The drawings had to be quickly put on the charrette, and if the project wasn't finished, the student would jump on the cart and try to finish the project while wobbling down the cobblestone streets to the waiting jury of professors. *Charrette* has thus come to mean an intense effort over a period of time, like twenty-four to forty-eight hours, during which one goes without sleeping and one's mental and artistic abilities are concentrated into a creativity machine more effective than one ever could imagine. It is a great "high," a great feeling—one that my partners and I continued to experience as professionals, when, in an overnight charrettte, it was the only time that we played music—usually Verdi's gorgeous *Requiem*, over and over—until the project was finished and we had given Verdi a cha-cha beat. You can tell that most architects enjoy studio life and the charrette.

Let me tell you about Anna. I don't know how she got into graduate school, but when I met Anna in her first week, struggling at her drawing board, and asked if I could help, she said, "I do need help! Until last week I was an emergency room nurse." I noticed that her drawings were scratches, clearly her first try—and also that she was pregnant. How could she handle these classes? Young Professor Refuerzo demanded that every student in Anna's class make an A—and insisted that they earn it, too! So, somehow, by semester's end Anna had learned to draw, and by her third semester she had become so skillful that I had her teach a drawing class. Being a single parent, Anna brought her baby boy to the studio, where he took his naps in a neat little bed made between the rungs under her drawing table. After six semesters, when Anna had become one of the best designers in the entire school, I proudly brought our guest, the famous architect Bill Caudill, to see her work after his all-school lecture. Her design studio was a grand room designed in 1916 by Cass Gilbert, the architect of the Supreme Court Building in Washington, D.C. It was around 10 p.m. We found the great room full of students, cardboard models, stacks of tracing paper, coffee, and rock 'n' roll. They were clearly embarked on an all-night charrette. As Caudill and I were admiring the imaginative drawings on Anna's table, a smiling little face looked up from his bed and said, "Hi!" Her son, now age three, got a big hug from us, then walked around the studio to kiss all the students in the class goodnight, as he had done for as long as he could remember.

Even life outside the studio is intense

Students present their projects to faculty and visiting critics for review.

because architecture dominates so many discussions. Most schools have a lecture series of visiting architects and scholars several times a month; a vital school will have several each week. An ad hoc noontime forum in a packed seminar room may become the hottest venue for discussion. One forum may invite faculty and guests to explain their formal work. Another forum may invite a scholar to present a topic they are working on but haven't yet resolved. (These are often the best forums and can go on for hours.) A variety of architectural exhibitions and guest lecturers offer new ideas and create vitality around the school.

Eventually, graduation happens! Whether it's a boom or bust economy, or even if the world is at war, students graduate and expect to enter their profession. My early mentors graduated into the Depression or into World War II. I myself graduated into the Korean War; others after me graduated into Vietnam or into economic booms or recessions. A placement director I once knew called it "graduation bingo." As students graduated around the millen-

nium, they enjoyed so many opportunities that recruiters were offering hiring bonuses. Because the architecture profession plans new construction, it has been a bellwether of the nation's economy. It's one of the first indicators of decline in business activity at the beginning of a major recession and also one of the first indicators of an economic upturn.

The awkward gap between school and practice—the ideal and the real—is often bridged by the opportunity to work in an architect's office while in school. My first such opportunity came in 1948, when I had decided to skip summer school for a job as a musician. Instead, I received one of those life-changing phone calls. The caller said his name was O'Neil Ford, that he needed someone who could draw, and would I like to come work for him. I had never heard of Ford, but he was an architect and that's what I wanted to be, so off I went to his office in San Antonio. But this was no ordinary office. This was a large spread on the San Antonio River next to the historic eighteenth-century San Jose Mission, with a group of old stone houses, workshops, and barns forming a large courtyard. Outside were peacocks, guinea hens, chickens, dogs, and little children along with a collection of period automobiles in various states of repair. It was the magical world of Willow Way, where Neil and his family lived and worked and also where we draftsmen lived, next door to the drafting room. We were being shaped in quite a different way than we would have been in a corporate office in Manhattan.

My next training came in the last two years of school with another of the region's first Modernist architects, Charles Granger, who had trained with both Richard Neutra and Eero Saarinen. This kind of preprofessional experience is available in schools with professional residency programs offering academic credit within the curriculum.

A professional degree is just the beginning. Even with a degree that has taken five, six, or even more years to earn, you must become registered by a state before you can call yourself an architect. To be registered, you must complete a three-year internship with a registered architect, although in reality it's a normal employment without the regimen that accompanies a medical internship. Extensive experience in the office of a registered architect can no longer be substituted for a professional degree for registration in most states.

After internship, you can qualify to take the Architectural Registration Exam (ARE) given by the National Council of Architectural Registration Boards. The exam is in nine parts: Predesign, General Structures, Lateral Forces, Mechanical and Electrical Equipment, Building Design/Materials and Construction, Construction Documents and Services, Site Planning, Building Planning, and Building Technology. Each part requires three to seven hours on a computer in a test room. Any parts failed may be retaken in six months. The pass rate is around 80 percent, and some of the best architects I know failed at least one part and had to wait six months to retake it. Nowadays, good preparation courses make it just another hurdle, but it does require intensive preparation and at least a week to

complete. While you will be registered in only one state, this exam gives reciprocity possibility in other states.

Alternatively, it's significant that some of our best architects, past and present, have no professional architecture degrees. Three giants of the twentieth century, Frank Lloyd Wright, Le Corbusier, and Ludwig Mies van der Rohe, were not graduates of an architecture school, nor was Harwell Hamilton Harris. In the Southwest, for example, the foremost regional architects have done beautifully without professional degrees in architecture. (David Williams lacked one course and as a maverick refused to complete his degree. O'Neil Ford took some courses with the International Correspondence School. David Lake and Ted Flato completed four-year preprofessional degree programs and

The geometric structure of the Wilson House was of solid mahogany. Dallas, Pratt, Box and Henderson, 1959.

finished with an intensive apprenticeship with Ford.) All of them became registered when experience was an alternative to a professional degree. It's notable that each of these men excelled as an architect, making extraordinary architecture on the cutting edge, often published, and broadly admired.

When I took the four-day registration exam in New Orleans at Tulane's Architecture Building in 1955, I was a navy lieutenant about to be able to return to my career and needing to pass. Fortunately I did, whereupon I took my passing exam report to the Orleans Parish Courthouse to have my architect's registration recorded. There, a kindly gentleman climbed a ladder to the top of a bookcase and brought down a handsome red-leather volume with gold lettering that read *Registry of Midwives and Architects*. I think I was number 445, but I doubt that registry survived Hurricane Katrina.

Fulfilling oneself as a professional architect requires one to operate with three distinct personalities, each having its own separate value system. The architect is (1) an artist, (2) a technician, and (3) a businessperson. The values involved invariably conflict and must somehow be reconciled, however uneasily. A practicing architect spends more time in technical and business matters than in design matters. Isn't it amazing that we have symmetrical architectural trinities: Commodity—Firmness—Delight, and its parallel, Business—Technology—Art!

The practice of architecture is quite different from school. Success in practice has additional demands. It involves being well organized, possessing both business skills and people skills, having a flair for entrepreneurship, and getting some good breaks. If you want to open your own office, your questions will be: Should I open first, or should I cultivate potential clients first and get "known"? And how does it happen? In my case, my partner, James Pratt, and I had the good fortune to be known first—and in an unusual way. We had the audacity to do a study of downtown Dallas, using the occasion to promote some new urban design principles—new ideas for that time, anyway—that seemed to deserve vital discussion. After three years of work, we caught the attention of the national architectural journals. We had also won an international design competition and received a lot of press even though we were still young associates in other firms. Then our first client called, the one who asked us to tell him what he should do with his 6.2 acres of downtown Dallas. We negotiated a contract to design a high-density, mixed-use development, printed a letterhead, and opened our office with more courage than business plan. It grew to become known as Pratt, Box and Henderson for the next thirty-five years.

Being an architect is more difficult than becoming one. Our firm's interest in the design of places and things at every scale involved us in urban design, business and institutional buildings, houses, landscape, interiors, and furnishings. These were exciting times. Unbelievably, we worked even harder than we had in school. After that first big commission, we designed a small, one-story office building that sorely tested our knowledge and experience, because we had each been working only in firms that were doing skyscrapers. Our experience had also not prepared us for designing a large house for an old Dallas family. My being from a little town in East Texas, and my partner from a little town in West Texas, we didn't know how to design a fine home because we had rarely been in one. As luck had it, though, our client was patient and instructive. We lavished time on the design and construction. All of us were delighted with the result—in fact, in 1990 it was named one of the fifty best houses ever built in Dallas, still extant. Next came a private school for mentally retarded children, two exciting churches, and a large market building—projects that would put us in the magazines and even a few books.

We stayed involved locally with community service and internationally with design competitions, through which we could see how our ideas compared with those of other architects. We took time for travel to see the great architecture of the world. (How can you design a great building if you've never seen one?) Our small firm conceived a plan whereby the three partners would each take a three-month trip every three years at the firm's expense. We traveled on shoestring budgets, but among the three of us we saw most of the great architecture of the world.

One of the excitements of construction is to work with new or unusual materials coming either from advancing technology or from extraordinary natural materials found at an affordable price, such as a particular brick or stone or just the right type of glass. One such example for me was in a

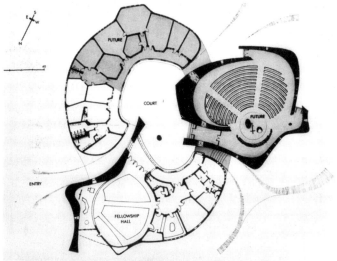

large residence where we had designed a complex roof geometry of exposed wood structure, for which we planned to use the most economical cedar available. A former client, himself in search of a good buy on cedar, alerted us to a boxcar of dense furniture-grade Honduras mahogany that had to be sold at a big discount. So we made the house as a piece of mahogany furniture within the original budget! The geometry of the three parts of the residence came together in a way that I could not draw well enough to explain to the carpenters how to build it, so I had to climb up on the second-

TOP: Interior of St. Stephen United Methodist Church with walls of Archilithics. Mesquite, Texas, Pratt, Box and Henderson, 1961.

BOTTOM: Plan of St. Stephen United Methodist Church, conceived to serve the liturgical processions of the congregation at worship, sat freely on a prairie in Mesquite, Texas, Pratt, Box and Henderson, 1961.

floor roof and piece out the rafters at the correct angle.

Once, while looking for new materials on the edge of technology, we got ourselves invited to watch a contractor's experiment with a new material composed of Portland cement, fiberglass roving, and a secret admixture for a material eventually called Archilithics. The cement mixture and the fiberglass roving were to be shot separately out of a two-nozzle gun onto a steel armature to make economical thin-shell concrete structures and other fluid shapes. At the end of the demonstration, the remaining concrete mixture was shot onto a row of concrete blocks about four feet tall by six feet wide. Several days later, we returned to see the dome experiment. For some reason, someone happened to kick over the wall of concrete blocks, and it stayed together like a solid wall. The cement with the admixture had bonded to the block while the fiberglass roving for reinforcement held the blocks together. Eureka! We suddenly had ourselves an inexpensive wall that could be shaped in curves without formwork by common labor rather than by masons! We asked a testing service to set up a strength test on a ten-foot-high wall sample, one-third of which had no foundation under it. Weight was applied to the cantilevered end of the wall, stressing it to failure. This yielded evidence of a very high stress resistance on the strain gauge. Our design was the answer to how we would build a church we were then designing that was composed of continuously fluid shapes. It was quite successful. It won several design awards and was published here and in Europe—even in a book on archi-

tectural fantasy. Unfortunately, because of legal problems with patents and ownership, the material was not used again, much to our loss, but it was a forerunner of the fiberglass-reinforced stucco now in common use on buildings of many types.

Practice has many surprises, such as when the American Institute of Architects asked me to write a book on the architecture in and around Dallas. Having avoided history and English in both high school and college, I found this a task that required help from every friend I had. We produced the first credible book on the subject, *The Prairie's Yield: Forces Shaping Dallas 1842–1962* (New York: Reinhold, 1962)—and I had my first glimpse of another facet of the discipline of architecture.

Our firm eventually grew to employ over thirty architects and handled large projects, such as college dormitories, office buildings, wholesale markets, apartment buildings, schools, churches, a community college campus, and several urban design projects, specialty shopping centers, and even an amusement park. We wanted the large office because it provided us with a base for doing significant projects, but it was a big risk; we have since learned better ways to do significant large-scale work (chiefly by associating with other firms). We won a number of design awards for our work, and all three partners, along with most of the long-term members of the firm, were honored by election to the AIA College of Fellows. A career high came in 1968, when we began design on a thirty-two-acre mixed-use project in downtown Dallas with a flagship building that would

Model of Griffin Square and Tower with I. M. Pei City Hall in foreground. Pratt, Box and Henderson. Dallas, Texas, unbuilt, 1961.

be both the tallest concrete building in the world and the tallest building of any kind west of the Mississippi. The thrill of that dream kept me awake at night and intensely engaged during the day, working sixty billable hours a week with a large design team for three years. Lots of flattering press came out of it, even a front-page story in the business section of the *New York Times* and articles in several European journals.Our New York partners ultimately changed, however, and our grand project stopped. But for three years I had the fun of thinking I was actually designing one of the tallest buildings in the world, exploring leading-edge technologies, and helping shape a city.

As an architect I have found the design process thrilling and the construction process challenging, but the lasting joy comes when the client loves the building and uses it in beautiful ways that I had not even imagined. An empty building is just a piece of real estate, but when it is given a place in the community and when landscape, furnishings, art, books, music, and food are added, or when a business or educational enterprise flourishes, it provides a satisfaction far stronger than seeing one's building in a magazine or receiving a design award. It gives meaning to the work beyond its architectural aspirations and makes a contribution to the community. On a personal level, being an architect allows you to acquire and enjoy many skills. It provides a rich sense of accomplishment. It allows a growing intellectual understanding of how and why architecture evolved as it did, together with a sense of participation in it. If you're fortunate, your works will live in their communities, in books, journals, and the ephemera of scholars—or at least in the memories of you and your colleagues.

| THINKING LIKE AN ARCHITECT:
THE DESIGN PROCESS

When I am working on a problem I never
think about beauty. I only think about how
to solve the problem. But when I have
finished, if the solution is not beautiful,
I know it is wrong.
BUCKMINSTER FULLER
(1895–1983)

Dear Ms. Van Zandt:

The alternative to hiring an architect or becoming one is learning to think like an architect and getting the help needed to make architecture. You have said that you want to build on your own account. Assuming that you wish to invest yourself in the process, I should first say that thinking like an architect differs from thinking like most other professionals because the architect is a generalist seeking to produce an art that is in service of people's needs. Its range of activity is broad.

The first time I thought like an architect was probably in Miss Klimer's first-grade class when she had us build a house—a real, full-size house with a roof and stucco walls—in an oversized classroom at East Texas State Teacher's College Training

School. The three small rooms were made of orange crates covered with chicken wire and plastered by the hands of seven-year-olds. Miss Klimer taught us to grow vegetables in a garden out back, then take turns cooking lunch and living in the "house." That project was so successful that she had us build a barn out of cardboard carpet rolls, like a log cabin, and bring in pets from the farm. The thinking I remember was the awe of seeing that big shape appear from the stuff we had had on the floor and how good it felt to press plaster into steel mesh. That teacher and those two buildings plus her stories of Mexico must have set my future.

If you draw to think or if you build useful things from your thinking, you have a core of architect-like thinking at work. John Ruskin described architecture as, "An art to learn because we are all concerned with it."

The readers I hope to address here design large and small buildings. These people are developers, engineers, building contractors, professional homebuilders, and active architecture aficionados. Large buildings require the seal of an architect or engineer to protect health, safety, and welfare in most communities. Small buildings and personal residences don't require a professional seal.

Thinking like an architect suggests that some kind of magic will happen. True, the design process is the magic, fundamental to the architect's work—a straightforward, logical quest for information, inspiration, artful resolution, and a means of expression. You can think of it as *creative problem solving* made into art—art contained and defined by functions. While approaches

and methods of design process vary, I'll describe the way I think about it and the way I have taught it.

Making shelter for people, things, and tasks is a basic human need; architecture is in the service of those essentials as a servant art. Building designs can be scratched in the sand or sketched on the back of an envelope in minutes or formatted from available sources and printed within hours. But the design of true architecture takes time, patience, knowledge, skill, and a will to make it happen.

You begin the design process by exploring three worlds that are about to meet: One world is the site, a place in the community or landscape; another world is the program, the owner's list of needs and desires; and the third world is the budget.

The site will be visited, explored, walked over, driven around, flown over, read about, and studied in maps of topography, geology, traffic, and weather. The geography, urban planning issues, building codes, zoning codes, and subdivision restrictions that are the physical and legal realities of the particular piece of property—all these need to be absorbed. Learn the site; have a picnic on it.

The program is a statement of what the building is expected to do, what it will contain, how it will function, for what group of people, what role the building seeks to play in the community, and how it can relate to the urban fabric. If it is to be an income-producing building, its financial pro forma becomes part of the program.

The budget is a prime reality of the project. It controls. It is value. When your project is finished, no matter how good the architecture, it will be only real estate to much of the world. I've never known of a budget that was too large. Yet a wonderful client for whom I designed a large house with solid brick walls, solid walnut cabinets, marble floors, and nothing ersatz anywhere, said at the end of the project, "Hal Box is the only architect in the country that can exceed an unlimited budget." A great quip, yet within a year he asked me to add to the house a twenty-five-meter indoor swimming pool. Budgets must be realistic for the proposed undertaking. They can change as objectives and resources change, so they are not fixed—they're just a fact.

Programming in the 1970s became an art form in itself with intricate procedures. William Pena, in his book *Problem Solving, Program Making*, described an excellent procedure that could be used by large firms working with complex corporate organizations to come to an understanding of the client's needs, record them accurately, and agree jointly that the decisions made in the programming phase represent what it is that is to be built. As you can see, such a process is very reassuring. Since that time, special consultants provide programming services sometimes even before an architect is hired. Although the program is an essential beginning to the design process, it is not the final arbiter. During the design process new factors will be discovered, priorities may change, and the program will be refined.

While the program presents the reasons *why* you build the building, many restrictions and ordinances will tell you *how*. Design of architecture is complex because there are always so many competing vari-

ables—and, tougher still, they all seek to be reconciled simultaneously and artfully. Mathematical formulae or computers can't make these kinds of decisions because each variable has a value judgment placed on it by each individual designer.

The challenge can best be handled with visual problem solving, in which diagrams of program requirements are made and solutions are tried. You make "bubble" diagrams of various functional parts of the building to organize relationships, functions, and proximities; then you begin to set limits and work with the messy body of information intuitively, by trial and error, to find workable relationships of progressions from one function to another as well as an organization of the whole. Some variables have a higher value and get priority consideration. It's like solving a puzzle.

Eventually a possible organization for all these variables becomes apparent. As you work with the diagrams you can see relationships emerge and patterns form into a composite that can be made into a building. In a complex building type or unusual site, early discussions with consultants may suggest that some organizations are better than others and may even be controlling factors because of cost.

With site, program, and budget in mind, you can begin to place each part of the project in a hierarchy and give it preference in size, orientation preferences, location, and functional proximity. Soon you will begin to see possibilities for actual physical form and develop a progression of spaces. This is visual problem solving. From the sketch diagram in plan form, visualize moving through the spaces; find axes that can help you organize spaces. Find a long wall that might become a reference plane to help organize the spaces around it. If it's dull, twist it, overlay it, reverse it, manipulate it. Find progressions through the spaces. Look for ways to create mystery and surprise on discovery. Begin to visualize roof shapes and sculptural form, but don't be too quick to adapt a roof form.

After you get a schematic diagram that seems to work, see if you can do a better one by starting all over, adding new considerations such as thinking about how the building might be organized in cross section (a cutaway view through the building) and in elevation (a straight-on view of one side of the building or room). Think about how you will put a roof on it.

Because each design problem is different, it's reasonable that you might do it better the second or third time. Yet we are told by Malcolm Gladwell in his book *Blink* (New York: Little, Brown, 2005) that our first idea is likely to be the best, even before we go through a lot of reasoning. An experienced client once told me at the beginning of the project, "I don't want to see a lot of sketches or process, I just want to see what you propose." Luckily my first schematic design was on target, was built, and was successful on all counts. On the other hand, I think it's good to check yourself by trying several schemes. Design problems differ from mathematical problems in that they don't have one right solution.

What you are working toward in this phase of the process is an architectural concept in which functions and budget are resolved in a preliminary way as you begin to create forms of the building in your head. The architectural concept will help you to define the form, the spaces, the light, the movement, and such, and it will become a schematic design that you can develop and refine.

Students ask many questions before finally understanding what defines a concept. It's your visualization of what the building seeks to be. It can be a sketch of the floor plan idea, or a small sketch model, or a sketch of the building sitting on the site, or any other means of describing the building in your mind—even a written description of the concept.

With thousands of variables to be reconciled in the design of a building, and with each variable susceptible to a broad range of values, the magic of visual problem solving will surpass the ability of today's computer. The computer can hardly be expected to create art out of a building program. The computer simply cannot make aesthetic decisions or creatively manipulate functional aspects, yet it can compute many alternatives for you to pass judgment upon. For now, the task of conceptualizing a design remains in the mind of the designer.

It's the architect's responsibility to develop an architectural concept that will satisfy the client's program of need, desire, and budget in a way that will enhance rather than damage the surroundings— and do so in a way that will make the client, user, and public grin with pure pleasure. My mentor, O'Neil Ford, said, "It's not enough to make a client happy; you must make them ecstatic."

Sketch of an architectural concept.

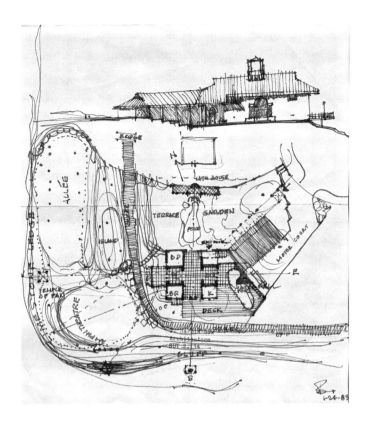

In the design process, my first rule is the same as the doctor's injunction from Hippocrates: "First, do no harm." In other words, don't damage the neighborhood, the streetscape, the natural environment, or the budget.

Test the concept to see that it satisfies the client's program, that it can be built within the budget, and that it meets the requirements of the regulatory agencies involved. Then, you want to see if it provides the maximum delight to the users and people around it. That last test will require a number of trial designs to see if you have chosen the best. You will want to look at other buildings of similar criteria, either in person or in the library. You will want to visualize the completed and occupied building to see if you wish to proceed with this design or seek another. The con-cept is your most important design decision. Make it. Test it. Pin it on the wall in front of you and work toward it. Verbalize it if you can and write about it under the concept sketch—a simple list of adjectives can give direction. Let it set for a while.

If you find that your architectural concept is inadequate, restart the process and develop one that's better. Keep the old one pinned up because you may go back to it.

As you work on the design and make decisions about it, keep the chosen concept in front of you and in your mind. It will help you make coherent decisions. Visualize it as a completed building rather than a design on paper.

An element of design to be balanced and adjusted about here in your process is the matter of scale. Scale is the relationship of the building to the human body or to the size and scale of the buildings nearby. Is it too big or too small or just right? For example, a tall doorway that dwarfs a person near it is out of scale. A McMansion next to a small cottage is out of scale on the street. Scale can make a setting be monumental or cozy. A client once requested that a single person or couple feel comfortable and at ease in a room that seated two thousand for dinner; for this we designed protected niches around the perimeter of the room that could be intimate spaces within the larger space.

A second matter of relative size is that of massing, the proportional relationship of one mass of the building to another and to the whole building. Complex masses become the solids and voids of sculptural form. This is where an accurate three-dimensional model is needed. A virtual model that can be rotated on a computer screen is a useful substitute.

Remember, most buildings are inherently ugly—often not as attractive as the natural landscape or old buildings they are to replace. So, unless great care is taken in design, a new building is apt to actually diminish the quality of the landscape or streetscape. Hence this axiom, which I either heard or made up: "Make sure that what you build is better than what you're replacing."

Zoning ordinances, building codes, fire codes, environmental standards, insurance requirements, and other legalities tell you the minimum requirements of how to design the building and must be learned and recorded in your drawings as well. The realities of structural systems, mechanical and electrical systems, as well as the physi-

cal aspects of the site, are assimilated into your concept. These realities are expressed in lists or narratives, or as you begin to get visual in your process, these facts can become diagrams that might relate well to your physical planning. When all this comes together, it is like a big pot of stew which you stir up and boil in your head, draw out portions of it periodically and test it—testing it in a sketch, a drawing, a cardboard model, or a computer model.

The building's complexity will determine the specialized knowledge needed from consultants, who will form a team with the architect to work on foundations, structure, heating and air conditioning, plumbing, electrical, lighting, interiors, landscape, and perhaps much more. The primary consultants will be major participants in the early development of the concept, working with the architect, who is a generalist—one of the last in this world of specialists—with training to work creatively with many specialists. The early phases of design require the generalist to make many overarching subjective judgments using incomplete information that is awaiting refinement by the specialists. The untrained designer will make even larger leaps that will need adjustment.

The basic tool in design thinking is the pencil. I use a pencil because it allows me to change my mind and my drawing easily—I erase almost as much as I draw. Others use ink and draw definite ideas; my ideas are usually too tentative to be recorded in ink. I admire those who can think so clearly, but I tend to suspect they may be arriving at form too quickly and missing the subtleties. More and more designers use only computers and have a computer skill that is as miraculous as a fine drawing skill, to which is added the advantage of the computer's memory. Today's students are extremely facile in computer graphics and use it as a basic design tool. Digital drawings look so perfect that you may not bother to think of the reality of the actual full-size building. A freshman design class can now produce what look like wonderful designs for buildings, yet when you take the time to visualize the reality, it may be an unfortunate or inadequate design decided upon too early because the graphics looked good.

I admire those who use the computer with such fluidity that you think they used a free-flowing medium like vine charcoal. In discussing the medium used in design, Bill Caudill, the distinguished architect and educator who spanned the era from watercolor renderings to digital design, claimed to be able to discern from looking at a building which medium was used in its design: charcoal, pencil, ink, chipboard model, foam-core model, clay model, or computer. Sometimes the medium used for design is readily apparent as you drive down the street.

In whatever medium, find the form that might be developed architecturally. The technique of laying a piece of cheap tracing paper over your previous drawing to refine your sketch again and again, or emulating that process on the computer, can lead to a magic synthesis of your objectives. Think of personally occupying the design, feeling the presence as intimately as you would in your own home.

Creativity in the design process, like creativity in anything else, can be honed by working through a cycle that I paraphrase from the highly regarded poet and planning futurist Betty Sue Flowers.

Prepare with a thorough investigation.
Focus intensely, obsessively, passionately, as an eccentric genius.
Dream and play, release cherished notions, and explore new ideas.
Seek a "flash of insight" by visiting the site, discussing ideas, assessing precedents.
Work effectively to develop the ideas into a design that solves the problem.
Assess your work; if it's not wonderful, repeat the cycle, perhaps from a different point of view, until you reach the result you seek.

The architecture you create must be expressed in drawings, models, or images, not fantasies in your mind. Yet drawings can deceive you; you can fall in love too soon with your own drawing. The architect Edmund Bacon, an exemplar of a twentieth-century city planner, cautions that "architects are often too quick to form." Be cautious. First of all, drawings must be to scale for reality to be visualized and assessed. A scale like $1/4$-inch equals 1 foot gives an accurate representation for visualization—smaller scales are used for concepts. A drawing not to scale will lie to you, leading you to wishful thinking and unworkable decisions. When possible, I like to draw the basic plan full-size on the site with stakes and colored tape. When you draw to scale on paper or computer, remember to visualize the full-size reality. Avoid the architect's trap of making "paper architecture," something that looks good on paper but is not right for the project.

As you put design ideas on paper, the visual problem-solving process prompts one image to lead to another, as ideas feed off of themselves, enabling you to create something more complex and satisfying than the idea you first conceived. This process repeated again and again, as you trace freehand over each idea to improve it, makes the design process work. As you are developing plan concepts, you must be looking at the building in section and elevation so that you understand it three-dimensionally and are adjusting to how the building will look and feel.

If your design is not working as well as you would like, remember that you are not alone with that piece of paper; its lines are not set in concrete and it will take suggestions from anywhere. There is wisdom in Emerson's words, "Every man is a borrower and a mimic," so admit it, look around, inform yourself, get inspiration, and work from there. In beginning design studios, some teachers will have students select an architect they admire and have the students emulate that architect's work in a design project. Mimicking good design informs us and enhances our own design.

Complexity enhances design by relating many disparate parts to one another and to the whole. Seek to form many interlocking relationships among parts of the building in its spatial organization. Manipulate the geometry and the interlocking proportions of the parts of a façade to make it visually richer in unexpected layers of delight.

Complexity is not to be confused with complication. Confusion signals that you should go back and readdress the basic problem, find a better solution by examining the elements and putting them in another order, reexamine the program. Try eliminating a variable. Seek complexity; avoid complication.

Models help you visualize and record design ideas sometimes even better than drawings do and are useful for people who lack drawing skills. The limitation of careful models is that they are time consuming to make and to revise and improve, so use something easy like cheap cardboard and Scotch tape to do rough models that show the masses, spaces, and light—don't try to make them look great; they are for you to study so that you can refine the design by making informed decisions. To view a model, put your eye at the eye level of the scale building and visualize it, as you would see it on the ground—that's much better than looking at a model from above, as only birds would see it. The internation-

Cardboard study models of masses and spaces are thinking tools—easy to modify and refine.

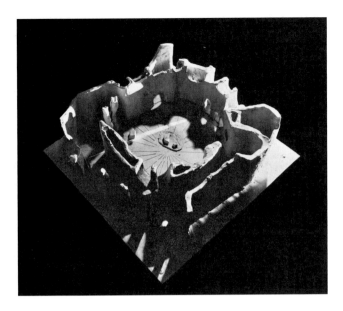

Clay modeling is like sculpting space. You concentrate on the space rather than on the walls.

ally acclaimed architect Charles Moore would give a building committee a site plan and a pallet of model-building materials—colored paper, Scotch tape, cellophane, soda straws, wire, candy Lifesavers, Fruit Loops, and rocks and vegetation from the site—and ask them to build a model of the building they envisioned. The committee would create models expressing what they wanted in the building. Moore would elaborate on the ideas in their Scotch tape model and create from it the sophisticated forms that expressed the clients' aspirations for the building. The design process absorbs all the knowledge and skill you can muster. And design doesn't stop when the drawings are finished. Design values are important in the bidding process, as you decide on what to take out or add in, and design continues throughout the construction as details are being built.

Your design will be constantly up for grabs on the construction site as a lot of people you never met before come to the job site to do something to your building.

Excavators, form builders, steel men, carpenters, masons, plumbers, electricians, painters, foremen, and inspectors descend on your site with nothing to guide them but a set of plans, their estimate of material, labor, overhead, and profit, and a few kind words from you. The plans, together with the written specifications of materials and methods, and a contractual agreement are the instructions on how you want to have the building built and how it will be paid for. The architect is much like a teacher. The architect's drawings seek to teach the builders how this particular building is to be built. This is an essential process of communication because, obviously, the architect can't build the building alone. Construction requires people with different skills—it takes a team. The classic example, Thoreau's cabin, is an exception worth considering, and that is why his *Walden* is on my Reading List. Wittold Rybczynski's *The Most Beautiful Building in the World* offers another sensitive insight into a person's intimate relationship with design and construction.

Conceiving a design requires both conceptual skills and basic knowledge. For example, I need to organize the site in my mind and begin to orient the building. For me this involves many considerations: knowing exactly where the sun is at different times of the day and the season; understanding the direction of rain and wind (both the good directions and the bad ones); understanding the effects of cold, heat, and shade, all of which affect comfort and energy consumption; finding the possibilities for vistas, axes, and spatial progressions; exploring the requirements for both privacy and community; and understanding the relationship with surrounding buildings and landscape so as to appropriately marry this new object with its environment. Notwithstanding this long list of considerations, one must keep primary the reason for the building in the first place: *to satisfy the client's program within the budget in a timely manner.* This is all exciting stuff.

The thrills of the art come from knowing how to manipulate the elements of design: space, light, progression, movement, proportion, scale, rhythm, and color. Thrills also come from determining the influences of the site (the qualities of a city fabric or a natural setting), mastering the nuances of the location and "lay of the land," understanding the social purpose of the building and its symbolism. The continuing quest of the design process is to find the appropriate relationships, the economy of means, the expression of purpose—all the while seeking an aesthetic that bespeaks beauty, charm, and comfort, a mellow background, an inspirational space or exciting place, or combinations of the above. This involves experimenting with different ideas and choosing one with the confidence that it's the best.

Needless to say, the budget and the constraints of zoning and building codes quickly become basic controls of this process. Because ignoring any of these realities imperils the project, you must be clearheaded about what can be done. Yet you must examine the opportunities. It may be that not enough money or land was allocated to the project; or it may be that the project is actually on an inappropriate site or doesn't have all of the programmatic ingredients needed for success, either financially, socially, or aesthetically. Zoning and building codes may need to be challenged. The budget and the financial objectives are principal elements of the design to be managed and will control some aesthetic issues. Moreover, in any income-producing project, profit too is a matter of design. For example, in designing private dormitories at colleges, I discovered that part of the profitability of the project was in design issues under my control and that with a detailed pro forma in hand, I could find revenue-producing space, improving profit centers to provide either a lower building cost, a larger profit, or a bit of both.

As the design process goes back and forth among functional issues, building systems, and aesthetic issues, it can be effectively guided by formal design theories—many of which are overwhelmingly dense. But it is clear what Moore meant when he described how he used a theory he called "the Goldilocks Theory," in which Goldilocks would find something too large, too small, or just right; too high, too low, or just right; too bright, too dark, or just right; and so on. The design quest, the theory, is simply to make things "just right." And that's one way to make art.

Regarding what's just right, Mark Twain said, "The difference between the right word and the almost right word is the difference between lightning and a lightning bug." One will ask, "How do we know when it's 'just right'?" Well, it's for the trained eye to know that it's "just right," in the same way that the ear of a violinist knows that she has the sound "just right."

Of course it's subjective. All difficult decisions are subjective—formulae or computer code can handle the others. How does a court know whether to say "guilty" or "not guilty"? It's by the same kind of process. The best design theory I know is to keep thinking about how to make something that is "just right."

The next most simple and complete design theory is the classic that demands that buildings have "Commodity, Firmness, and Delight." We would have much better buildings if everyone would use this basic architectural test first established by Vitruvius, the first-century BC Roman architect and theorist. Here, "commodity" concerns a building's functional aspects (how it satisfies its program); "firmness" concerns its vital properties (structure, drainage, mechanical, electrical, plumbing, energy use, and such); "delight" concerns our perception of the building's aesthetic qualities. Achieving delight is normally the most difficult of the three and the one that most demands the architect's talents. Accountants and planners can ensure the commodity of the building, and engineers can ensure its firmness, but the delight is the special effort of the architect—when achieved, it sometimes rises to the level of art.

Delight enters the design process in many ways. The strongest delights, of course, come from our perception of space, light, proportion, and form—the basic art form of architecture. Yet there is much more. Delight continues with seeing the architect's skillful manipulation of design elements: handsome proportions, rhythmic sequences, richness of form, balance

of composition, dramatic events, stimulating color, and delight in the fine details of the building. Louis Kahn said, "God is in the Details." Other senses thrive on delight: the sounds of the building: water, wind, footsteps, and the quality of voices; the touch of a building's handrail or doorknob and the texture of a wall or a floor; scents, both pleasant and unpleasant, also have effects. Moreover, anticipated delights of the tastes to be sensed in the building add to our overall perception. The design process includes everything you can imagine that will delight all the senses.

Much of the satisfaction during the design process comes in creating a design idiom for a building. The design idiom is developed in the synthesis of ideas for the form, materials, and particulars of purpose placed into a style or manner of artistic expression that the designer uses in manipulating the design elements. The design idiom will show itself to the observer in myriad ways—for example, in the way windows and doors are detailed, the way intersections happen, the way handrails and grills and columns are

Design projects can be as large as city blocks or as small as doorknobs; this one in bronze is by James Pratt.

The Villa Rotunda, one of many villas designed and built near Venice by Andrea Palladio from 1540 to 1580.

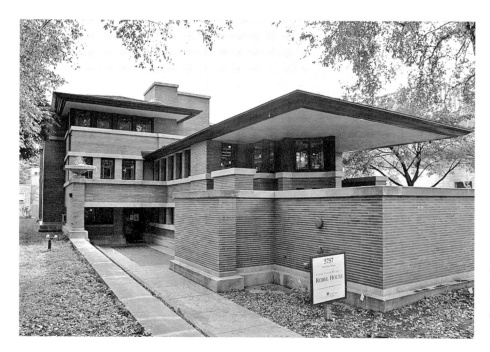

Wright's Prairie School houses used a consistent design idiom with slight modifications.

detailed, in the use of materials, and in hundreds of thousands of detailed design decisions.

Some architects, like the Italian Renaissance master Andrea Palladio, formed consistent design idioms that influenced centuries of architecture around the world.

On the other hand, Frank Lloyd Wright, a genius of invention, created a new, consistent, integrated architecture composed of many original design idioms—such a comprehensive set of idioms that it formed a design philosophy for the last century and affected the way almost everyone lived. Other important architects like Eero Saarinen sought to develop a new design idiom for each building; his inventiveness was responsible for much of the refinement of the Modernist movement. Some of today's architects have been successful in creating a consistent idiom that becomes inherent in all their work. The architect Richard Meier is an internationally known

master of his idiom of white rectilinear forms and their layering. Harwell Hamilton Harris, O'Neil Ford, Frank Welch, and Lake and Flato created regional design idioms that continue to influence buildings in their regions. Some idioms are based in technology, some in craft, some in geometry, some in traditional design, some in invented form; all are a part of one's individual creativity.

An exciting way for an observer to understand an architectural work is to be able to "read" the building, and in so doing discover and enjoy the idiomatic aspects of the design. Design idioms can be found and savored by the knowing eye just as the ear savors classical music, its motifs and variations evolving during their exposition, development, and recapitulation. These motifs or design idioms are at the heart of both music and architecture.

Reading an existing building's design idioms can be a rewarding experience and

The consistently elegant and crisp details of Richard Meier articulate the surfaces of the Rachofsky House, Dallas, 1995–1996.

Eero Saarinen developed a new design idiom for each project.

useful in developing your own design idioms. Start by looking at a window. How you look in or look out are major events in experiencing the building and an essential part of the architecture as seen from the outside: the façade. Notice the edges of the window. How are they made and of what? How deep is the reveal, i.e., how far is it set back from the wall? What surrounds the window? How is the window divided? What are its proportions? How does the designer relate it to the other windows? Is there something special about this window? Is it the right height when you look out of it? What supports the weight above it, an arch, a lintel, something invisible? That specialness may indicate the design idiom. Look at the doors in the same way to see how they relate. Look at the roof and the cornice. Is the edge thick or thin? Is it flat, sloped, or shaped? What's the roof made of? How is the roof held up? By walls, beams, arches, or does it appear to

hover? Look at the walls and see if there is something special about them. What materials? How many different materials? How does the mass meet the ground, meet the roof? Is it a load-bearing wall or a visible structural frame with infill? Is it a local material or exotic? What is the color palette? Look at the massing of the building—have the parts been articulated or expressed as a single mass? How do you perceive from the outside what is going on inside? How does the building address the street, the sky? Does it have authenticity—does it look real? Is it derivative or innovative or both? Does it have classical proportions and composition? Is the composition random, symmetrical, or asymmetrical? These observations can help you know how the designer developed various idioms to solve design issues. In designing, when I can find the right idiom for a particular building, I feel that I have a way to solve most of the design issues without reexamining every condition—let the idiom help you work through the building in the design process. Place examples of your design idiom next to your concept sketch and it will guide you. Getting the right design idiom is almost as comforting as getting the right concept. It's like Goldilocks finding the right chair.

What if you don't like what you've done? It's not right. Take action, seek inspiration, go to books and journals that you respect, and explore new ones. Look for ideas that might improve your almost right design. Scan architectural journals to assess the current design directions. That architecture is not necessarily good; it's simply the editor's choice of the newest and most

unusual work available in the magazine's office at the time of publication. A richer collection of good examples may be found in your bookstores and libraries, where the editors, the designers, and the public have had more time for assessment. Aside from the inspiration your search will give you insight on how other designers solved problems like yours.

When you decide that your schematic design has resolved all the major decisions regarding architectural concept, size, cost, and construction type and that this is what you wish to build, you are ready to be specific by refining all of this in the design development drawings.

The design development drawings, as the words imply, will develop all the architectural aspects of the building—the structural, mechanical, electrical, plumbing, communications, and other specialties, including interiors and landscape. These drawings will be the basis for the detailed preparation of the technical construction documents.

You have several ways to go with the design development and construction documents and the actual construction, depending on how involved you wish to be. It will depend on your skills and on the level of design you want in your building. One, you can take the results of your design process to an architect and work with him or her to review, refine, and finish the job, carrying out a full or partial professional service. You may want the architect to begin at the beginning, using your work as input to the program, or simply to complete the technical aspects of your design. While many architects are unwilling to do the latter, there are continuing relationships of architects with nonarchitect clients that produce good results time after time.

With varying objectives, building contractors often have their own in-house people who will "draw up" your design. Hand your drawings to a contractor or builder, make a written contractual arrangement, and start construction with a general idea of what to build and realizing that most of the decisions will be made by the contractor on the job. The risk here is obvious. In this scenario, the assurance you need can be gained by looking at previous work of the contractor or builder and understanding the level of design, materials, and details you can expect.

Another bold choice is to work through it yourself, getting the help you need in various stages and working with a contractor that you trust to realize the project. Reading construction documents is less difficult than reading some books. These are the drawings used by the architect to communicate to the building contractor exactly what is to be built. You can understand what is intended when you focus your mind and vision, starting by locating the outlines of the walls and, by looking at the dimensions, visualizing yourself there.

Buildings are designed and built by successful developers with various combinations of "design-build" that can produce good buildings. This works best, from a design point of view, in building cultures in which architecturally viable building traditions are still in place.

When you think of the skills involved in the design process, the difference between professional architects and nonarchitects is large. The professional has the advantage from university-level design studio courses of over two thousand classroom hours of instruction. He or she will have studied in a succession of design studios for five of six years, five hours a day, three days a week, and have taken a lot of technical courses. So, lacking the professional training, the nonarchitect must be patient—explore and refine, don't be daunted by your lack of experience; you are gaining experience rapidly when you take the time and get tutelage throughout your project. To design is to redesign. There are hundreds of thousands of design decisions to be made.

We've just begun our work on the design process, but for now, know that your aspiration for good architecture needs your audacity and dedication: the audacity to find the best solution and do it, the dedication to get it right. Make it a well-behaved building, courteous to the street and to its neighbors.

CHAPTER NINE

VISUALIZING WITH DRAWINGS AND MODELS,
PENCILS AND COMPUTERS

*If we are to devote our lives to making build-
ings, we have to believe that they are worth it,
that they live and speak and can receive
investments of energy and care from their
makers and their inhabitants, and can store
those investments, and return them aug-
mented. Bread cast on the water comes back
club sandwiches.*

CHARLES W. MOORE

(1925–1993)

Dear Haley:

Visualizing and drawing are the keys to
the architect's work—as important to the
quality of the work as its construction. You
ask, "How does one visualize a design and
capture it in a drawing or model?" Visualization is at the heart of creativity; it's the
mechanism that enables your imagination
to focus. It is an essential tool.

I was first able to visualize a building
full-size in my mind late one evening while
working on a second-year studio project to
design a small museum. I had sketched
several perspectives of the building and
realized I couldn't visualize from my sketch
what the building would actually be like. So
I built a small cardboard sketch model.
That helped a bit. Then my roommate said,
"Be real! Go out in the street and try to see

it in your mind full-size." The Austin street outside our place was quiet and empty, but contained lots of trees, streetlights, wires, and such, so that I could use them in visualizing roofs, walls, and parts of the building full-size. My imagination formed an image in my head of a real, full-size building that made it real enough to allow me to make design decisions with some confidence. This image was then easily transferred to a drawing—in this case, a perspective drawing of what I had visualized in the street. From there the plans and elevations developed. The final project earned my first commendation from a design jury. Visualization had really proved its value.

Visualization tools were also needed in the design of the Great Hall of the Dallas Apparel Mart for Trammell Crow in 1964. As big as a football field—sixty feet high and programmed to seat two thousand for luncheon fashion shows—it was surrounded by one million square feet of showrooms. One end of the space could hold every building my partner and I had ever built. We couldn't visualize the reality of such a huge space, so we built a model at the scale of 1 inch = 1 foot, large enough for two people to stick their heads through holes in the model floor and look around so that we could sculpt the space from inside. To visualize dimensions full-size— for instance, the size of a cornice sixty feet in the air—we measured comparable features in the only room we could find that size, which was Grand Central Station. When the building was completed, we found the visualizations accurate except for one dimension. When the scaffolding was finally removed to reveal the finished

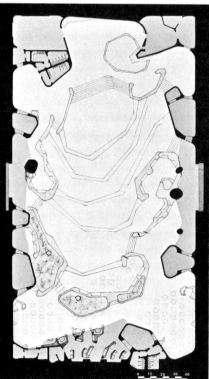

The Great Hall of the Dallas Apparel Mart required a twelve-foot-long model to design the 300' x 120' space. Pratt, Box and Henderson, 1964.

Plan of the space shown above.

space, and we walked into it, it appeared much wider. I had not realized that my head had taken up twenty-four feet in the model.

My point, though, is that you need to do whatever you can to invent devices that will help you visualize so as to get a realistic image of your project.

Visualize and draw. Draw and visualize. Saul Steinberg, of *New Yorker* drawing fame, said, "Drawing is a way of reasoning on paper."

I want to empower you with the knowledge of how to realize your design on paper by offering some simple directions on how to get started. Drawing is really not complicated. Dispel the fear that you cannot draw. You can, I assure you!

Design starts with a thumbnail sketch or a "napkin sketch"—that is, a sketch on whatever's handy. With a scrap of paper, an idea, and a pencil, you can do wonders. In fact, you may do the most important drawing of the entire project at this stage, since it may help you capture a seminal concept. Find something to draw on as soon as you have a good idea. On an airplane, for example, airsickness bags have proved better than napkins and far more durable. The important thing is to start drawing your ideas.

One of my freehand drawing teachers offered this simple but very useful tip: "Start with a dot." By that she meant, "Put the dot of a pen or pencil anywhere on the paper other than the center, and start drawing either what you are looking at (say, a still life) or what you have in your head, recording as best you can your vision. So what if it's awful? You have a wastebasket.

Try some more, until you get a drawing that begins to communicate your idea."

Computer programs do a great job, too, provided you have good computer skills or the time to learn them. I suggest you start off with a simple beginner's program. A professional program like Auto-Cad may require far more time than you want to give to become facile enough to design. While most architects' offices use Auto-Cad extensively, it demands much training and regular practice. Follow the instructions with the software or take a class, but keep in mind the design process I suggest here. When using the simple "Build a House" programs, ignore the unfortunate architectural realizations they show. It's easy for the computer to give you a false sense of security because it draws without thinking and it draws very well. Most architects I know agree that it's best to begin your designing with a pencil. Some architects, however, don't use a drawing board at all, opting instead for Auto-Cad. After years of practice they can do subtle, fluid, lyrical work on a machine that one would think would make it rigid. Today's students, who've grown up with computers, definitely have a head start when it comes to developing excellent design skills on the computer. Computers are already shaping advanced architecture in ways that would be impossible without them.

To give you some insight into how drawing is an essential tool of design, I will spell out how to get started.

I love the pencil, and no pen or computer will ever come between us. I myself favor the 2B for sketching and the HB for hard-line drawings, but your first step in drawing can be with whatever tools you have at hand. As you get caught up in the process and as you need to get specific about your building, you will probably require a few special tools.

If you intend to get into the design process, rest assured that you can get the basic tools for under three hundred dollars. Go to an architect's supply store or blueprint shop and buy some simple equipment. Here's my shopping list: buy a 24" x 36" or 20" x 30" drawing board with a built-in parallel bar. (The Mayline brand is best because it has a reliable bar, and the folding feet are handy when setting the board on your desk or dining table.) Also buy a 45° triangle and a 30°–60° triangle about 10" long. Buy two mechanical pencils (Mars brand) with HB and 2B lead and a pencil-sharpening grinder. Your constant companion will be an architect's scale— use either $^1/_8$"=1'–0" or $^1/_4$"=1'–0" for plans, elevations, and sections. Buy two kinds of tracing paper: a roll of cheap tracing paper 12" wide, to sketch on, and about ten large sheets of 1000h Clearprint or K&E Vellum (expensive stuff, but you can draw and erase on it forever). Also get a pack of drafting dots for sticking the corners of your paper to the board. Finally, buy a good white eraser in a plastic tube, like the Pentel Clic Eraser, plus a kneaded eraser and an erasing shield. I myself erase so much that I use an electric eraser.

While you're out shopping, I suggest you purchase two tools of a different nature: a small ten-foot tape measure and a Swiss army knife—one with a corkscrew. These are tools of *reality* that will remind you that what you are drawing wants to

become full-size. Keep these in your pocket or purse and you will be surprised how often you will use them around a construction site.

When you are all set up, think again about what it is you want to design. Can you state it simply? You'll need to. I used to come up to my draftsmen or students, all hunched over their drawing boards, and ask, "What are you doing?" They'd typically give me a rambling, unfocused reply. I'd come back with, "OK, tell me what you're doing in one sentence, in the English language." This magically focused both of us on the most important task at hand. (You'll see an example of this when I describe the concept for the hilltop house discussed in Chapter 11.) So I urge you to challenge yourself to *put your intention into one sentence*. Actually write it down! Now, if what you've expressed is what you really want to do, you have made a big decision and are ready to start.

If you have a piece of property to build it on, you will want to get specific. Not so much as to encumber your vision, mind you, but enough that you can get all the qualities of your site into your vision without misleading yourself. So, without losing any of your fantasies, stick the plot plan of your property onto your drawing board, overlay a piece of the expensive tracing paper, and start putting on that paper the critical information that you know. Of course, you will do most of this by drawing—tracing the outline of the property, for instance. You may need to have the plot plan photocopied to change it into an architect's scale. Don't let the expensive paper intimidate you; draw and change—that's

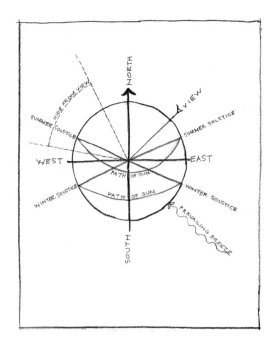

what your eraser is for. (I've drawn, erased, and redrawn so much on one sheet of good paper that my first drawing ended up being used in the final construction drawing after months of work.) Use pencil, never ink, because the pencil drawing is so easy to change when you spot an improvement you can make. Isn't this simple? Here you are learning about your most important asset, the site, as you learn how to draw!

Your inexpensive sketch tracing paper, meanwhile, is for trying out ideas. You will use a lot of it, maybe fifty feet on a good day. The expensive paper is for recording facts and decisions; the cheap paper is for exploring new ideas.

First, trace the boundaries accurately, draw a precise north arrow, then add any site features that must be kept (like trees) or avoided (like cliffs or boulders), as well as the directions toward attractive vistas you wish to see and any unattractive ones you want to hide. Draw the surrounding buildings so that you can relate form to them and know what you see of them; know what sun they may block. Draw the all-important building setback lines (your city building inspector will help you determine these along with any parking requirements, maximum lot coverage, and maximum building height) and any other information you consider important. Trace the topographic contours (your survey should already show them) with a light dotted line. Then embellish the north arrow into a compass circle (called a compass rose) and draw arrows toward the views, as well as the solstice angles to help you visualize the sun's path as it rises and sets. Now you are through with the preci-

sion of facts for a while and can begin to consider subjective issues. Heed this crucial maxim: "Decide first where *not* to build." Draw lines to define those places where you will not or cannot build. Now you have drawn a base site plan depicting a true representation of the facts of the site. Keep it handy—it is the representation of your property.

Next, before making any assumptions about the plan of the building, draw several sections through the site, looking both crossways and long-ways, if the building is on a hill. If these will fit on the edge of your plan drawing, put them there, for it's convenient; if not, put them on a new sheet of good paper with enough room above the ground line to draw the building. Now you have two base drawings: a site plan and a drawing of two site sections. Keep them, understand them, and experiment with both of them together so that you understand the three-dimensionality of the site.

You should also consider building a topographic model of the site. It will definitely help you visualize it. There is a simple way to make such a model: use layers of cardboard cut to the outline of each contour, then glued into position to match the contour map. Use a cardboard thickness that is the same scale as the map.

You are now beginning to get this special place, your parcel of land, in your mind as well as on paper. You have converted your eyeball perspective of the land from the street into a perfect and usable abstraction of the land—in a drawn *orthographic projection*. That architect's term, by the way, describes three types of drawings: plans, sections, and elevations. A plan is a bird's-eye view, looking straight down on the building. A section is a drawing that depicts what you'd see if you were to slice right through the site or building. An elevation depicts the sides of the building—in this case, the exterior sides—when viewed horizontally and without perspective. There are typically four exterior elevations, one for each wall surface.

Third, just for starters, make some assumptions about the best site orientation for your building relative to the information on the compass rose you drew showing sun angles, prevailing breeze, views to enjoy, and views to hide. Then draw, always to scale, the single most important room of the building, putting it just where you think you want it on the site. It may be wrong in size, proportion, and location, but it's a place to start. You are now using your mind to connect the drawing of the site to your vision of the building. This is the way to visualize: full-size on the site, recording

it and manipulating it on the drawing from the vision in your mind. (See Chapter 11, "Building Architecture: An Example," to see how you lay out full-size rooms on a site with stakes and colored tape—remembering that those stakes can easily change as well.) To bring your mind, your drawing, and your site into reality in three dimensions, also draw the room into your site section drawing. Keep that visualization of your concept and the reality working as you progress.

After doing the careful factual drawing, assess it and play with it to see what can be done creatively. Give yourself permission to cut loose. You have the facts on paper, so now you can explore any fantasy you want. Do some freehand drawing to loosen up. Maybe try drawing a bowl of fruit or part of a garden. Start with a dot near but not on center and go from there. You may want to take a life drawing class at a local museum or gallery. The famed Spanish architect Antonio Gaudí is said to have taken a life drawing class every week, even into his mature years!

Now go to the cheap paper, overlay the base drawing you made, and make some trial diagrams of how other rooms relate to the most important room you have already located. You may already have a start on these, but try them with this new information on the base drawings. As these spaces and relationships become more and more realistic and workable, you can add them to the base plan drawing and the section drawing.

As images of the organization of upper floors evolve, see how walls line up with those below, as well as where stairs might go, and begin to think about structure. The most important thing to know about structure is that everything has weight, which goes straight down to the foundation in the ground through walls and columns. Load-bearing walls—typically the exterior walls and walls of major rooms—carry most of the loads. Be aware that rooms over fourteen feet wide require some extra structure like deeper joists and beams or trusses. Openings more than six feet require some special beams. There are always exceptions, so you will want someone to confirm your structure and modify it, if necessary, to work properly.

You can learn a lot by mimicking a good model, so I suggest you find some architectural drawings of a building by an architect you relate to and study them. This may be the time to start buying some basic architecture books or exploring the holdings of your local library. (Later, you can learn a lot by studying and mimicking actual working drawings, as I did.) They'll help you understand the fascinating symbols and the language and conventions that architects use to efficiently describe construction details to the builders. These details are communicated through what are called working drawings or construction documents, but that is more technical than what you need right now.

Eventually, you will study the elevations critically. Start by drawing a section or two through the building. This is where everyone, amateur or professional, has work to do, because this is where designers are on their own, determining what the building will look like. Be patient and forgiving of yourself as you draw the outlines and begin to place the windows, doors, roof, and other features you have tentatively placed in your plan. It may not be very good, so lay over it with cheap tracing paper and work on the proportions and composition until you have an understanding of the physical reality of your building. Because it won't be wonderful on the first try, even for a professional, think about how to improve it. Do you have an idea of how you want it to look? Go to some of your favorite precedents and see if you can get an idea that will help. You will want to draw and compose an elevation of every surface of the exterior as well as every wall of every room of the building to know that every view has been designed visually. But for now, simply know that you can draw and that skill will come with repetition. You may later want to have someone redraw and refine what you have begun. At every step you will want to stop, look at the design in front of you, and criticize it. See how you can improve it. See how it relates to the other parts of the design. Pin up several trial drawings on the wall and ask others what they think, then select the best. You also want to make sure it fits with your original concept and budget, or maybe you'll want to redefine your concept. In fact, you may want to start over. It will take time.

Conceptual models can help you visualize spaces and masses. They give you a small-scale abstraction in three dimensions rather than the two dimensions of drawings. Models come in all sizes. I say, the bigger, the better. But you can start with a real miniature no bigger than your thumb. Believe it or not, I've seen students start with a model that small and present their entire concept with it. Use whatever materials are available—cardboard, modeling clay, balsa wood, thin pieces of metal, even toothpicks. The miniature model, only a few inches long, can help you find an image for the building that fits in the landscape.

Of course, you also need a little model of the landscape to fit it in. You could then photograph it and make a montage with a photo of the site, by cut and paste, or by computer with Photoshop or some other software program. The miniature model presents ideas of mass or image. But the most helpful model is one that is large enough to visualize interior spaces.

Modeling of space is best done with cheap cardboard and Scotch tape—something easy to work with and easy to cut up and change as your ideas evolve. Understand, this is not a presentation model made by a professional model builder; it's a study model—a really rough draft or rough 3-D sketch. I like to use white cardboard because it renders light well—light and space being the ingredients with which you are working. Use scissors or a metal ruler and an Exacto knife to make the floor plan just like your drawing (maybe a photocopy), and paste it on cardboard. Cut the walls and tape it all together. Then take it outside into the sun, or else put it under a single light bulb in a dark room to simulate the sun in the proper directions for different times of day; start noticing the effects of shade and shadow. Visualize yourself inside the model

by putting it at eye level. This gives you a far more realistic view of your creation than you'd get from a bird's-eye view that no one will ever have. Show it to others; change it. How can you make it better?

You will probably have noticed that it is hard to put a roof on it. Roofs are such a difficult design problem that you may want to start over and consider the roof first. I always keep the roof shape in mind as I am designing, and sometimes I'll even start with the roof shape and work everything in relation to it as a sculptural mass. Here you see one of the big advantages of the model: it demands a complete shape, a roof.

Having a 3-D model you are pleased with, go back to the drawings and incorporate the changes. Don't fall in love with your drawing or your model until you have tried another design of the same program for the same site—it may be better. It can be a new path to follow in design or it will simply confirm your first idea, which is often the best. I normally try out several ideas before I decide to put all my money on one. When several people are involved in the decision making, it may help to have alternatives to discuss, such as: What are the merits of Scheme A versus Scheme B? Usually new ideas will be generated, but compare them to your first concept to see which is best. You have to prove to yourself that the concepts you have chosen are really sound. There's no better test than through a critique. We'll explore this phase of the design process next.

Architects should learn to study not merely minimum requirements, but maximum possibilities; to learn not only how to economize space but how to be extravagant with it; to learn not only to use space but play with space.

JOHN SUMMERSON

(1904–1992)

Dear Hannah:

How do I know when my design is "just right"? you ask. You say you are designing a small but elegant studio in which to display your work and need to make some important design decisions. No matter what your background or experience in architecture might be, you want to know, Is this design exciting architecturally, tastefully boring, or plain awkward? Is this really the best I can do? Does the plan work? How about the section, and the elevations? Are the composition and proportion right? How am I doing? These are all good questions. You're ready for a critique!

Deciding design issues requires a generous conversation between yourself and others. You want deep testing of your design before you commit to it with time and mortgage. You want to bombard your design with different scenarios, making reality checks such as, Does it work for a group of two hundred? or What if we expand? or Is there a better structural system? Such questions, and thousands more like them, indicate that you could use help.

Even though you have already done a lot of self-criticizing as you developed your design, you will benefit greatly from a critical review by those knowledgeable about the project. The professional architect as well as the student uses the critique as a basic process to test, to vet, to evaluate, to gather new ideas, to confirm thinking, to call into question, or to propose a new direction. The critique is not an exercise in negativity or a review by an art critic. Rather, it is a way of assessing and reviewing the design, its effectiveness, and the quality of what is proposed. For example, when my partners and I reviewed each other's designs with respect to visual concerns such as composition, proportion, and form, we would pin up the drawings on the wall and evaluate. Often we would pin up three or four variations and discuss which was best and what could be done to improve it, then take the best, draw it up, and try to improve on it. The eyes make this kind of choice; there are no numbers.

The one-on-one critique is the basic method of teaching design. It's also the basic method of teaching music, painting, sculpture, and most of the arts; it's even used in business schools on business plans. In acting or sports it's called coaching; in writing it's called a critical reading. Yet in architecture, where so many subjective decisions are required, the critique offers an effective way to explore alternatives and make the subjective decisions—that are always more difficult than the objective decisions of calculation. Clearly, this is not a time to be defensive; it's a time to grow.

In architecture school, a critique happens either at the student's desk or via a formal design jury composed of faculty, students, and professionals to whom the student presents his or her design in drawings and models in a crowded exhibition room. Each jury member discusses the design's attributes and its unresolved problems, perhaps makes suggestions, and offers an overall assessment with a response from the student. It's much the same in professional practice except that it is in the form of a conference in which several specialties present their points. Each critique, properly taken, helps you reach a new plateau of refinement. The critique is your friend.

Client conferences resemble jury critiques in that you present to a client, they respond to you, and then you go back and forth to find the right answer. When you're both the client and the designer, take the client's role and look objectively at the designer's work and make notes.

Design conferences with consultants are a sort of collaborating critique in which a mutual solution that's better than either individual solution evolves. A favorite process of mine is to work creatively with an imaginative structural engineer, who is dealing with hard facts, and together come up with something both exciting and sound.

Quite different from the design conference and critique are the many reviews by public agencies demanding your compliance with local, state, and federal laws, or by financial institutions loaning money for the project or insurance. Such a review can be a prolonged and controlling process. But it's an essential process, or at least an inevitable one, so my advice is, work creatively with it rather than grudgingly against it. Often the reviews—for zoning, building codes, fire department regulations, environmental regulations, historic preservation laws, disabled access, traffic, sustainability, and such—are so technical and time consuming that consultants have to be brought in as facilitators and expediters. This is true for professionals and non-professionals. Unfortunately, in some cities this process has become so labyrinthine that you might spend more energy, time,

and money on the approval process than on the design process. There is rarely an architectural review of design quality, though. That's up to you.

Hard-won knowledge of the codes, plus early reviews by specialists, will inform the creative process. Indeed, the codes are a set of realities, similar to your budget, that contain and define the project. Join them to the design process creatively and they will simply become another part of the equation to be solved.

Before going forward, consider this checkpoint: *If you don't love it, don't build it.* The most expensive mistake is to build something you don't like. I also like this advice from the great Winston Churchill: "When you get a thing the way you want it, leave it alone."

CHAPTER ELEVEN | BUILDING ARCHITECTURE: AN EXAMPLE

It is something to be able to paint a particular picture or to carve a statue, and so to make a few objects beautiful, but it is far more glorious to carve and paint the very atmosphere and medium through which we look. . . . To affect the quality of the day—that is the highest of arts.

HENRY DAVID THOREAU
(1812–1862)

Dear Jim and Betsy:

In your last letter you said that you wanted to know what to expect in the design and construction of your house on the hill, as you think about whether to do it yourselves.

My purpose here is not to tell you "how to do it." It's more "how to *think* about doing it." No one knows a perfect way to design architecture—that's why the profession is called a *practice!*—but it helps to have a reliable map to guide your way. As an example of a guide, I'll try to tell you how I myself design as an architect—the kinds of things I think about during the process, and why. My colleagues, of course, have their own variations of this process, and many think in different directions. And you yourselves will surely have your

own, too. I am simply offering you one way. A house makes an excellent vehicle for describing design, in part because we all know about houses. After all, we live in them! Since you're going to be building a house on a hill, I'll walk you through my own experience designing a hilltop house overlooking the Austin skyline and the silvery strip of river that runs through that city of evergreen oaks.

The site is on the very top of Nob Hill, the first hill of the fabled Texas hill country as you come up from the coastal plain along the Gulf of Mexico. These uplands help distinguish Austin from its flatland neighbors. The Balcones Fault that formed all these rolling hills and the river below has been inactive for thousands of years, leaving a tranquil setting for chickadees, cardinals, mockingbirds, doves, and herds of whitetail deer. Covered with live oak, mountain laurel, and ash juniper, the site slopes up from the southeast and faces both the prevailing breeze and the view, a fortunate synchronicity which is pretty

breathtaking. This particular piece of land, basically a hunk of limestone, poor in topsoil yet rich in native flora, had never been built on—it's a great place to design a house.

My wife, Eden, and I began to have the kinds of fantasies one has when making a place to live. We spent hours thinking about how we wanted to live at this time in our lives, now that the children were grown; retirement was nearing for me, although Eden was still an active executive. For starters, being a classical music lover, I wanted some room that would be large enough to accommodate chamber music concerts. Eden, meanwhile, yearned for a bath and dressing room that together could function like a morning office so she could begin her day on the phone while dressing for work. We also each wanted a room of our own for a studio/office. Plus we wanted space to entertain large groups, even though it needed to be a small house. Of course we had hundreds of minor requirements, too, that would emerge more insis-

Distant view of skyline from the site for the Nob Hill House. Austin, Texas.

tently in the course of design and construction. Deciding on how you want to live leads you to entertain ideas outside the ordinary, where you can create your own special world in your very specific place. Keep in mind, your house need not resemble anyone else's house—and probably shouldn't!

Being both the architect and half of the client at Nob Hill, I can make the description of my design process simpler than it would otherwise be. For here I'm free to use an open, ad hoc process, workable only for small buildings that don't involve a lot of clients, users, and consultants. It involves simply thinking through all of the functional factors and design variables, using what I imagine to be common sense along with experienced aesthetic judgment after inserting the realities discussed in the preceding chapter. Then it involves

rethinking the design, again and again and again, until it feels "just right." I hope I have persuaded you that good design is labor-intensive—successful only when a clear, appropriate, and exciting concept can be developed.

My approach to developing the architectural concept for this program and place seems simple on the surface. On the half-acre Nob Hill site, there's a grove of live oaks and a heart-filling view southeast, showcasing the shining Colorado River and the city skyline set in a sea of green trees. It's obvious that the grand view will be dominant in any concept and that the drama in the place will come from celebrating the view. Once I arrive at a promising concept, I make a sketch that depicts it, as I understand it, and pin it up on the wall in front of my desk. I then work toward that concept as the objective. If I change the

Topographic plot and site plan of the Nob Hill House, by author, Austin, Texas, 1992.

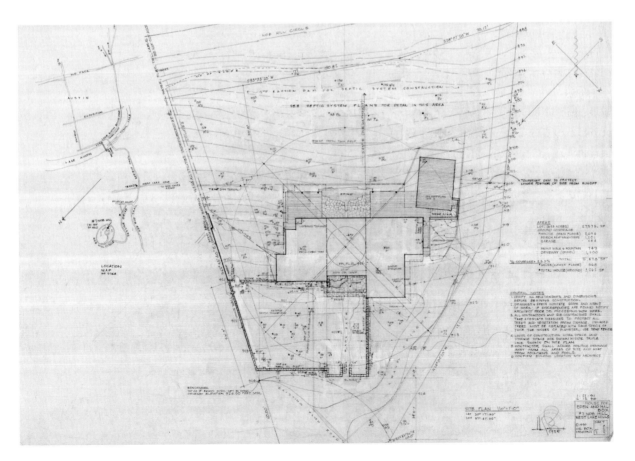

concept for what I think is a better one, I change the sketch in front of me. It's the target at which I'm aiming.

When you think about how to develop an architectural concept, know that it may take days of study, reading about the place, exploring its physical and cultural history, and of course, pondering the way you want to live there. I build the visual information in my head using all kinds of visuals—contour maps, aerial photos, photos of the surroundings, and photos with the new building mass sketched in or simply with a drawing glued onto the photo. Photoshop makes images that can do wonders to help you visualize and assess outcomes. Color copies, cut and pasted, also help in visualization, both for you and anyone else involved in the project. Conceptual ideas expressed in words help capture the idea, too. I try to abstract the major elements to find an obvious concept so fitting that it seems inevitable. I go to the library to look at my favorite buildings and seek out the latest ideas in journals to look for precedents that will inspire me—the opposite approach from the way I was taught as a Modernist ("Begin with no preconceptions").

With these thoughts in mind, I walk the site slowly to assimilate the place, to discover and to map all the assets of this special piece of the world. It's fun and informative to have an afternoon picnic on the site and then a morning coffee to see the site in different light; a visit at midday, the most unattractive part of the day with its harsh glare and dark contrasts, is also instructive. Seeing the site in the rain and during other extremes of weather helps

too. To get to know the lay of the land, I use some simple surveying instruments—a hand level and a Brunton sighting compass on a tripod. They help me understand the engineer's plat and also give me an accurate bearing on the objects I might wish to screen out, as well as those I want to feature as views from the house.

To make the most of the view from the various rooms, I map and imagine how to view the dome of the State Capitol, the Tower of the University of Texas, an extinct volcano on the horizon, and the foreground profile of the live oaks, knowing, after hours of observation, just as in my first look, that the primary object in the view— the centerpiece of it all—is the path of the curving Colorado River and its reflections of light. The only bad view is really bad: a huge water treatment plant that mars the peripheral vision and must be masked by a part of the new building plus trees that could block the view. Additionally, I want to find the most advantageous way to look at the close-in landscape. I note a few intrusive views of neighboring houses that I'll want to hide. But the site itself has never been built upon, so there are no unattractive or damaged parts that need to be healed or built over. I know, of course, that there will have to be a treeless area for the septic drainage field, but wildflowers should grow well there.

Obviously, building on the part of a site that's damaged is a good place to build. But more than once I have seen people buy a site that they considered beautiful because of its great trees and then, finding it difficult to work around or with the trees, cut them down to build their building. They ignored the Hippocratic injunction; they did harm.

You will want to be alert to your building's orientation. It is critically important to comfort, energy conservation, and the drama of natural light in the building. For energy conservation and comfort in warm climates such as Austin's, you'll want to face the long dimension of the building to the south and avoid windows on the west. In cold climates, open up to the west, so you can warm up the building in preparation for the nighttime cold. These orientations need not be precise, though. Staying within five or ten degrees will suffice for this purpose.

If you enjoy astronomy, as I do, you may want to get some accuracy in orientation to the sky. I take an accurate compass, the bearings on the survey, and (best yet) accurate alignment with the north star to locate true north and lay out some stakes to visualize the sun angles. This lets me determine the location of the sun's light and the shadows it will create. I visualize the morning, noon, and evening sun on the days of the solstices of summer and winter and the equinoxes of spring and fall; using these as guides, other days can be imagined. This allows me to understand what the light will be in the rooms, terraces, and patios on those days of the year and to consider the effects of solar heat gain. My interest in astronomy and cosmology—an outgrowth, I suppose, of wanting to know where I am in the world—leads me to align the building precisely on the cardinal points of the compass so I can enjoy predicting and seeing the paths of the sun, moon, and stars. If such things interest you, consider lining

up with the cardinal points, or the diagonals, but don't compromise the desirable sun orientation or views.

Back to Nob Hill. I next make a few trials, on the site, of a possible ground plan, using yellow ribbon and wire pegs and a sharp machete to find the best envelope for the building, particularly the major room. I make these observations and initial decisions about the "site's sights" before I do more than a quick sketch. I don't like falling in love with a drawing before I have a good idea of what all the design issues are. Then and only then can I seek a concept that will solve all the design criteria.

Next, on a drawing board, just as I suggested earlier, I lay a sheet of tracing paper over the carefully detailed surveyor's drawing, which shows all the boundaries, setbacks, easements, and trees and significant plants, along with any other special features of the site, such as interesting rock outcroppings or evidence of ancient habitation that I'll want to preserve. Deciding where not to build will be clear. I note on my drawing all of the initial observations and decisions I made while on the site. I draw arrows indicating good and bad views and circle areas that offer special opportunities. In short, I make a preliminary sketch full of information that will help me design—this being all part of what architects call visual problem solving. The brain can somehow synthesize the information on the drawing and direct us toward forms that solve all the design problems simultaneously. If it doesn't, it's back to the drawing board.

You may think this prep work is tedious, but it's actually fun. I now take my prelimi-

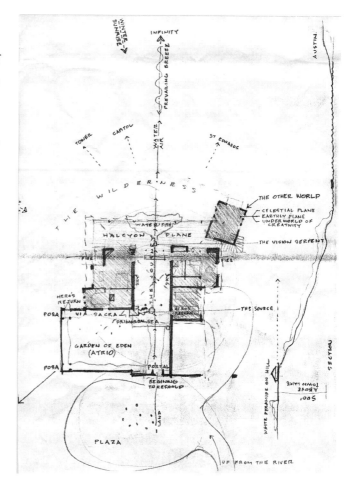

nary site drawing and a mental construct of the concept back to the site and visualize in more detail where to place various functions of the building. In a dense urban site with party walls there will be fewer choices, but the steps remain pretty much the same.

At this point in the design process, I am also being a bit of an amateur landscape architect and interior designer, since I'm not calling in these professionals for early collaboration the way I would on larger projects. Later, though, I will want consultation on plant materials, garden plants, and garden organization and on specific interior colors, furniture, and fabrics that will enhance the concept. These specialists in interiors and landscape are essential for design refinements, and on most projects they are just as important for concept development.

My next step on the drawing board, after understanding the features, light, and views of the site, is to loosen up after assessing all those facts. I find a soft pencil and get creative. Now I want to accomplish two things at once: (1) find the best places for the functions, and (2) begin visualizing the spatial-design possibilities that will make this a true piece of architecture. Materials, structure, and character, so far, are considered only subliminally.

Architecture being a functional art, unlike painting, sculpture, and music, we must include many issues beyond the aesthetic, like the forces of gravity, of rain, building codes, sustainability, program, and budget—all while trying to make art. The poetry can still come in, though, in the artful creation of the spaces, progres-

sions, and forms. Like painters, we must design two-dimensional surfaces of walls, floors, and ceilings; like sculptors, we have three-dimensional masses of the exterior; yet the architect's dominant medium, the three-dimensional space formed inside and around the masses, is our own special challenge. We see most buildings from the outside, but that is not how we experience a building. To experience it, we must use and explore the building just as we would take time to appreciate a painting or a symphony or a book that we may think looks good on the outside but inside loses us in a labyrinth of confusion and dulls our interest. So you will want to design movement and spaces from the inside out.

Concept sketch of the Nob Hill House, landscape, and views sketched on the back of a meeting agenda. By author, Austin, Texas, 1991.

Soon the concept emerges in my mind and on the drawing board clearly enough to abstract in words: "A stone wall on the street with a thick portal through which you can see, past a garden, all the way to the distant river, horizon, and skyline by looking through a central space formed by two stone masses under a broad pyramidal roof." There, I've managed to get it all into one sentence! Everything else will work to serve that concept. The space between the two walls is the 22' x 36' main living space of the house, with a 14' ceiling and skylights lighting the stone masses; within the two stone masses flanking it are, on one side, the master bedroom suite and, on the other, the kitchen complex and garage. In reality the concept evolved into a Texas Dog Run House by serendipity rather than by following a precedent.

I decide to place both the guest room and the studio in a tower detached a few yards from the main house. Like Carl Jung's symbolic tower, ours will have three levels: a lower level to promote deep creativity (my studio); a middle level—level with the main house—to serve as an earthly plane (the guest suite); and, on top, a lovely roof terrace for entering the celestial plane—a great place to stargaze from a hammock on a summer evening. Such symbolisms add personal meaning—and I like them. As the design progresses, I expect to add still other meanings and mythic elements when I see the opportunity.

In a simple building like this, I design the furniture placement before settling on the locations of the walls, confirming all this with my beloved client Eden, who is giving helpful critiques as we go along. On the site and on the paper plan, I locate the main seating group of the living room to maximize the views in two directions and place the dining table for similar views. I also locate the bed of the master bedroom, the breakfast area, and the kitchen sink and bathroom sinks so as to optimize their views, too. These are all places where people will spend at least some time gazing out the window. By the way, that awareness of interior space dominates my thinking. I learned early in my practice the importance of drawing an elevation of every wall, inside and out, so that I could know what it would look like and prevent any surprises. The only times I have been surprised occurred when I forgot to draw an interior wall elevation.

(Let me confess something here: You may think it overkill, and it was, but I developed seven trial concepts to a quarter-inch scale, my reason being that we expected to live in this house a long time. One concept was developed into a set of working drawings before I found a better one. In these trial concepts, all the furniture remained in the same location relative to the views. On one attractive and complex scheme, I employed a colleague to build a large-scale model about six feet long, showing all the interior spaces with a multifaceted removable roof. It was a beautiful model and an exciting example of deconstruction, a buzzword in everyone's thoughts at that time. But as my wife and I brought reality into its visualization, we decided to go back to basics, agreeing with the architectural gold medalist Fay Jones, who once said about a new design trend,

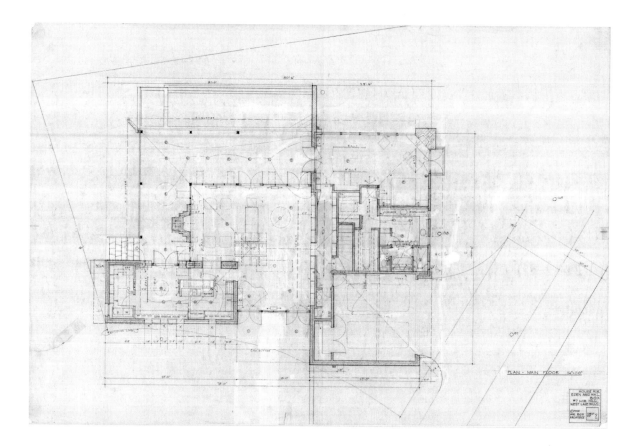

Plan of second design for the Nob Hill House developed in construction drawings but not built. By author, 1991.

"I think I'll sit this one out." After the seven iterations, the one we decided to go ahead with looked very similar to the first trial. What had we gained? Conviction: the sure knowledge that we had explored at least six other ways and chosen the best. There's likely not another scheme out there that we would rather have built.)

Designing the building inside while looking out, I give first priority to places to eat, because when dining, one has the time, several times a day, to really see and think and chat. Working, meeting, and sleeping places are second in line for good relationships to the outdoors and the prime view. If one has a special private place to meditate—a place I like to call a "bliss station," as in Joseph Campbell's "Follow your bliss"—it might get the prime view. In a house, as in a restaurant, dining happens at specific times of the day, when natural light can be predicted, just as church services happen at particular times, allowing the space to be designed for the light at just those times.

Personal spaces of modest size benefit any habitable building. Such spaces, to which Virginia Woolf gave a resonant name with her novel *A Room of One's Own*, can be minimal, including only a desk and chair in a niche with or without doors. As you continue to develop the design, seek intangibles that give meaning, or give personal or corporate expression, making each room—each room!—a special place.

One of the most important functional and spatial decisions, for me, is how to approach the building—the entrance

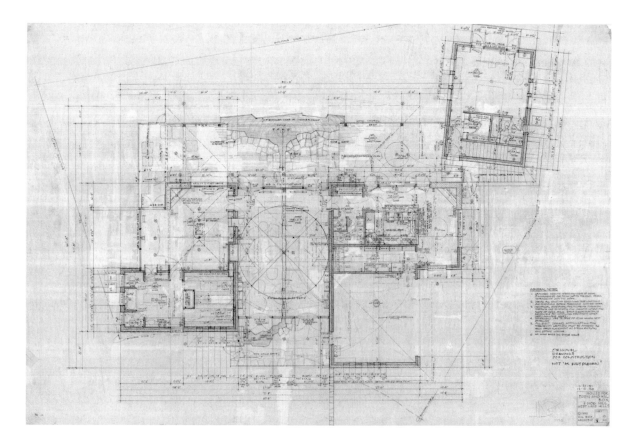

Construction drawing of the Nob Hill House. By author, 1991.

sequence—as well as the subsequent movement through the spaces inside and outside. Christopher Alexander's classic architectural manual *A Pattern Language* describes this sequence beautifully in many details and concludes with the following advice:

Make a transition space between the street and the front door. Bring the path which connects street and entrance through this transition space, and mark it with a change of light, a change of sound, a change of direction, a change of surface, a change of level, perhaps by gateways which make a change of enclosure, and above all with a change of view.

In the Nob Hill House, I employ a Mediterranean approach through a patio surrounded by tall walls instead of the more conventional American or English approach, where you come directly off of the street or front yard down a walk through a grass lawn. (The tall walls were against the zoning ordinance, but we felt them so important that we sought, and fortunately got, a variance.)

It should be easy to understand that space formed by walls, structure, and landscape is the driving force in the search for spatial form. I begin here by considering how spaces and light will occur on this particular site. Of course, if the site involves difficult terrain, or if there are other special considerations, one will have to think of structure first, yet the structure is easier to manipulate than many aspects of the building and consumes a small percentage of the budget compared to finish materials, mechanical/electrical systems, and equipment. Even so, if designed with appropriate simplicity and clarity, structure determines much of the architectural quality of a building, helps provide an elegant spatial solution, and usually costs less. I enjoy using here an elegantly simple, barnlike structural solution that enhances the spaces and their architectonic aspects. This will be a simple masonry-and-frame house organized within the mass of a square pyramidal roof. The pyramid is a strong sculptural and symbolic image. And thanks to its simplicity (no corners or valleys), it sheds water well.

Whatever building we make, comfort and security are always our highest functional priorities. The reason we build shelter at all is to make a secure and comfortable place—safe, dry, and neither too hot nor too cold. We require quality drinking water and sanitation. We also want a choice of light or darkness and all of the convenience and entertainment that technology (and our budget) can afford. These support systems should be civilized, arriving and leaving the building without visible wires and meters. Some architects really like the industrial aesthetic. I enjoy it myself but only in an industrial setting, unless it is immaculately and artfully crafted. The distribution of services, particularly hot and cold air, requires a lot of space both in plan and section; supply and return air grills can be intrusive, so all are best hidden from view.

You can be sure that I visualize the environmental systems, heating, air conditioning, and lighting by drawing overlays several times during the project because they can get out of control visually as well as out of budget, accounting for 20–30 percent of total building costs. A reflected ceiling plan is a good way to understand what is going on with lighting and air conditioning and also a good way to control their appearance. You draw a reflected ceiling plan by laying a sheet of tracing paper over the plan and drawing the ceiling as if you're looking into a mirror on the floor, and you design the ceiling just as you would every other surface. I insist on drawing all of the surfaces because the pain of drawing something ill-composed or poorly proportioned will cause you to revise your drawing. AutoCad and other software create these elevations and plans readily so that you can examine and refine them; your eye will instinctively catch awkward composition and proportion or plain error. It's better to see it first on the paper than in the building, when it's too late or too expensive to change.

Finding a way to hide every air conditioning supply and return grill makes an interesting game well worth pursuing. The toe space under cabinets and bookcases, for example, is a perfect place to hide air conditioning outlets. I also ask experts to look at these things with me. Architecture school doesn't try to teach the novice architect how to do all of the engineering; instead, it teaches just enough technical knowledge that the architect knows how to work intelligently with consultants and to challenge

them in a collaborative effort. Good engineers are exciting to work with creatively.

At Nob Hill, I base the design on design traditions of the region, just as my mentor O'Neil Ford had taught me, and use those design idioms with full confidence in their value: a big, simple roof that gives generous shade to all the walls as well as the porches; the local stone—Austin limestone—for walls and floors; natural wood for doors, windows, and cabinets; thick walls with lots of insulation; deep windows; tall 8' doors; niches cut into the masonry; and high ceilings (mostly 11' high) with light coming from above in all major rooms.

In the plan, I devise special sight lines for distant vistas and interior enfilades. ("Enfilade" is a concept borrowed from artillery; it's a sight line through several spaces down which one can shoot—or, in this case, see.) The plan is organized for communal spaces with long views and private spaces with intimacy and sound-proofing.

The main living space, the traditional "dog run," is given much of the area budget at the expense of other rooms, so that it can make a significant-sized space in a smallish house. (I think the failing of many buildings is that there is not one large room in which to gather.) The nine-foot dining table will get a place of honor in the main room at the prime position for the view. The fountain that starts in the front courtyard will come through the living room symbolically as a dark green slate inlaid in the limestone floor to emerge on the porch as a fountain into a fishpond.

The fireplace, the hearth, is typically used to center a seating group for conversation, yet much of a family's normal activity in this part of the world is around the television, so a conflict is created between hearth and TV; a group cannot face both. Here, in place of a log fire, I decide to install a large TV behind an ornamental fire screen. (The TV turned out to be unused except for special events.)

Our most used room, I anticipate, will be the covered porch. It will provide a sense of being in nature, as it faces southeast toward the river and city. Eighteen feet wide and sixty feet long, it will be big enough to accommodate a seating group at one end, a six-foot diameter dining table for twelve at the other end, and a long, irregular-shaped fountain and fishpond in between. Texas weather will allow the porch to be used at least once a day except on the few days that prove too cold.

To give the kitchen special character, I seek the look of a "cantina," an informal Mexican bar with barstools where men go to drink and sing. The working part of the kitchen—shallow and splendidly compact, everything reachable in three steps—will go behind a long, thick wood bar, the counter of which I plan to construct out of a great, glossy slab of local ash juniper. The lucky person behind the bar will get to enjoy facing not only his guests, but also, beyond them, a broad skyline view. Warm colors, hardwood floors, and unexpected ornament such as a zinc, copper, and brass image of the hill as the vent hood will give a nonkitchen look to this space so that it can be used inconspicuously during parties; a large preparation area will get tucked right around the corner from it, out of sight but readily at hand. Also off to the side I will have a cozy breakfast alcove—a very special place. It will feature banquette seating for six and a severely dropped ceiling sloping to 6' at the several small square windows on its two sides.

As for the master bath, I aim to make it more of a real room by giving it a look of spaciousness (actually 11' x 15'), comfortable seating, and a hardwood floor, set off with an Oriental rug. Matching doors for the water closet compartment and the shower compartment and windows with views in each of them will lend the bathroom symmetry and make it feel more like other rooms in the house. The clothes closet, meanwhile, I design as a large (11' x 14'), tall, walk-in dressing room with wall-sized mirrors and track lighting so that it will look more like a stylish dress shop than a closet.

I don't avoid idiosyncrasies that I believe will enhance the architecture. Some people will advise you to build the typical, most common house plan in order to ensure the best resale value, but I believe that if the idiosyncrasies are good design, they will only enhance the value. At least that has been my experience when houses of my design have sold. So I let in the idiosyncrasies. The main atypical elements of this house will be the 8' wall, creating a courtyard, rather than a front yard, as a central part of the concept, and the separate three-story tower outside of the pyramid, requiring one to leave the main house via a large back porch. Walking outside before entering the tower, though, will provide a separation, both real and psychological, for my studio; it will also provide more privacy for the guest room and the roof deck, the latter being a place where one can literally get away and enjoy a 360-degree view.

In an earlier, more idiosyncratic house that I designed in town, I had separated the master bedroom from the master bath, requiring one to cross the library that was open to the living room. It sounds bizarre, but my aim was to capitalize on the drama of a Palladian plan that created a large central living space with a dome 38' high. In that house, as in the Nob Hill House, the idiosyncratic design proved effective. When sold, each house brought the highest dollar per square foot that a house had sold for in that city at that time.

Building your design can give you even more goosebumps than designing it—or maybe even than living in it. During construction I went by Nob Hill almost every morning because I enjoyed the workmen asking me to help make decisions in their work. My attitude was that I wanted to be there to answer questions, and the workers seemed glad to see me because I was trying to help them. Some architects will come on a site and begin telling everyone what to do, triggering quick resentment. I did this only once. On my first visit to a big job as an architect, I tried to tell a brick mason how to lay brick. I learned quickly that I didn't know how to lay brick, but I found enough resilience to get across to him my idea of how I would like the brick laid if it couldn't be done the way I had drawn it. Together we came up with a better detail than either of us had in mind.

You cannot build the building by yourself. You don't have the time, and you don't have the skills. The contractor is potentially your best friend, although many young architects think he's the enemy. He can make a beautiful building, if you have designed one—or he can make a mess, run up the cost, delay completion, or all three. What you can do is describe to all involved how you would like it built through plans, specifications, shop drawings, and on-site conferences. Then focus on working creatively with everyone. My test of whether I'm doing a good job on the construction site is if the contractor is happy to see me and has the problems ready for me rather than solving them in his way. The general contractor selected for Nob Hill was a man I had worked with before on several jobs, and the nine

months of construction went apace in a pleasant and logical sequence.

The typical sequence of design and construction goes through several phases. The program described why you would make this architecture. The site selection determined where you would build it. The design process defined what you would build. The work then progresses in this order: The construction documents will describe in precise detail what and how you wish to build. (The nonarchitect will need help here.) The bidding and negotiation will decide who will build it, when it will be finished, and at what cost. The selected contractor and subcontractors, together with the owner and the architect, will make it happen. There are a lot of variations, but this is a typical progression.

I would like to add two comments that have to do with money. The better the quality of the contract documents and the more carefully thought out the drawings and specifications, the more they can minimize costly changes. I always use AIA contract documents for general conditions of the contract and the actual contract between owner and contractor because they have stood the test of time and are updated annually. Changes during construction are disproportionately expensive and time consuming for everyone involved. Minor changes can happen without cost and improve the final result, often saving money. It's important to know that should you ask the contractor, "How much will this change cost?" and he answers, "Too much," that is not a valid answer— you need to know how much so that you can decide how much is too much. The change may be minor, but it may make a great improvement over what you had visualized in the drawings. The second money matter that can make for a happy job is for the owner to hold back a secret 10 percent of the building budget beyond the contingencies that might be available in the contract.

The finished house at Nob Hill, completed more or less on budget, had such a strong visual form that it could be seen fitting into its hillside from five miles away. Because we had placed all of the furniture during the design process, there were few surprises when we moved in. An architect friend once asked me if, after living in the house, I'd have made any changes. "Yes," I told him, "I would have added twelve inches behind the dining table, and I'd like to have afforded a standing-seam metal roof." But the house proved to be a joy in which to live and entertain. Magazines published it, garden clubs from miles away came to visit it, chamber music ensembles played in it, and it was used for museum, symphony, university, and political events—even though it was only a thirty-six-hundred-square-foot house on a barely accessible hilltop.

CHAPTER TWELVE | ADDING MEANING

Better the rudest work that tells a story or records a fact, than the richest without meaning. There should not be a single ornament put upon great civic buildings, without some intellectual intention.

JOHN RUSKIN
(1819–1900)

Dear Gail:

Designers are always looking for ways to help determine the form of their work, be it a function, a style, a theory, a structure, a precedent, a geometry, a sustainability issue, a moral imperative—anything, really, that helps create form. We seek to validate our newly created forms visually, intellectually, and emotionally. We want them to be stamped "special." We want people noticing them and admiring them and being eager to inhabit them. So your concern about wanting to make your compound "more than just bricks and mortar" is a valid one. So many buildings seem forgettable, even soulless. A few, though, somehow manage to feel alive and "just right." They have the magic of true architecture.

In many cultures of the past as well as
in some present ones, myths, particularly
those of a spiritual nature, have been the
dominant form-giver. Architecture is
intrinsically romantic. Myths of a spiritual
tradition were expressed in architecture
through the use of special progressions of
spaces, by specific forms, by light, by the
arts of sculpture, painting, and music.
These forms begot cultural traditions and
symbols. Thus, many of the great buildings
have a spiritual content. Of course, in
Rheims Cathedral, spirituality is the whole
purpose, yet nonreligious buildings can
have qualities beyond the aesthetic that
affect the spirit. This is true even of a
house. So, being aware of this dimension,
I experimented with the Nob Hill House to
see if I could create a level of extra meaning that would enrich the experience of living in the house as well as help me give
form to the design.

You may wonder about how this will be
of value to you. But follow me, if you will,
as I describe this experiment with the idea
that buildings can tell the commonly held
stories we call myths. The hypothesis is
that a connection can be made between the
architecture and the person experiencing
it, provided they are open to it. Architecture's form, space, and iconography can
communicate ideas, tell histories, evoke

emotions, enhance spirituality, and create a sense of place. The stories have beginnings, middles, and ends. They help give form to the building. Think of these myths as metaphysics (i.e., going beyond physics), going beyond architectonics.

Some buildings are dumb, with nothing to say, without voice—simple physics; others just make noise; still others may tell a fool's story of pretension and ostentation. Architecture, once considered the Mother of the Arts, integrated painting, sculpture, music, and drama into the whole—a concept that generated great ritual art and architecture through the collaboration of the artists. The Beaux-Arts architect, who was arguably more of an artist than today's typical architect, collaborated with painters and sculptors to present an iconographic program in the building, where artists would bring in sketches and plaster maquettes to the architect for possible inclusion. After centuries of successful integration of art and architecture, the iconographic program disappeared with the onset of Modernism. Should it be brought back?

The ancient myths of Egypt, Greece, Rome, and the Maya, as well as those of medieval times, the Renaissance, the Enlightenment, and even the 1930s industrial period gave form to the art and architecture of their time. In some cases, the myths were the sole reason for building, as in a monument or religious building. Kingdoms like the Maya had much of their power embedded in buildings that symbolized a connection with the sun and stars. Myths were dramatized, empowered, and perpetuated by architecture and art. Much of the popularity of Disney's theme parks is built upon stories that have become popular myths.

Myths embedded in architecture give information, communicate ideas, explore mysteries, provide guidance, imply meaning, and provoke thought, even awe. The architectural iconography of some civilizations is the only evidence left to tell us their story. Buildings can represent a history of human events that took place within them. What speaks to us skips nostalgia and goes directly to the vitality of the human spirit. Monuments communicate and perpetuate the myths. Simple everyday nonmonumental buildings can also express myths.

Some of today's architecture seems bound up in the search for form following fashion, becoming empty once the fashion passes. It's said that early Modernists searched for basic spiritual expression in their abstractions, although the Modernist movement later gave little notice to expressions of myths and meanings that a building might communicate. Is it true that users and clients, finding little mythic content in the new architecture, have found less need for architects?

Architecture determined by function, structure, and theory leaves a blank page rather than a story. This blank page can invite many abstract ideas; yet missing is the dialogue with the user about spiritual or mythical aspects of his or her time in the building, leaving us with only the designer's stylistic and personal expression. Architecture wants to be more.

Should one wish to explore this, know that myth telling in architecture can enter the design process at each of its phases. In conceptualization, one can think about cosmology, orientation, directional elements (fire-water-earth-air), iconography, symbolism, place, or a specific story. Painting, sculpture, and the decorative arts and crafts have always been the most direct way of telling a myth, as they are integrated with the architecture. Some of the architectural devices include spatial progressions of high and low, wide or narrow, light or dark, color and texture, quiet or reverberant, hot or cold, events along the way. Design devices of the architect's craft can work to dramatize a story. Designing for the rituals of everyday use and special festive ceremonies gives cause to elaborate on the myths. The myth becomes stronger with each experiencing, each telling. Celebrations of a birth, a wedding, an anniversary, an Easter, a Passover, a birthday, a Christmas, a Hanukah, a christening, a reunion, and a graduation are the kinds of continuing events that extend the myth. Myths explore such questions as, Where am I? Who am I? Why am I here? What is my journey? What is my place in my world? These are timeless, universal questions incapable of precise answers; they engage body, mind, and soul. For those who believe there is no soul, please read on. There's probably another name for it.

Recent history, up until World War II, saw iconographic programs in post offices, courthouses, stock markets, banks, utility companies, and office buildings. The iconographic art gave meaning to many of the major buildings of New York City. Visualize the Woolworth Building, Rockefeller Center, the Metropolitan Museum, the New York Public Library, the Chrysler Building, the Empire State Building—they all have icons

embedded in them that made them more than just functional buildings. After World War II such iconography became rare.

To explore this additional layer of design, let me lead you through the design of a simple building. The design of the Nob Hill House involved intangibles that I didn't mention in Chapter 11 because doing so would have confused the other issues. Indeed, I believe these second thoughts of intangibles add something of value to the experience of the building.

The iconographic program here is *the Journey*. It will have several stories within it. The first story comes in defining the place, the location uniquely yours in ways

The architect Cass Gilbert used hundreds of icons on the exterior and interior of the Woolworth Building in New York City, built as the tallest building in the world in 1911.

that own the place beyond the legalities of the deed. On a typical street pattern, in a row of buildings, this requires both imagination and invention. However, in this example, the mythic journey begins thus: A road spirals up around the hill to the place, the *genus loci*, the *axis mundi*, the center of this particular world—visible from miles away near the top of a hill. Looking out, one senses this place as the beginning of the Texas hill country, with the Colorado River flowing toward the Gulf of Mexico connecting us by water with the rest of the world. I know exactly where I am: Earth, Latitude 30° 17' 50", Longitude at 97° 47' 55", altitude 922.2 feet above sea level, a physical place that I want to make also a metaphysical place.

The historical and geological story of this place on a hill extends into the human story viewed in the skyline of the modern city: the dome of the Capitol of Texas, the towers of the universities, the tall buildings of known and unknown enterprises. Vitruvius tells us to locate the building on high ground with salubrious breezes; Frank Lloyd Wright tells us to locate it near the brow of the hill rather than on the top. I had to go with Vitruvius because of the small site. Any primitive builder seeking to build a ceremonial site would relate to the hills, orient to the stars, perhaps the cardinal compass points, and focus toward an important distant object to give meaning to the place. In this case, facing due southeast would relate to the cardinal points, the direction of prevailing breezes, and the view down the glistening Colorado River.

One objective here is to make this place the center of a personal world. Where do you start? When possible, I like to start with the concept of a clearing, a contained space under the sky, sheltered by simple roofs. It seemed perfect here to start by placing a square, pyramidal roof facing southeast, the diagonals of the square on the cardinal points of the compass; and to angle the ridge of the roof so that one can sight up the roof ridge to see Polaris, the North Star. This mythic locking-on to the cosmos makes this roof seem "just right" intellectually. I thought about what was built in simpler times, when one related to the land and the climate before air conditioning allowed overwhelming architectural pretense, and I thought of how I might articulate the space under that roof as a "dog run," the space in between the stone masses and under the apex of the pyramid. That reinforced the architectural concept; in the Beaux-Arts era it would have been called the *parti*.

With this parti anchoring the pyramidal roof on the side of the hill, enclosing a central space, a clearing, I have a concept that can be metaphysical as well as physical. I can use the historical vernacular forms of the region to help the myths unfold and develop a clear, specific sense of place, a place in the cosmos and the topos—it connected.

With place established, other myths can be engaged: myths about time, life's journey through time, the future, spirituality, sense of self, and many levels of meaning and celebration beyond that of comfortable shelter. The myth of a Texas hill country architectural idiom is expressed in limestone, metal roofs, broad overhangs with thin roof edges, porches, small openings

against the west sun, and a clear search for shade and breeze. These are icons that enhance the myths of central Texas buildings. A steamship company pamphlet given to nineteenth-century German immigrants bound for Texas gave instructions on how to build a shelter in the harsh Texas climate: "Face into the southeastern breeze. Build a basic cabin, later a second cabin, one for cooking and eating, one for sleeping; separate the cabins by 10 to 20 feet to form a roofed breezeway (dogrun) and add a porch to shelter the house from the sun." This is the parti of the Nob Hill House described here—to which I added glass walls at each end of the dog run to allow for air conditioning. The myth of the harsh Texas summer is responded to by the maxim, "Find a breeze and get in the shade." Make shade with porches and overhangs; orient for shade and breeze. Air conditioning makes this irrelevant today in Texas unless one delights in natural settings, feeling breezes, and sensing weather's variants before it gets too hot or too cold—five good months a year. One can celebrate at least one meal on the porch on most days,

even in harsh temperature regions. The stone walls and floors, sheltered by a thin-edged metal roof, made people ask, "Is this an old house?" That's evidence that this parti possessed authenticity.

A clearing in the wilderness creates a place. In a forest, the clearing would be an enclosed space, a place of light. Primitive tribes would mark the center of their world by making a hearth of three stones or a mound of five stones. Other cultures would place a pole as the *axis mundi*—their world center. The Maya created a sacred clearing by building a group of three pyramids to form a ceremonial space. This clearing becomes the central space. In every building I have designed I have made a central

TOP LEFT: The front gate is a portal into the personal world of Nob Hill, where crossing the threshold begins a journey toward the distant horizon as part of the iconic program.

TOP RIGHT: Rather than a *front yard*, it is a Mediterranean patio, an atrio of a sixteenth-century church, a clearing in the woods, a Maya primordial sea, or simply an enclosed garden.

The snake looks toward a view of the remaining journey.

View from the house back to the front gate looks through the patio garden.

The cross axis as a transept with the dining table as the alter.

OPPOSITE PAGE BOTTOM: The view and path continue through the house, as does the slate image of the watery snake, symbol of the *journey*, heading toward the distance.

clearing in the form of a patio or a large central space.

Joseph Campbell, an authority on myths, advises that they "help us experience the rapture of being alive." One's own personal myth becomes one's largest mystery, more important than goals or plans or possessions. Imbedding this myth in a building can help one understand the journey. "Journey" and "time" can be sensed in linear progression through spaces. A circular path of spaces gives unending repetitions. The linear mythic journey expresses a beginning, middle, and end or extension to infinity.

In the Nob Hill experiment, the journey is a story that begins as one spirals up to the top of the hill, where a small plaza is edged on two sides by stone walls. A portal in the stone wall opens with a thick wooden gate to make the threshold into the private world marked by a walled garden courtyard, expressing in a mythic sense the beginning. The courtyard is the beginning of the journey—as in the Garden of Eden with its biblical icons. In a different mythic system, the space formed by temple-mountains in the Maya creation myth represents the primordial sea, the underworld, where the Maya gods and ancestors live. The Maya ceremonial space represented by this garden advances historically to represent a third mythic system, the sixteenth-century Spanish/Mesoamerican ceremonial space of the Atrio (churchyard) with Posa Chapels in the corners, a Via Sacra walk around the garden-atrio, a Tree of Life connecting the underworld with the heavens, and a representation of the gathered faithful by post oaks and cedars in the center of the garden-atrio.

The Nob Hill interior can be read as a sanctuary nave with cross axes arranged like a church transept leading to the Green Chapel (master bedroom) and the Red Chapel (the kitchen). Fireplaces anchor each end of the transept. The altar of the nave serves as the dining table; the view through the glass is the retabla. The journey ends in infinity.

Sighting up the roof ridge to Polaris sets the scene to watch the constellations circle the house through the night.

You can enhance the experience of progression through a building by using the idea of *chakras*, the mythic Oriental meanings related to seven areas of the human body. Thinking through the chakras can give a particular focus to each event along a linear progression through the body of the building. The first chakra roots the building to the rest of the world. The second chakra represents the beginning, the entrance. The third chakra represents the navel as the connection to the world of energy and knowledge, symbolized here by a round reading table laden with books. The fourth chakra represents the heart, symbolized

here by the seating at the center of the clearing under the apex of the pyramid. The fifth chakra represents the mouth and throat, in this case the dining table. The sixth chakra represents the eyes and the other senses, represented here by the distant view. The seventh and final chakra, called "spiritual energy beyond," is the view of the sky and clouds, the river, the skyline, sometimes a rainbow. I have used chakras to articulate events along a progression and help form an idea of what should go on at each place to reinforce the experience.

One has to include Feng Shui because it can be another form-giver or modifier when you take time to understand it or work with a Feng Shui master as a consultant. I've found Feng Shui ideas to be helpful. See the Reading List.

It's the historic myths of a building that are easiest to understand—connections to one's past as giving value to one's experience of a place. Things remembered, such as ideas of the clearing, the frontier cabin, the plaza, atrio, nave, transept, cloister, recollections of architectural typology, diverse cultures, hero myths, and natural landscapes—all give meaning and involve myths. Add to the house or building the family stories or institutional history, and there is a recollection of myths of the place expressed in the iconography of objects, paintings, photographs, favorite things, heirlooms, and spaces.

Bernard Berenson in *Definition of Culture* asserts,

The effort to build a House of Life where man will be able to attain the highest development that his animal nature will permit, taking him ever further away from the jungle and the cave, and bringing him nearer and nearer to that humanistic society which under the name of Paradise, Elysium, Heaven, City of God, Millennium, has been the craving of all good men these last four thousand years and more.

In building such a "House of Life," many things or places have commonly understood symbolic meanings as icons: the hearth, the bed, the stove, the table, the reading place, the listening place, the viewing place, the talking place, the thinking place, the workplace, the cozy place, the public place, the cleansing place, the dressing place, the attic, the basement, the sunrise place, the sunset place, the lunch place, the winter place, the summer place, the other-world place, the underworld place, the earthly world place, the celestial world place. All are places, objects, and times to be celebrated. These are more than functions for form to follow; these are the stuff from which the myths of Paradise are made.

In the Nob Hill experiment, I tried to see if I could tell a story that would communicate the journey. But who would read the several mythic themes and progressions? For me, it completed my consciousness of the house. I thought I might be the only person who could read the iconography. But when the poet Betty Sue Flowers and, later, the Maya anthropologist Linda Schele visited, they found the meanings instantly.

While the experiment was still new, another reading came when the noted architect and author Christopher Alexander visited the house. I was intrigued to see how he would perceive the house and what he might say because I had followed his advice in *A Pattern Language*. He wandered in through the gate, then through the courtyard, looking down, seeing only the paving. But as he approached the front door, he stopped and said, "What's going on here?" I told him that I was trying to tell a story through the spatial progressions and icons along the way. He looked around, perceived a bit of what I was trying to do, and excitedly said, "Have you written anything about this?" When I said no, he asked, "Have you not had the time or have you not had the courage?" We spent the rest of the evening talking about how buildings could, and perhaps should, tell stories. We recalled that important architecture used to have an iconographic program as well as a functional program and thought that it might again. His challenge caused me to go into such detail here.

To summarize, my objective in these experiments was to find ways to design that enhance a sense of place and purpose, but this only scratches the surface. In reaching beyond function, style, theory, and personal preference, I found the myths to be determinants of form that add intrinsic value to the architectural experience.

Absence of mythic content in architecture is a missed opportunity. Of course, all the myths and meanings could be ignored in this experiment and one could simply describe this house as real estate in a classified ad: "Charming 3 bedroom, 3 $^1/_2$ bath, stone house on a hill with a view."

*Always design a thing by considering it in its
next larger context—a chair in a room, a
room in a house, a house in an environment,
an environment in a city plan.*

ELIEL SAARINEN

(1873–1950)

Dear John:

Your project for a lakeside resort sounds exciting and sounds like a welcome addition to the coast. As a developer/builder you already know how to approach the design process, so I want to offer a handful of practical guidelines that I've found useful in making the myriad design decisions involved in a building. Whether dogma or personal preference or style, they will give you a point from which to begin. Some of these guidelines I describe here are broad and conceptual; others address the hundreds of thousands of design details encountered in building. It is important to know that every guideline is subject to question, because the exception often proves to be the best solution.

1. *"Decide first where not to build."*
This injunction came from one of my mentors, the city planner Sam Zisman; it's similar to "First, do no harm," and it's the key to intelligent site planning because if you decide first where not to build, the choices of places to build will reveal themselves. Evaluate your site so as to respect the best part of it by not building on that part. Instead, consider building on the worst part to cover it up. The same applies at other scales: for instance, in a room decide where not to place furniture, and in a garden decide where not to place plants— these places are the best spaces for people.

2. *Make a place.*
Places are spaces that get fixed in your memory and become part of your life. Life takes place. We cherish memories of the sensations of place and seek the discovery of new places. A place can be a city, a neighborhood, a park, a lake, a street, a garden, a house, a room, a chair, or a paragraph in a book. All form a personal hierarchy of places that exist—in fact or illusion—in your memory.

3. *Form a space.*
Planes—the floors, walls, and ceilings of buildings—form architectural space and give it shape. On a larger scale space is created between buildings. Space and area differ. Area is flat and two-dimensional. Space is the three-dimensional substance in which we live. Spaces leading up to and around the building create the presence of a building. Groups of buildings form spaces that can create a courtyard, a plaza, a campus, street, or, in the absence of design, a wasteland. Inside the building, the three-dimensional space is designed to form rooms, interlocking spaces, and connectors, held together in movement as a spatial progression. The art of space is the substance of architecture. It is to be shaped, related to other spaces, and assembled in progressions.

4. *Locate for the senses.*
Consider each of the five senses in locating the spaces of the building.

   1. Consider what your eyes see: the light, the views of near and distant points of interest, and the visual relationship to neighboring buildings, spaces, and landscape. Focus on views of a distant object, a mountain, a river, or a tower, if you are so fortunate, or gaze at an urban or natural landscape.

   2. Orient the spaces so you will feel the breeze and sense the heat of the sun or cool of shade trees or nearby water. When possible I orient the longest or most inhabited side of the building facing south because that light is the most available and the most controllable, whereas east and west sun that penetrate the building at low angles can be harsh and difficult to manage. North light is less intense, cooler in color and diffused, desirable for some conditions. When you want sunlight to enter all rooms, consider orienting the building on the diagonal of the cardinal points, with the principal spaces facing southeast. Outside spaces, gardens, patios, and spaces

between buildings are an integral part of the whole. The outside space formed by the buildings may be the most important room in which to be.

3. Screen and protect from sounds that bother, such as sounds of traffic and noise from the neighborhood. Find or create delight from sounds like splashing water—it can also screen unwanted sounds.

4. Avoid the fumes from traffic, industry, and nature that smell bad. (Offensive sounds and smells are often uncontrollable and may be such an irritation that a different site should be found.)

5. For the sense of taste, just find the most desirable location for meals and snacks.

I enjoy orienting spaces to precise cardinal points of the compass to help me know where the sun will enter rooms, to predict where to see sunrise and sunset at equinox and solstice, and to follow the stars.

5. Orient for energy conservation.

An aspect ratio of length to width of 2 to 1, with the long dimension facing south, limits exposure to the sun on the harsh east and west sides of the building while still having a good area-to-perimeter ratio. Sun on south exposures is easier to predict and control with overhangs. North provides a diffused light and puts no direct light or radiant heat into the building. Exceptions to this rule are when the topography or view dictates, or when you need to protect from excessive sunlight architecturally or with landscape. *Green architecture* and *sus-*

tainability are terms given to a broad range of concerns in the building and its operation, efficient energy and water use being the most critical. In cold climates, consider an orientation for light and heat in a sort of square plan oriented forty-five degrees off the cardinal points because all of the rooms will receive sunshine at some time during the day. The many issues involved in orientation and sustainability can be explored in the Reading List.

6. In a hot climate, make shade. In a cold climate, bring sunshine.

This may seem self-evident, but keep it primary in your thoughts. This alone will bring you better comfort and lower energy bills.

7. Trees are great assets.

Trees shade the building from the sun and screen unwanted views, offer a sense of shelter, and provide texture, color, and mass, as well as being one of nature's great delights. A mature tree cools the air around its base by eight to ten degrees during the summer months. Designing around existing trees and placing new ones can create a special setting for the building. Trees can extend or shelter the building, screen unattractive views, and create outdoor spaces related to the building. Do every thing in your power to avoid cutting down trees; add as many as you can. In most cases it's more pleasant to see a tree than a building.

8. Organize the plan to give rooms a lively natural light.

Southern exposure is generally the most

preferred for all rooms. North is desirable for diffused light in galleries or work spaces. East is good for spaces used mainly in the morning and for shady terraces in the afternoon. West is an undesirable orientation in hot climates, desirable in cold climates. West exposures are best used for windowless rooms such as storerooms and garages in hot climates, or, in cold climates, for rooms used mainly in the late afternoon or evening.

9. Shape the building by considering the organization of inside spaces as they create outside spaces.

Conceptually, begin by shaping the plan of the building in relationship to its surroundings, buildings, trees, and landforms, seeking to shape both inside and outside space. Manipulate the shape of the organized inside spaces to form the outside spaces and bring light and air into the building. Shaping the three-dimensional open space gives particular form at both the urban design scale and the private garden scale. These shapes become the sculptural forms of the buildings and spaces—the solids and voids. Yes, voids have sculptural form too.

10. Shape the building by organizing functional spaces.

Organize functional spaces in a two-dimensional floor plan, working back and forth with your spatial objectives. Controlling this effort will be the detailed functional elements of the building, so start with the functional plan diagrams. I find it useful to think of the simple geometric forms that yield desirable spaces and natural light. Consider the possibilities of these abstract plan forms.

11. Plan forms.

The simple rectangle is the most economical shape, as demonstrated by the archetypical cabin in the woods and the archetypical commercial office building cereal-box

Most plans that are rectilinear fit one of these footprints or can be rotated to make angles as well as intersections and combinations.

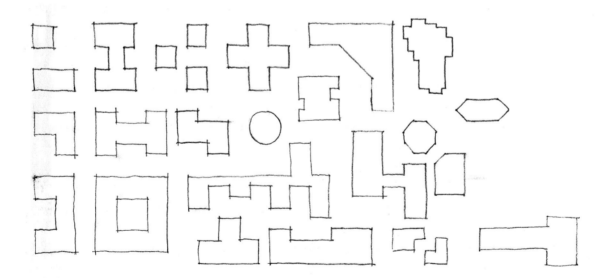

form. It is an object on a ground plane or an object connected to an urban mass. It has a limited capacity to form outside spaces or to provide spatial progressions or desirable orientations.

12. Design what the eye will see.
Visualize walking through the site and the building by mentally walking through the floor plan, visualizing exactly what someone will see on a path through the building. That is how we sense the spaces, surfaces, and vistas in a building. Concentrate on the design of the views of what you want to see and minimize the rest. There is a theory that the Greeks designed their visually rich panoramas in such a way that from your viewpoint you will see an object or a building corner at each fifteen-degree increment as you view the scene. I found it satisfying to see from my favorite spot in the garden at about fifteen-degree intervals, starting with a framed mirror, then a large pot of bamboo, and on around to a bed of flowers, a garden gate, a bench, and a fountain. Try this and see how it works for you from your favorite viewpoints.

13. Express the character and scale of the building in a way that communicates its intentions.
Is the building to be monumental, intimate and cozy, or something in between? Does the scale communicate monument, religious aspiration, prestigious corporation, effective government, substantial school, or comfortable, secure homestead? Each will have a different proportional relationship with the size of the human body that will be indicated by the size of spaces and elements

in the façade, such as the height of the entrance. Character is expressed by the use of scale, form, materials, icons, and nuances reached by design study. Your eye and your critical faculties will be your guide.

14. Design a roof that makes shelter and shade: it forms the shape of building.
Sometimes it's good to design the roof of a building first, and then get under it. Make sure that flat roofs are not flat—a slope of at least $1/4"$ to a foot is needed along with plenty of routes for the water to get off the roof without damaging anything. Roofs can get complicated; keep them simple, because each change of material or intersection with another roof plane or wall invites a leak.

15. Make your building look like gravity is working with it rather than against it.
Dramatic exceptions of the Modernist movement defy gravity with extraordinary grace, using the structural finesse available to our era, and can create the illusion that a building is hovering or cantilevering over empty space. For this, use caution; gravity is the *Great Resolver* in aesthetics as well as in engineering. I find as much or more comfort in seeing gravity calmly at work than seeing the modern expression of a cantilever demonstrating great stress to hold itself off the ground.

16. Express the structure.
Let materials do what they are meant to do. Structures have four kinds of forces: compression, tension, and their combination in bending and torsion. Stone and brick work in compression in walls, arches, and

domes, where the stones or bricks are held together by gravity to support the load above it; stone will span small openings as a lintel. Wood and steel work with all forces, usually as linear elements in a frame or truss. Steel works well in tension, as in cable structures. Steel-reinforced concrete can do most anything, including columns, beams, slabs, rigid frames, and many sculptural shapes. Metals and carbon fiber plastics can carry all forces within stressed skin construction used in airplanes and cars, and more recently in sculptural architectural forms. Because most of today's buildings are concrete or steel frames covered with a thin veneer, expressing the structure may not be necessary, but our eye still wants to see what is holding up the building. The exceptions are seen in the new architecture of *blobs* and *wobbly* buildings, whose legitimacy is in the fantasy they can evoke.

17. Manipulate the structural system.

This can create unique spaces and complex sculptural form. In addition, it can express ephemeral lightness of high technology or the eternal mass of earthy solidity. The extremes are dramatic: Calatrava bridges versus Romanesque churches and stone fortresses. In my year in jet aircraft structural design we sought to make the structure as light as possible so as to use less fuel, carry more payload, need less aerodynamic lift, and fly faster. A team called Weights and Measures would come by each designer's desk and ask, "How much weight do you have in your assembly?"— like Buckminster Fuller asking the museum director, "How much does your building weigh?" Lightness is a fascination of our time—to leave the earth, become suspended, fly. On the other hand, heaviness has its reasons as well: permanence, stability, security, compression, and identification with Earth. That's what seduced me in Mexico, where the timeless technology depended on heavy walls with simple arches and domes—all in compression. You can go light or heavy, or juxtapose their contrasts. Of course, both of the systems are hard to imitate in wood frame, sheetrock, veneers, and ersatz materials of the kinds now generally used.

18. Walls do most of the work.

Use walls to form space, to define, to give security and shelter, to enclose, to screen, to divide, to give privacy, and to sit on as low benches. Give them color, texture, thickness, and proportion. Make them high enough to contain more than an area but to contain, visually, a three-dimensional space.

19. Foundations come first.

Foundations are invisible, and while one may not want to spend money where it doesn't show, the investment is essential to structural integrity. Test holes by qualified laboratories and foundation specialists can assure the client and the designer that the investment in the building will be secure structurally. Because the substrate of a site is not seen, several test holes are needed. On a site in Oregon near a millrace, there had been a single test hole made that showed good bedrock at five feet, so we scheduled another series of test holes closer to the millrace, but we were on a fast track to finish the five-story college dormitory before school started, so we were well along in design when the soils report came in. Bad news: the test showed that the bedrock fell off toward the millrace to a depth over ninety feet. Our brilliant engineer redesigned the foundation to put half of the building on piers to bedrock and the other half on pilings that would hold the building up by friction on the silt, both sides balanced by measuring the weight of each half so that each would subside at the same rate along an expansion joint through the building. The floors are still level at the joint.

20. In selection of materials, consider first the natural materials indigenous to the region.
Compare these with the new processed synthetics or materials from other regions. The natural indigenous materials may last longer, be cheaper, and use less energy to manufacture and transport. On the other hand, look at the latest technology to find the best possible material choice for the particular situation; just be cautious of new materials. I've made this comparison ever since the failure of a new material that I used caused a lawsuit.

21. Water goes downhill.
Water runs either into your building or away from it; owners do not tolerate water running into their building from the ground or the roof—and shouldn't. Every exterior surface, no matter how small, should slope away from the building at $1/4$" per foot, or $1/8$" per foot if on smooth paving—that includes little things like copings, ledges, and windowsills.

COMPOSITION AND PROPORTION HAVE SIMPLE ANCIENT RULES THAT OUR EYES FIND SATISFYING.

1. Compose objects in groups of three rather than groups of two or four.
Two objects can present a dichotomy, opposing elements that may or may not be the desirable message.

2. Columns are best in pairs, rather than threes.
Always have an even number of columns making an odd number of spaces in between. Ever see a Greek temple with three columns? A column in the middle is to be avoided. A lovely exception is a Gothic entrance or a Moorish window with double arches.

3. Avoid putting objects in the middle of a space.
This restricts movement and can make the space static rather than dynamic. Remember that the space not consumed with objects is the place where people can be.

4. Compose an arbitrary division of a line or plane at its "third point" or "center."
This is a good place to start for a quick eyeball judgment. It may be either dull or powerful; for proportion, you must decide and adjust to what seems like the inevitable location based on your eye.

5. Symmetry brings order.
Symmetry can be strong and assertive, even monumental, and it seems like an easy way to compose. It presents the familiar and pleasing kind of balance you see in the human body. But the limitations of symmetry are that visually, it may make the composition static and uninteresting, and functionally, it often doesn't work well. Asymmetry is a useful composition tool and can be dynamic or balanced, giving emphasis to a particular element of the design. Your eye must work out the balance.

6. Once symmetry enters a composition, it demands to be continued.
So, continue the symmetry or go into dynamic symmetry, where things are visually balanced but are unequal.

7. The best-known proportion is the Golden Rectangle, a ratio of width to length of 1 to 1.618.
This historically satisfying proportion approximates the proportion of a 35 mm slide or a 3 x 5 card. To use this proportion, simply multiply the width of the rectangle by 1.618 to get the dimension of the length or height. For example, a window 1 meter by 1.618 meters is found in many cultures. Use this for windows, doors, sizes of rooms, façades, anything—it may not work but it's a good place to start. (Notice that this is the first mention of math, and this is no more math than you would use in the grocery store.)

8. Another useful proportion is the "square root of 2," the ratio of 1 to 1.414.
This ancient proportion was easily constructed in primitive cultures by using a rope to measure the diagonal of a square and rotating that length to become one of the sides of the resulting rectangle. Use the proportion ratios in both plan and section.

9. The simplest proportion is the square.
And a very powerful one—a square room, a square wall, a square window are used to make something special. A cube is super strong. Again, as with symmetry in a

The most used proportions: square, square root of 2, Golden Rectangle, double square.

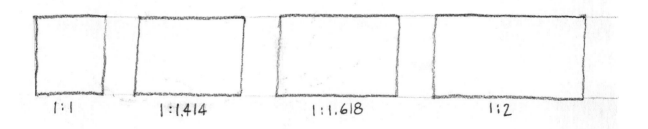

1:1   1:1.414   1:1.618   1:2

façade, when you start it, your eye may insist that you continue it as a design idiom.

10. The double square and the double cube are useful proportions and also good organizers of space.
They are less overwhelming than the square or cube.

11. Use the circle as an organizing device.
The circle has the magic of containing the most area with the least perimeter. It has so many symbolic and geometric complications when used in walls of a building that one must use it thoughtfully because it is one of the most demanding forms. It is useful as an invisible tool for composition.

12. The 3-4-5 triangle can be used to make a right angle.
It's a useful tool of ancient geometry. This is what Antonio Gaudí, the famous architect of Barcelona, was speaking of when he said, "With two rulers and a cord one generates all architecture."

The 3–4–5 triangle made with cords has been used since primitive times to determine 90 degree angles. The cord is also used to determine a vertical line or plumb line, the force of gravity pulling at the end of the cord.

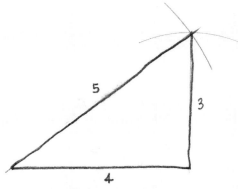

13. Color can make or break a design.
It amazes me to see how colors affect the appearance, the size, and the ambience of a building or room, and how an expert can manipulate the infinite number of colors in the visual light spectrum. A color has a hue that can be changed by mixing several colors and can be made lighter or darker by adding white or dark. Color is perceived through three variables: the actual color on the wall, the color of the light that illuminates the color, and the receptive characteristics of each person's particular eye sensitivity. See the Reading List.

USEFUL GUIDELINES FOR REFINING THE DESIGN OF A WALL OR A FAÇADE

1. Façade studies require many trials before finding the one that is "just right."
Review that procedure in the chapter on design process. This is a good place to remember that a little knowledge is a dangerous thing—get critiques.

2. Determine the geometric composition of parts of a wall.
This is determined by how they relate to each other and the whole, as described in Jonathan Hale's "The Old Way of Seeing" (Boston: Houghton Mifflin, 1994).

3. Visualize how sunlight will fall on the surfaces of your building.
Light and shadow create patterns as strong as fixed elements of the surface and cause the surface to have varying patterns.

4. In the design of a wall, draw absolutely everything that you will see and compose it as a whole.

Look for those things that you do not want to see, such as electrical switches, transformers, trash containers, electrical wires and entries, meters, scuppers, and vents.

5. A garage door hurts any street façade.
There's no place to hide it. Find another place for the car.

6. Glass is rarely transparent.
When one looks at a façade from the outside in daylight, glass more often reflects surroundings, makes glare, or appears as a dark hole. Glass becomes transparent only when the light is brighter on the side opposite the viewer, as when one is inside looking out on a sunny day or looking through glass into a lighted interior space at night.

7. Windows happen.
Windows are major elements in design; they are the difference between a building and a solid sculpture. We can hide the windows behind a glass skin, part transparent and part opaque, as in a glass-box office building or a sophisticated sculptural geometry of glass skin. But for the most part, we must deal with the composition and detail of windows as major elements of the design. The size and shape of the window expresses what's going on behind it. Vertical windows suggest people are in a room standing up; horizontal windows suggest that the people are lying down or in motion; a large central window suggests the major space or function of the building.

INVENTION DEL VIGNOLA

Designers using traditional forms and details need to use proper sources, such as this example in works by Giacomo Barozzi da Vignola.

8. The use of columns and moldings has very specific precedents.
Columns and moldings can guide you if you will take the time to really study them or take extra care in their invention. If you can't do moldings or any other period ornament correctly, don't do them at all. There are thousands of excellent historic examples to copy.

9. Should you wish to design a façade around classical or traditional details, go to a good firsthand source in a proper book.
This is preferable to casually looking at an example and trying to approximate it. From the proper source, copy or have someone copy it precisely with only minor modifications for your design. Build it carefully. The suburbs are full of unfortunate, thoughtless, inaccurate borrowings such as the front door as tall as a Triumphal Arch that shouts its ignorance in a McMansion.

10. The entrance makes a statement about the character of the building—the introduction to this particular building—where the spatial progression begins.

The entrance can be dominant in the façade, minor, or even hidden, but you usually want to make its location obvious. Sounds easy, but on many student projects—oftenbeautifullysophisticateddesigns—I have to ask, "Where's the front door?"

SPACE AND LIGHT (THE ARCHITECT'S RAW MATERIALS)

1. Ceiling heights are best when higher than ten feet, preferably eleven feet in normal rooms.

And to be commodious—or for acoustical reasons when music is played—ceilings should be at least fourteen feet to eighteen feet, determined by design in section drawings. (Builders' houses became standardized by the postwar FHA minimum requirement of eight-foot ceilings, which instantly became the dimension of manufactured wallboard and the ceiling height of most U.S. homes.) Another way to determine height is to set it at three-fourths of the smallest dimension of the room. The ceiling height is not necessarily proportioned to the size of the room; it is proportioned for its effect on the feeling of space. Consider variations in ceiling height along the progression of spaces.

A reference plane, a wall, can help organize the composition of objects and masses.

2. The shape of ceilings and volume of the room define the space and the way we sense it.

For example, barrel vaults, domes, exotic curves, trusses, sloped rafters, and beams shape a space. Treat the ceiling as a vital element of the space. Great rooms have distinctive ceilings. People who enjoy architecture always look up.

3. Create lines of movement or axes that start and end.

Have the axes pass through openings in layers of walls along the way. A long axis or enfilade can increase the apparent size of the spaces. Design the walk through your building as if you were doing a movie and the camera is the walking observer.

4. Establish one wall of a space as the reference plane, then organize space and objects in relation to it.

A reference plane can help compose spaces. It can define a limit or suggest movement.

5. Dimensions that seem spacious are useful to know as you go about laying out rooms.

My rule is that a room needs to be at least thirteen feet wide, but sixteen feet is better, and the major room needs to be at least twenty-one feet wide. (It's amazing how many English country houses and French chateaus are about twenty-one feet wide. A generous outdoor terrace or porch needs to be at least fifteen feet wide. Major corridors are best at least seven feet wide—furniture can be accommodated, and they will seem like more than passageways.)

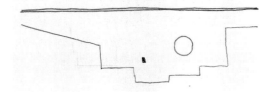

6. Hide light sources.

You should never see a light bulb. Lighting only the paintings or objects will probably light the entire room without any additions except for task lighting. Supplements will be needed to add an overall incident light and to vary the mood or setting of the space. Glare is the enemy.

7. Natural light makes spaces come alive.

Balance the light in a room with light on two sides, three if you can; four is better. A colleague once described his ideal light for a room to be like what one sees while sitting under a large spreading tree on a sunny day, with light all around and dappled light coming from above through the leaves. Consider using skylights to give an effect of light sliding down a wall, or a skylight in the middle of the space like an oculus to give a centering light. This kind of natural light often distinguishes a work of architecture from a building.

8. In the absence of natural light, the "three-lamp rule" provides a good balanced light for the average room or office.

The lamps should be arranged in a triangle around the perimeter of the room. Often this provides enough light to both light the room and light reading tasks in a residential size room.

9. Keep the light balanced with a low brightness ratio (the ratio of the brightest area to the darkest area).

It's more comfortable on the eyes. A bright window on one side of a room needs to be balanced by a window on the opposite side of the room or balanced with light from above. Windows that let light shine on adjacent planes, like deep window reveals or on ceilings or walls, spread and diffuse their light around the edges, reducing the brightness ratio. Curtains and blinds can mediate brightness. Because lamps or ceiling fixtures may also be too bright, important spaces should have their lights on dimmers. When needed, a high brightness ratio, like a spotlight, gives drama.

10. Use mirrors to expand space.

A mirror on the full face of a door or window or an entire wall can give desirable effects. Mirrors in frames appear a bit like holes in a wall, which may be desirable for expanding the space but works against containing the space. A mirror placed so that a person cannot see himself but sees instead another scene from an angle is a playful trick in a garden.

11. Sound can be as important as light in some spaces.

The sounds one hears in a room indicate the size of the space. Acoustics can make or break a building. The sounds of a beautiful concert may be lifeless if there is a short reverberation time, or chaotic if there is too long a reverberation time. The noises that can't be isolated and are so loud that they cannot be tolerated must be silenced, or the room should be relocated; the space where music is performed is a musical instrument itself that brings music to the listener. There was an acoustical challenge in designing for the sound of the Great Hall of the Apparel Mart that was to seat two thousand people. We sought excellent acoustics for concert quality music even though it was not a requirement of the program. The forms of the walls were shaped for live acoustical reinforcement. A well-known acoustician was employed to advise us, yet we felt that his recommendations would make the reverberation time too short for music. The acoustical consultant proposed hanging huge loudspeaker boxes from the sixty-foot-tall ceiling to alleviate the concern that performers would be bothered by the echo of their own sounds. To test our design against that of the acoustician, we had a loudspeaker suspended on a crane sixty feet above a vacant lot. My partner and I then sang an aria and discovered that no echo could be perceived. Because of its acoustics, the Great Hall was a good venue for concerts; the Dallas Symphony played their summer series there.

DETAILS

God is in the details.
MIES VAN DER ROHE

1. Use natural local materials.
This will give authenticity, compatibility, and a sense of belonging and will probably save money and energy. Transporting materials can be costly.

2. The number of building materials used can have an important effect.
Use only a few building materials to give solidity and formality (a Gothic cathedral used three: stone, glass, and lead). Use a lot of materials to loosen up (the Bilbao Guggenheim used many).

3. Two materials meeting in exactly the same plane tend to create a messy joint.
When changing materials in a wall, consider a reveal or break of $1/2$ inch to 3 feet—whatever seems right. Moldings can also be used at the juncture of two materials to mediate the intersection. The exceptions to this rule are beautiful, especially in marble, in Italy.

4. Create wall thickness.
This refers both to real thickness and the illusion thereof. It makes the building seem more substantial on the interior and exterior and can hold a lot of insulation. Wall thickness can be created by the placement of bookcases and closets near major doors and windows. Deep reveals at windows help mediate the brightness of the incoming light by reflecting light on the side walls. The current preference for superthin walls can be appealing in a well-crafted work.

5. Deep reveals at windows and doors serve several purposes.
They give a sense of substance, provide a layering effect with more shadow, and help keep out driving rain.

6. Doors are better when they are solid and substantial.
Interior doors are best as inch-and-three-quarter solid core, which adds an unexpected sense of solidity, much preferred over conventional doors that are thinner

and hollow. Think also of the possible need for wheelchair access by widening the doorways—required in public buildings and advantageous in residences.

7. Using double doors that swing onto thick wall openings allows the door to be out of the way when open.

When a door is needed but a large swinging door would not work, use double doors.

8. The height of the windowsill affects the feeling and visual experience of the space inside.

There are several choices: at the height of a table or a desk, about thirty inches above the floor, or at the floor where the floor plane extends to the outdoors. To give a sense of the outdoors but more sense of security, use a sill height of sixteen inches.

9. Consider the window treatment when designing the window.

Visualize the need and possibility for drapery, shutters, or blinds to control light and privacy—this is critical to the success of the room. Window treatments are better not left to chance.

10. Stairs must be generous, unless they're only service or fire stairs.

A generous stair has a shallow slope, long treads, and short risers that give dignity to movement—ease and safety too. Minimum dimensions are 9" tread and 7.5" riser; an often-used ratio is 10.5" tread and 7.25" riser. Grand stairs will use a longer tread and shorter riser, such as 6" and 12". For outside stairs be more generous: a 14"

tread and 5" riser is max, and 4" is better. In an elegant hotel, I was surprised when I walked up two stories without noticing it—the stair had a slow and graceful ratio of 13.5" to 5". When you feel comfortable or uncomfortable on a stair, check the ratio of tread to riser and make note of it.

11. Moldings can be key ingredients of a design.

Most designers today have had no training in moldings and often make awkward use of them, yet moldings can provide important transitions between walls and ceilings and around certain doors and windows. I remember seeing Michelangelo's moldings in Rome at the Campidoglio for the first time. I was amazed at how they caught the light with such grace and balance, and when I felt them with my hands it was an emotional experience—this was genius. Moldings are sculpture, so think of them as such rather than as pieces of trim.

12. Place light switches on the wall level with the doorknobs, at thirty-six to thirty-nine inches above the floor.

Why? Because this is where the resting hand will be, and it's out of our field of vision, so a wall switch won't distract from a nearby painting. Also, the switch plate lining up with the doorknob gives a small degree of order. (Switches are placed high simply for the convenience of the electrician who is installing them.)

13. Plan the furniture arrangements before planning the walls.

Figure out where and how you want things

to happen by placing the primary functional furniture groups before placing walls. You can even mock this out on the site. Figure out where you want to be at various times of the day, what you want to see, where you want to eat, and where you would like to read, play games, watch television, and such. Example: When I was designing a lake house, the clients showed me where they always had their picnics on the unbuilt site and said they spent a lot of time at the breakfast table, so I made a dining alcove on the special picnic spot that became the most important room of their house. Another example: In a house I visited, there was not a comfortable, well-lit place to read, watch television, or work on a computer; the house was wonderful for entertaining a hundred people, yet it worked poorly for the activities of one or two people. Not placing the furniture in the plan of the room will cause some disappointing surprises when the room is built.

ROOMS IN RESIDENCES

1. The entrance is the transition between inside and outside, public and private, bad weather and shelter; it introduces the building to the visitor, receives coats and packages, is a place to exchange greetings.
The part of the entrance that's outside needs shelter from the rain, a place to sit and wait, a place to wipe feet, and it must be of a size that accommodates several people standing at the door. The part inside needs a place to sit and wait or hold coats and packages, a place for mail and messages, art, and flowers. The space can be intimate or grand, making a contrast with the ceiling height, sound, and light of adjoining rooms. In Mexico, this kind of space between street and courtyard is called a *zaguán*.

2. The kitchen is the center of many homes.
The kitchen is not only the place where we cook, eat, and read the paper and sometimes watch television; it is also the place where the children gather and play and where guests gather informally. It is often the actual living room. It can be designed as a large room with a couch and armchairs and a fireplace, or it can be a small, functional unit related discretely to a living or gathering room. Hide appliances like the fridge by placing them around a corner, or disguise them by special doors. A U-shaped plan is the most efficient arrangement for a kitchen because it can place the sink-dishwasher-stove-refrigerator ensemble close together. I like to use the three-step rule, which states that you can get to everything within three steps. My favorite arrangement allows one to plant one foot and reach sink, stove, dishwasher, and fridge without moving the foot, and still have a large room.

3. "A living room confronts each visitor with a style, a secular faith; he compares its dogmas with his, and decides whether he would like to see more of us" (W. H. Auden, "The Common Life," a poem from About the House, *p. 107).*

Most buildings have what one could call a living room, whether it is a reception room, meeting room, sales floor, or other space where people congregate. The residential living room has a long history and sometimes has been called a parlor, sometimes a drawing room, and recently a family room. Lifestyles cause many choices, yet to me the most important thing is that there is one large room that can be used to gather one's entire extended family or friends or organization, be it formal or informal. The living room needs to be of appropriate size, have light on several sides, and have seating groups, a view or at least a focal point, books, places for conversation, eating, meeting, and all the other things one would like to do in a group. Other rooms can be made smaller so that this main room can be large. This budgeting of space is useful in every building or suite of rooms because it builds a sense of place for a home, a business, or an institution. On a larger scale, urban living rooms are the special places in cities where people gather—an Italian piazza, a Mexican plaza, or a village square.

4. The bedroom can be a personal sanctuary for a couple or individual.

The bedroom has a wide range of expressions, from monastic cell to a small living room with a couch, fireplace, books, perhaps television, a writing desk, and a reading chair or two, in addition to a bed. Cluster the bathroom/closet/dressing room so that they are a unit apart from the bedroom, through a single door. Feng Shui suggests no television in the bedroom. Natural light entering the space in unusual places can give the room mystery.

5. A bathroom is best when it doesn't look like one.

The combination of dressing room/bathroom/closet is very much a social part of the house. It is where couples visit while getting dressed for the day or preparing for an event—important opportunities for communication. Add a chair. Put a window in the shower. Put the water closet in a separate room about 3 by 4.5 feet with natural light or a view, and add a few books.

6. Use alcoves in rooms to bring a personal scale to the room.

This is important for every room in a residence, but I found that alcoves are important in giving a personal scale to parts of a large public room. Once a client said, "I want this room to seat two thousand people for dinner but be comfortable for only one person." The room was the size of a football field and had sixty-foot ceilings, but several alcoves made those places pleasant for one or two people.

7. The fireplace has become a symbol more than a source of heat.

In buildings with central heating, a fireplace draws heat out of the building for a negative effect on energy use. Yet our literature and our memory make the symbolic hearth a place, a social center, a visual focus, and an anchor signaling this is a place of power, security, and domesticity. Effective heating with a fireplace can best be accomplished by using a Count Rumford firebox design with effective damper control.

8. A wall of photographs describing a corporation or a family helps make a significant place in a building.

It tells a story. It provides depth and substance to the experience of the building.

9. The outdoor room can be the most-used room in the house at some times of the year, be it called a porch, a loggia, a portico, a terrace, a patio, or a sale al aire libre. Make it useful for conversation, eating, games, and parties—even cooking in a fireplace grill. It can be no less than ten feet deep, good at fifteen feet, and best at twenty-one feet, like a major room in the house.

A list of this sort could be endless, and if it's useful to you, look at two important "lists" from two very different architects that offer wonderfully insightful design paths that can inspire and guide you.

Christopher Alexander, in his widely acclaimed book *Pattern Language* (Oxford: Oxford University Press, 1977), codified many of the simple, traditional, appropriate design issues in the making of buildings, neighborhoods, and cities. He offers a thorough understanding of many typical design issues, each of which is an excellent starting point for solving your particular design problem. Alexander's landmark book does not enjoy the wholehearted endorsement of Modernists. In fact, I heard a Cornell architecture professor say, "Whatever you do, keep the students out of Alexander's book." Nonsense. I say it is a great place to start.

Charles Moore and Donlyn Lyndon "assemble a set of observations on the composition of *places*" in their extraordinary book *Chambers for a Memory Palace* (Cambridge: MIT Press, 1994). Their themes are so well stated that, when teaching, I give a copy of the table of contents to each of my design students to pin up at their board. I want them to read it when they're confused or wondering what to do next. I use the ideas to help me enrich my design process, as a sort of checklist to help me go further, to make things "just right." Take a few minutes to think through each one of the chapter ideas and imagine the pictures. Here they are:

Axes that Reach/Paths that Wander
Orchards that Measure/Pilasters that
    Temper
Platforms that Separate/Slopes that
    Join/Stairs that Climb and Pause
Borders that Control/Walls that Layer/
    Pockets that Offer Choice and
    Change
Openings that Frame/Portals that
    Bespeak
Roofs that Encompass/Canopies that
    Center
Markers that Command/Allies that
    Inhabit
Light that Plays/Shadow that Haunts/
    Shade that Lulls
Rooms that Define/Space that Leaks Up
    Into the Light
Types that Recur/Order that Comes and
    Goes
Shapes that Remind/Ornament that
    Transmits, Transforms, and Encodes
Gardens that Civilize/Water that Pools
    and Connects
Images that Motivate

As the authors say, "The Chambers are meant to help assemble thoughts about places . . . to nurture sparks in the designer's consciousness . . . starting points, aids to the imagination." I suggest you find the book, read it, copy the contents page, and pin it up where it may help you design.

Remember, the exceptions to these guidelines could be the best, so keep your mind open for a better idea. When you discover more guidelines, add them to your personal list. May it be long and useful. But we're just getting started—design, in concept and in detail, comes from a rich set of ideas on style, taste, and design theory.

| STYLE, TASTE, AND DESIGN THEORY

If you foolishly ignore beauty, you'll soon find
yourself without it. Your life will be impover-
ished. But if you wisely invest in beauty, it will
remain with you all the days of your life.
FRANK LLOYD WRIGHT
(1886–1995)

Dear Oliver:

You expressed wonder at the influence of style and taste on design. You had not considered it, as an engineer of large construction, but you say you are now considering putting up a small office building in a residential neighborhood and need to take a closer look at design.

Design inevitably brings up the sticky matter of preferences. People's preferences—some would call them our prejudices!—have a huge effect on design and decision making in making architecture.

Even close friends can have spectacularly different ideas about what's attractive, can't they? For example, several years ago, while having lunch in the dappled light of a giant willow tree in a Mexican garden ripe with lilies, bougainvillea, scents of flowers, food, and wine, a friend and I sat at a table next to a dismal shack soon to be replaced by a house of my design. The friend, Latané Temple, my midlife mentor, took in the lush, colorful scene and remarked, with his typical frankness, "Were it not for your vanity, you could be very happy here."

It was true. Latané was a poet and painter. From his viewpoint, the place was charming—beautiful even—despite the rustic shack, or maybe even because of it. But from my own viewpoint, the shack was ugly, the product of no design, and it fit none of my aesthetic preferences, so it marred the entire scene for me. If this was vanity, so be it.

We're all concerned about what we see around us. When we are planning something new, we have questions like, How will it look? and How would I love it to look? Even if you are unaware of it, what you design or choose will exhibit your own sense of style, your own taste, your own notion of enlightened design theory, and something of your own time and place, too, plus your measure of the result on some ultimate scale of beauty, however vague. And, if you're attentive, you will doubtless discern these omnipresent qualities embedded in every building or object you behold. Volumes of scholarship have been written on these qualities, and some of my own colleagues are prominent authors of them. I hope they will forgive me as I offer you some of my own possibly heretical thoughts about these design qualities.

As you work through your design project, with or without an architect, you will become involved in matters of style, taste, design theory, and concepts of beauty. Let's start with beauty. What will you mean by that word *beauty*? And what will your architect mean by it?

You might be surprised to learn that it's a word I rarely heard around architecture schools. It wasn't out of mind, no, but it was almost unmentionable there. Even though we invoke the idea of beauty daily to describe people, nature, music, and objects—and even though we live in a culture virtually obsessed with beauty—it's rarely discussed in architecture circles, even today. Why? I think one reason is that the heavy intellectualizing and moralizing of Modernism overwhelmed the values that, to my mind, make up beauty. In the early years of Modernism, beauty was superceded by function and a rhetoric that didn't include it.

Beauty excites sensuous aesthetic pleasure; it stirs emotions; it is an aggregate of qualities in something that gives delight or exalts the mind and spirit. It applies to all aspects of life. But somehow it lost its relevance in the Brave New World of twentieth-century architecture. Some critics even used it contemptuously, as a nasty word, a word signifying an obsession with superficial values. Yet even when form is following function, it surely can be argued that one function of architecture—in fact, a vital function—is to provide beauty for the human spirit.

Can beauty be pinned down, or is it ineffable? Is one person's beauty ever any better than another person's? We've all heard that beauty is in the eye of the beholder, and who can deny it? But it seems pertinent to ask, How well educated is that eye? There is no absolute here, of course. But I believe a case can be made for the value of sensitizing the eye to compositional elements through education and ultra-attentive observation. Compositional elements, such as symmetry, proportion, rhythm, and unity, not to mention the materials and colors one has chosen, strongly affect people's sense of what is satisfying. So the better we understand them, the better we can manipulate them and adjust them to achieve a "just right" appeal to the discerning eye. Our understanding of them comes partly from good theory (i.e., plausible explanations) and partly through very attentive looking. Studying images from architectural history in books, museums, and travel trains the eye. Everything around us—everything!—affords us lessons, positive or negative, in what makes for satisfying compositions. And often the best lessons come from nature itself.

The "good eye," innate in some, definitely can be trained in others. Many who, like me, grew up with little beauty around them except in people and nature have developed their eye and mind to appreciate beauty and have made it a major quest to be more sensitive beholders.

Our beholding, our personal preferences, influence our every decision. One of my college roommates, a brilliant man, once remarked, "We build our lives on a set of well-honed prejudices." By which he meant that we learn to appreciate certain things and depreciate others. We become

liberal or conservative, nostalgic or futuristic, high tech or low tech, Ford or Honda. Some of these prejudices are well-informed, carefully positioned points of view, and others are simply personal preferences that have more to do with familiarity or ignorance than with careful thought. As we like to say, they're a matter of taste.

Speaking of taste, here is another concept that bears discussion, even though such a discussion would be even more rarely heard in architecture schools and offices. In business, in writing, in painting, in any creative endeavor, a person's taste determines myriad decisions, large and small. You may find that if you say to an architect, "Such-and-such building is in bad taste," he or she might well reply, "There's really no such thing as taste." How would you respond? I would respond, "Do you like escargot?" Taste, as I see it, is an amalgam of individual preference, critical judgment, discernment, and appreciation; in art circles it could perhaps more accurately be called design judgment. But *taste* is the common term. Taste also may be innate in some people, whereas in others it's a result, once again, of education and attentiveness. Taste is akin to connoisseurship—a skill that is developed over a long period of study and experience. Some people are widely considered to have good taste or a good eye for design. Others have no eye for design and may cheerfully admit it. Still others are said to have poor taste or bad taste and are mentally sent off to the corner. The whole question of taste is one that is good not to get defensive about; taste develops at different rates for different people. I've found it useful to be quiet and learn.

We have to know that the dictum "I don't know much about art, but I know what I like" can trump the opinion of the most highly acclaimed connoisseur or professional. Also, we know that a person with strong convictions about art—or architecture—can overcome any sensibility and walk around with blinders on, seeing only their convictions. Prejudices can be inviolate. So what do you do? To reach the highest degree of lasting satisfaction, you acquire knowledge and experiences in art and architecture—you read, see, discuss, learn.

The difference between "good" and "bad" taste is set by how well considered one's point of view is, how experienced one is, and how aware one is of elements of design. Some fortunate people simply are gifted at birth with the good eye or ear, just as others are incurably tone deaf, while some others are, shall we say, taste impaired, even though they might be highly intelligent. In architecture, one consideration is, How much true architecture has a person seen? Also, how carefully have they assessed it? Are they a connoisseur or simply opinionated? Some think the difference between good and bad is ambiguous. In fact, though, it's not only palpable, it's almost measurable—by awards, publications, and the writings of distinguished critics.

Aesthetics, of course, is finally subjective, not a value to fit into mathematical equations. But the design problem to be solved in architecture will always include aesthetics, won't it? It is a basic criterion for solving design problems, as when we must decide if some element feels wrong, almost right, or *just right*.

Unlike the education of architects, the formal training of engineers seems to ignore aesthetic values as forming no part of their responsibility. Yet engineers are responsible for many of the structures we see in the public landscape. And many of those structures damage the landscape and affect the quality of life for all that see them. On the other hand, some of the most appropriate civic design of the early 1900s was by civil engineers. And today some of the most exciting physical design has been the work of engineers. Foremost at this time is the work of Santiago Calatrava, the Spanish architect/engineer who creates, in his structures, a high art form near a peak experience. So it's partially a matter of intentions.

Let me explain by telling you a story. A common excuse for inept design is cost, and sometimes aesthetic considerations will indeed cost more; one has to decide for one's self and one's community, Is it worth it? What are the intentions? Some years ago, when a bridge over the river that forms Lake Austin was proposed as an ordinary highway bridge, a group of us went to talk to the people in charge at the Texas Department of Transportation. We were led by Ann Richards, then a county commissioner (later, governor of Texas), and voiced a plea for a special and significant design for this important, perhaps even symbolic, bridge. The engineers in charge said, "Anything other than the least possible cost is a waste of taxpayers' money. It would be irresponsible." They wouldn't budge. But we pointed out that their typical bridge design would create a public-safety hazard because it would put pylons in the river into which pleasure boats might crash, especially at night. Seeing an opening, I sketched, on the back of a road map, a long-span bridge with a unique character that eliminated the hazardous pylons. And that is more or less what was built. Fortunately, the redesign considered the aesthetics after all, but the engineers' decision had been on a safety criterion and perhaps a newly felt responsibility for a larger social need. Because of its aesthetics, though, the bridge has become an almost sacred place for Austinites, celebrated as a symbol of the city to be seen on billboards, postcards, advertisements, and letterheads—all because a small percentage of total cost went to aesthetics for the human spirit.

The concept of taste separates the aesthete from the clod, but one can find several comfortable levels between those two extremes. Clearly there are opportunities for learning fresh preferences. Preference, or taste, is readily apparent, especially in a building, where one sees it in everyday life, inhabits it, or just walks through it. There, someone's design preferences are in our face; we either like them, dislike them, or try not to care.

Grossness, bad taste, and the blatantly ugly have from time to time become popular models in fashion design, and they inevitably find their way into architectural design, too. Some fashion designers use bad taste as a starting point (as in "grunge") to manipulate it as something comical or cynical and bring it into high fashion; it signals a pride of ignorance, or anti-art, and is anti-intellectual.

But most people prefer good taste rather than bad—good manners rather than bad. I like for buildings to be what I call well behaved, that is, to respect their neighborhoods and landscape by fitting in, performing their function, conserving energy without pollution, and enriching the lives of people in and around them. Poorly behaved buildings, like poorly behaved people, become victims of their own bad taste. "Well-behaved" doesn't mean boring, by the way. Well-behaved buildings have character, but they don't scream for attention; they're not aggressive even if they're monumental—they're willing to be buildings we like to be with. Today, the architectural object that stands out as new and different may be highly valued by architects and critics but cause the public to shudder.

You may be aware that some architecture is considered by its author to be an *intervention*, a word that certainly sets me to shuddering. An intervention, by my lights, is an expression of a designer's ego placed inappropriately into an otherwise good streetscape. Such ego displays, aka "statements," rarely succeed unless the rare, true genius is involved. We are interested in the whole and what a designer might thoughtfully add to it, not blatantly defy. Whether in a landscape or an urban setting, it seems extremely arrogant for a designer to intervene. But it does make news. Journalists and critics love to call our attention to the offbeat, the bizarre; and of course the latest dramatic architectural intervention fills that bill. It will get bally-hooed for its novelty and then dignified for how it "expresses the chaotic times we live in." But why exacerbate the negative aspects of how we live? Shouldn't we seek to tame the negatives and contribute something positive? There are great exceptions, to be sure, such as the intervention of the Guggenheim Museum in Bilbao or the Seagrams Building in New York. These are genius buildings, both over the top and beautiful at the same time, contributing enormously to the world around them.

You and I both might think it important for an artist, sculptor, or poet to express the world's chaotic condition in their work. But their work won't be lived in. Buildings, on the other hand, are ever-present, all day every day, and can give comfort rather than exacerbate the chaos. Architecture can offer shelter from the harshness of today's complex life, as well as shelter from the rain and cold.

Style is another word that bears comment. Style is the manner in which you do the thing you are doing; style is the way you present the content. Curiously, it too is a word, like "beauty," that many architects still get huffy over. When my friend Professor Kevin Alter organized a major symposium on style in 1998, involving such notables as Tom Ford and Stanley Marcus, some of his academic colleagues wrote letters insisting that there is no such thing as style in architecture. Heresy, they called it. It's suggested by journalists and advertisers that "such-and-such is in style," meaning

currently popular or fashionable; this also has been denied by many Modernists because it's morally impure. That's unrealistic—things are popular and current or they're not. The adjective "stylish" can't be denied. So I hereby give permission to you, and to the hundreds of architects whose diplomas I have signed, to use freely the terms *beauty*, *taste*, and *style*.

By definition, style is a distinctive manner of expression or custom—a distinctive quality or type. It's from the Greek word *stylus*, meaning "column," back when various styles were named after the particular capital (i.e., head or top section) of the column—Doric, Ionic, or Corinthian, names taken from those same geographic regions where they originated. Today, there are distinctive styles for different people, places, and things: Asian, English, Chinese, French, Mexican, Moroccan, Southwestern, Southern, Californian, Italian, International, and on and on. Clearly, each of these implies different customs and preferences. You could easily add "-style" after each category above and find such titles in your local bookstore.

The beginning of the twentieth century saw many vigorous stylistic directions as adaptations of the architecture of the past: Romanesque, Gothic, Classical, Colonial, Beaux Arts, as well as the beginning of new directions by Frank Lloyd Wright, the Arts and Crafts Movement, the Modernismo of Barcelona, the Secessionist of Vienna, and stirrings of something new in Scandinavia.

Style is changed by new technology, new ideals, wars, and economics as well as by two other forceful engines of change. The most obvious are the ideas and images published in professional journals and popular magazines, in which fashions, trends, and styles are studied in order that both the designer and the consumer can keep current. Equally influential are the crosscurrents made possible by our exploration of different cultures. Perhaps the grandest example is when Europeans discovered the New World, where, within a few years, the Franciscan and Dominican friars were building, as nonarchitects, the hundreds of handsome sixteenth-century churches in New Spain. Describing this particular Spanish phenomenon, Elizabeth Wilder Weismann writes, in her *Art and Time in Mexico* (Austin: University of Texas Press, 1985), "When you . . . use amateur designers and builders who are more or less familiar with Classical, Romanesque, Gothic, Renaissance, Mudejar, Isabeline, Manueline, and the earliest Baroque styles in half a dozen countries—working with craftsmen trained in alien and exotic forms—it is obvious that the resulting artifact cannot be described by any of these names." Contemporary Mexicans have a word for that which fits no orthodox style; the word is *anastilo*, meaning "without a style." *Anastilo* might also apply to a straightforward design within a vernacular.

Changing much faster now are an art and technology greatly enhanced by digitization and fiber-optic cables, whereby designers and their works are readily transferred to other parts of the world. It's happening when Tadao Ando of Japan, can create a museum in Texas next to a museum by Louis Kahn of Pennsylvania,

and Louis Kahn can create a National Assembly Building in Bangladesh, and Balkrishna Doshi of India can build anywhere in the world as well.

Theory and history give us an intellectual basis for design. Architectural theorists give designers guidance and new challenges. Philosophers, as well, have given designers a lot to think about. All of this is in support of the creativity and sensitivities of pure art. When students and faculty as well as leading-edge architects began working with such notions as deconstruction, it was clear to us at the University of Texas that we needed a philosopher on our faculty for both architects and city planners, so we added Bob Mugerauer. His doctorate had dealt with Martin Heidegger, and he often spoke of Jacques Derrida and deconstruction. He helped us learn from the science of the mind during the 1990s as architects struggled to learn a new path.

As useful as this was, though, I myself prefer to see more simple design theories discussed in the design process—theories like Vitruvius's "Commodity, Firmness, and Delight," or Charles Moore's "Goldilocks Principle," which preaches the importance of getting things "just right." These simple theories I recommend as a primary basis for design, no matter how sophisticated one's abstract theories might eventually become.

The discipline of architecture is so rich, so well documented and discussed, that you can spend much of your life traveling to places where you can experience the architecture, and you can spend all the time you want enjoying volumes of descrip-

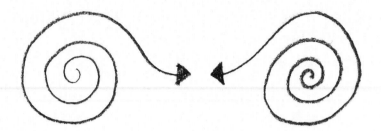

The designer and observer interact; the designer works to transmit an idea or image to the observer, while the observer can receive only as much information as his or her background will enable him or her to appreciate.

tion and discourse about the art.

We all look at things differently, yet there is a lot of commonality. Knowledge and sensitivity are enhanced by the exemplary cases found in books on architectural history, in monographs on architects, and in significant buildings and by traveling to look and experience the best architecture.

In experiencing architecture, the observer and the designer must both bring into play education, background, erudition, and, yes, taste. Is it good, bad, or mediocre? Do I like it or not like it, or do I try to ignore it? Was the project "well designed"? Is it innovative? Is it an asset to the community? Does it fit in? Does it add value to our lives? Everyone is a valid player in this drama of experiencing architecture. Develop it by study, travel, and participation in the design process.

PART THREE | THE UPPER LEVELS

*We shape our buildings; thereafter
they shape us.*
WINSTON CHURCHILL
(1874–1965)

Dear William:

As a real estate broker, you know that
where you build can be as important as
how you build. Your project's success will
turn on how well it connects with the
organism of the city. That organism of
transportation systems, markets, services,
shopping, schools, neighborhoods, arts
and entertainment, and utilities is the
realm of city planning.

You remember my telling you about my
first course on city planning with Hugo
Leipziger-Pearce. It was so dull that I often
slipped out the back door. Why learn about
city planning when I wanted to do architecture? I just didn't get it. But in his design
studio on neighborhood planning, I got it.
I became convinced that city planning
could vigorously extend architecture into

an exciting realm of ideas on a larger scale. The city planner's realm connects architecture with the neighborhood, the city, and the land. It holds the answers, along with land cost, to the question of where to build, but you won't find it in a tidy package of plans.

It's a cliché but no exaggeration that the three most important real estate values are location, location, and location. Obviously, the most uncorrectable building mistake is to build in the wrong place. The right place is where the connections work for you. These connections are basic matters of city planning. Some are as subtle as sidewalks.

Master plans, current plans, and analyses of planning issues provide a base of information developed by professional planners, administrators, and political processes. I think of a city as a large work of architecture. In this large-scale architecture, streets are corridors; open spaces are rooms; plazas and parks are courtyards and landscapes; buildings make the walls. The forms of buildings and spaces you see as you move along a street, walkway, or freeway determine how you feel about a city. You will see the inside of only a few buildings, but you will move through and see many streets. You will see undesigned wastelands and look forward to seeing thoughtful urban streetscapes.

What you see in the street and on the maps and plans of the city is the product of changes in long-term formative forces: the economic engines, transportation systems, utilities systems, populations, political dynamics, and design attitudes that are constantly forming the physical city. It can grow by design or by nondesign.

POTOMAC RIVER

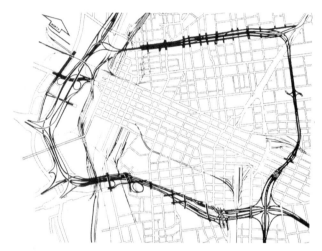

Location questions other than costs and restrictions are numerous. Some examples: What's the best situation for a particular building's purpose—the center of town, the suburbs, or the fringe? Where should the site be located for the best connections to systems of transportation, retail traffic, and schools? What is the right neighborhood? What is the right market area? What is the growth pattern? And, more important than you may think, can I walk to shops, services, schools, and transportation? These questions call for a discussion of what architects and planners call urban form.

TOP: The Baroque plan for Washington, D.C., by Pierre L'Enfant in 1792.

The freeway loop of Dallas, Texas, is typical of the freeway systems in most cities in the United States.

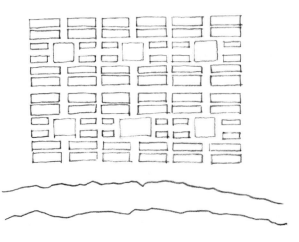

The plazas and fabric of Savannah, Georgia, designed in 1733 by General James Oglethorpe.

A look at the shapes of the city will help you visualize the kind of evolution that happens over time. Visualize an Old World city that began as a feudal village and grew in ways determined by commerce, transportation, religious ritual, defense, or all of the above. Formed physically by its hierarchy of power, circulation, and defensive walls, the village realizes a particular form. As the city grows, it will be remodeled: a larger public square for the church, new streets for newer transportation, and new public buildings. Remodeling is continuous as it accommodates changing transportation, commerce, and population. The rate of change in the growth of cities greatly accelerated in the nineteenth and twentieth centuries all over the world. Consider the dramatic change to medieval Paris when it was remodeled by Baron Georges-Eugène Haussmann into a Grand Design that reshaped winding medieval streets into broad, tree-lined boulevards and spaces shaped by the walls of buildings with special places for architectural landmarks. The city was transformed.

During the twentieth century, cities in the United States saw dramatic changes as the automobile began dominating our

lives. Even more dramatic changes came as high-speed highways and off-ramps impacted the growing city by increasing the distance and the speed of travel available. Alex Marshall, in his book *How Cities Work* (Austin: University of Texas Press, 2000), describes how cities adapted to all forms of transportation until the advent of freeways and exit ramps.

Concurrently, new planning concepts separated land uses in a way that caused long distances between housing, shopping, school, and work. Corporations began moving their headquarters out of the downtown and to the fringe of the city at the same time that retail shopping was moving from downtown to the suburbs. Distances became greater, speed faster, walking more unrealistic, and downtowns were left to struggle for new life. In addition, real estate development became a major economic engine in the city, as it provided needed services and facilities. Yet developers are sometimes at odds with planning because if the money is there, they will build—and build not to the market but build until the money runs out. It's like sourdough bread rising: you have to use the yeast or it will die. The oversupply of buildings spreads distances further.

As Marshall observes, the new high-speed, controlled-access freeways facilitated the new centers of activity and required a dramatic readjustment in people's lives because of a basic fault: no one could walk to work, to shop, or to play. The distances involved were so great that they had to go on wheels even if they were too young or too old to drive. That change in transportation affected everyone's lifestyle as well as the physical form of the city. It also facilitated new large-scale developments as destinations: regional shopping centers, megastores, industrial parks, and "edge city" communities at the ends of the off-ramps.

Accommodating the new scale of freeways, off-ramps, and parking lots is a major part of the intellectual and artistic struggle to create desirable urban form for this phenomenon. The objective is to find a way that gives us the modern benefits without taking away values of neighborhood, sense of place, and community. How can we avoid the loss of personal time to travel long distances, the loss of fossil fuel resources, the cost of massive concrete constructions, and the large amount of real estate used for moving and parking cars, all of which increased through the separation of land uses called zoning?

Speaking of zoning, why did it get to be so popular? It was originally meant to keep polluting industries in appropriate places. But zoning was extended into everything in the city. It made it easy to sell real estate and do mortgage packages in bulk at low rates. It made it easier to build freeways and major arteries around areas separated by zoning. It's now known that these systems choke traffic by clogging the few arteries available and make a worse traffic problem than the old gridiron plans that allowed more options for movement. And zoning practically eliminated walking.

Knowing that a city's form comes from its economic drivers, politics, nature, density, and its access to transportation, one might ask, What influences will cause the coming changes to be positive? How will

we balance individual rights and the free-enterprise system, on the one hand, and the quality of the community on the other? Can a city, historically laid out to sell real estate as a laissez-faire enterprise, pull itself together into an urban form that facilitates wonderful places to live and work?

Consider some familiar examples.

Visualize some of the fortunate cities that had urban design aspirations in their beginning: Washington, D.C.; Philadelphia, Pennsylvania; Savannah, Georgia; the French Quarter of New Orleans. Started in simpler times, these communities were more coherent because they could be guided politically by a strong design idea. Transportation systems shaped the development of the city. But it was the *urban form* generated by architectural geometries and hierarchies that shaped the streets and communal open spaces—plazas, piazzas, squares—formed by the walls of the streets. Conscious design helped make the town more livable and usually made of it an attractive, coherent urban fabric, sometimes beautiful, in which people could walk to the stores and services they needed. Some of these cities were also fortunate in being able to accommodate the new scale of the freeway without destroying their earlier urban qualities.

We have all kinds of cities in the United States. We have designed cities like Washington, D.C., and early Philadelphia and Savannah, rationally laid out cities like Salt Lake City, undesigned cities like Dallas, and historic cities like New Orleans. We have complex, dense cities like New York and sprawling cities like Los Angeles. More often than not, in the absence of a grand

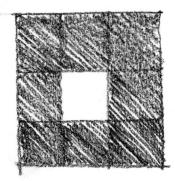 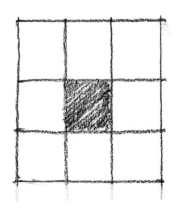

The geometry of nine squares within a square explains the use of land in a typical detached house with yards all around and in a house with common walls and an open patio in the center, which can increase density for walkability and shorten infrastructure and time for travel.

design, our cities are large areas of nondesign with a future foretold by signs that read "Pad Sites Available."

We usually see a modern city made up not of architecture but of everyday buildings. One will drive for many miles before finding something that would be considered architecture. Yet, when we go to older cities, we see a coherent, everyday architecture. What's the difference? Both cities have cars, people, thriving businesses, and some good architecture. What happened in the United States, the richest, most powerful country in the world? I will tell the story as I understand it.

The Modern City differs from the Historic City in ways that we should consider at the outset because of the effects on lifestyle and infrastructure. Colin Rowe, in his *As I Was Saying* (Cambridge: MIT Press, 1996), observes that the Historic City form is a solid with voids in it—the buildings are solids, the streets and plazas are voids—whereas the Modern City is a void with solids in it for buildings—the voids being the streets, parks, parking lots, and all the landscape area surrounding the buildings. The Historic City has walkable dimensions between functions; the Modern City has only drivable dimensions

between functions because of its concept of separation of uses (zoning.) The Historic City has a compact, economical infrastructure; the Modern City extends its expensive infrastructure exponentially, both in distance and cost. The Historic City has a density of population that can support retail services within walkable distances; the Modern City has low density and separated functions that require everyone to drive a car. In the past several decades the car has sped up to interstate highway scale even within the city, where off-ramps lead to vast areas of parking and superstores. Accretion of larger and fewer facilities (Wal-Mart versus the corner store) requires extensive driving at high speeds. One's style of life is completely different—as different as New York is from Los Angeles, or Rome from Houston.

The form of the Historic City, such as the French Quarter in New Orleans, makes the lesser architecture and everyday buildings more attractive because of the street form. The buildings are right on the street, giving the street space its enclosing walls. The continuous walls make the street a space, a communal open space for people as well as cars. The street space can curve

Historic cities tend to be walkable, as is the French Quarter of New Orleans, designed on the Spanish model.

and vary in width to make it visually special. Trees can be added for shade and ornament, softening the hard urban edges, making it a more pleasant place to walk. Everyday architecture is possible because the buildings are less dominant than the street that holds them all together. Because only the façade of the building is visible and attached to its neighbor, the architectures tend to respect each other. Most important, the building is not exposing itself to vacant spaces around it—it only shows its face to shape the street; its open space is the generous private courtyard or patio within, which forms the center of the building. When the density requires that cars be parked, parking facilities can be behind the buildings or under them rather than in front, so that the spatial aspect of the street maintains its integrity. As merchandising evolves, much of the retail and service stores may be replaced by Web-based purchases delivered to home and office by truck.

Consistent, everyday architecture as well as architectural high points are much easier to accomplish when the culture has a tradition of community rather than a tradition of independence—i.e., individual rights above all else, including the community's. It is also improved when there are traditional building forms rather than a complete individual freedom to build whatever. The U.S. city is shaped more by the entrepreneur than by a grand design for urban life; more by profit than for public good. It's a choice to make. The Modern City does not have the charm of the Old World or Third World that we enjoy seeing on vacations. That kind of environment is

now replicated and placed in a kind of museum, like Disneyland, where we pay admission to enjoy it as an entertainment event rather than enjoy it in everyday life.

I live in the mountains of central Mexico in San Miguel de Allende, a charming historic village with street spaces formed by gently curving building walls, a traditional everyday architecture, and a heterogeneous neighborhood without zoning. Every building comes to the street to form the wall of the street space. I enjoy walking to almost everything and seeing ordinary architecture of graceful heterogeneity. These buildings are individualized at every doorway, with no two alike because they're built by hand, paid for in cash, with no mortgage, no zoning controls, and only architectural controls. These qualities were begun in 1542 in San Miguel, now a town of ninety thousand. The architectural controls came in 1927, about the same time that zoning came to the United States.

That human dimension of walking is possible in fortunate modern cities, where one can live near the center of a million-

The high density of cities like Boston can provide a walkable neighborhood because of the proximity of a population that can support the services needed.

person city but within walking distance of Main Street, schools, restaurants, and services without using the high-speed freeways, off-ramps, or car parks. My other home, in Austin, Texas, has such opportunities for walking to the grocer, coffee shop, restaurant, cleaner, and to homes of friends. Proximity makes life so much simpler. It also dramatically increases real estate costs, as many are finding when they seek to move from suburbs to center. Should there be a change of intentions in how we live in cities, the change will require changing the zoning requirements for separate land uses, mixed-use neighborhoods with higher housing density, and rail transit systems.

There are ways of increasing housing density and heterogeneity that produce many of the assets of living in the city rather than driving from and back to its edges. One of the best ways is the secret of Colin Rowe's Historic City—the patio house, the Mediterranean house, the house with the courtyard in the middle. Its form can be useful in almost any building type. In Historic Cities the same plan form is used for offices, schools, hospitals, hotels, and shops; in San Miguel, even the downtown bullring has a street façade and portal on a narrow, walled residential street with small stores and an elementary school on the street. This building form—the patio in the middle and as many floors as are

San Miguel de Allende,
Guanajuato, Mexico.

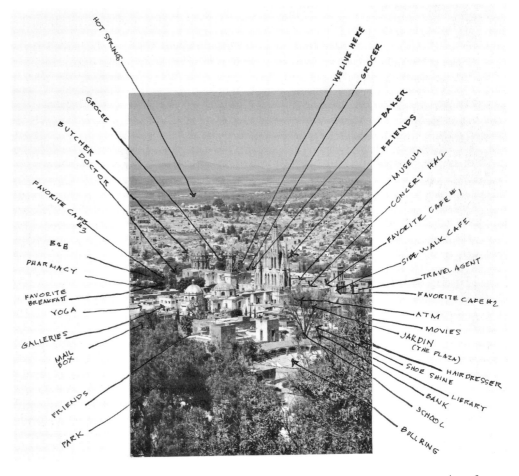

needed—allows disparate buildings to be close together, giving many types of services to the neighborhood. In an extreme example of mixed use, the San Miguel bullring, loud as it may be on certain days, has some of the best houses in town sharing common walls with it. Compare the advantages of the geometry: the Mediterranean house form surrounds the open space, giving privacy and security; in the U.S. house form, the open space surrounds the building, giving most of the land to front yards, backyards, and side yards on almost all building types—residential, institutional, and commercial. Similarly, the model of the New England village clustered densely around a common offers advantages in a less formal pattern. The accretion of such villages, as the city grows to a large population, can be seen in Greater London.

Importantly, the historic forms use less land and offer greater density so as to let families and services be close enough to reach on foot. The infrastructure, thus shortened, yields a great economy in utility distribution and street pavement because the distances are only a fraction of those in the Modern City. Certainly, the best part is the proximity of people and services that generate the activities of a neighborhood.

Where land is better utilized and neighborhoods are made possible by being dense enough to enable residents to walk to parks, services, schools, and friends' homes, there could be land remaining for communal open spaces, like plazas, becoming loci of the neighborhood activities in a nexus of social, residential, and business uses. These old ideas of the patio house and heterogeneous neighborhoods with plazas for people to gather would offer better lifestyle choices in the United States, except that such ideas are against the law in most cases. Architectural enthusiasts who travel and who have experienced urban forms might be the ones who will make such a change.

Even though cities in the past could adapt to carriages, trains, streetcars, and even automobiles, cities cannot handle well the speed and distances of the modern freeway connecting distant zoning-separated functions. Many Historic Cities lost their vitality when faced with the freeway; the time-distance geometry overwhelmed it. People no longer had to live where they worked or where they shopped or played; all were connected by car except in the few special older areas that still functioned as pedestrian neighborhoods. This is the con-

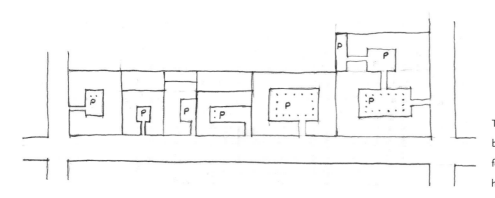

The building with a patio can be used in many forms and for purposes as diverse as a house or a general hospital.

dition in which the Modern City finds itself, where there is little opportunity for the face-to-face meeting in a communal open space of some kind. Such pedestrian places can still exist if they are protected. To achieve these urban concepts that support heterogeneous pedestrian neighborhoods, we would have to subsidize them, just as freeways are subsidized at a much greater cost than neighborhood modifications.

What happened to the city planners whom we might expect to give form to our cities? Once the activity of kings, emperors, popes, and then architects, planning as a profession is even newer than architecture. And it's a profession that has, in the past two or three generations, become devoted almost exclusively to policy planning, systems, and two-dimensional organization rather than involving the physical, three-dimensional forms of cities that we experience with our senses. There is a gap between the disciplines, and it shows in our cities.

The gap developed at an unfortunate time. Major changes were occurring in U.S. cities in the early twentieth century. The growth and change were accommodated, as I view it, by six idealistic concepts: two were competing architectural manifestos, three were public policies, and one was social change.

The first new concept was a set of dynamics that caused relocation. The city was considered the magnet for farmers and African Americans from the South. Moving in the opposite direction were corporations that sought to get out of the center city to build their headquarters in a parklike setting on the city's edge. At the

same time, other relocation forces were at work in city centers. Urban renewal legislation and land acquisition for high-speed freeways set a lot of people and patterns in motion. These dynamic migrations fueled the changes.

The second concept, the one that facilitated the other concepts, was a powerful new economic engine. The home mortgage programs of the Federal Housing Administration (FHA) set in place a machinery that would shape almost every life in the United States, and change the cityscape forever. It allowed the many to build and own their own home—but in a very rigid, separated, single-family detached house. The FHA also set minimum property requirements that became the pattern for making housing subdivisions. Zoning and the FHA helped weaken older neighborhoods and created the new homogeneous suburbs without retail stores or restaurants that could make possible the social structure of a true neighborhood. The two physical-planning concepts forced change: The physical-planning policy of zoning, which separated functions, exacerbated the need for transportation. And the easy facility of the FHA allowed rapid real estate development.

The third concept was a prevailing vision of the form these changes would take. Primary among these were the planning concepts of Le Corbusier's La Ville Radieuse Plan (1931), a plan to raze Paris and replace it with vast open spaces separating skyscrapers that would contain the functions of the city in a world of the future. Variations of that Modernist theme were expressed in the Century of Progress

World's Fair in 1934, the Futurama of the World's Fair of 1939, and in the magazines and movies of the time. The single-mindedness of the ideas gave them extreme power. This became a seductive concept, a zeitgeist as strong as the Nazi movement among planners, architects, and developers. They shaped the thinking on the Modern City more than any other model. The newer downtown area of Los Angeles is a partially realized example. Every city has its labyrinths of thoughtlessness.

The fourth concept was the vision of Frank Lloyd Wright's Broadacre City. Unveiled in 1932, it was a plan that would decentralize urban areas into a social ideal with no center—putting every home on a self-sufficient plot of land, spreading over the landscape to infinity without hierarchy. Luckily, the English New Towns and the Garden City planning of Radburn, New Jersey, by Clarence Stein and Henry Wright moderated the two "ideal cities."

The fifth concept was a policy, not a plan. In 1929, new laws were enacted to separate land uses by zoning, the original intent being to keep smoke-producing industry in the town of Euclid, Ohio, away from other parts of town. But zoning laws spread and began isolating every other urban use into discrete areas as well. What started as a protective isolation of smokestacks soon isolated every use into its own separate area. It sounds good until you analyze the results. Zoning destroyed any possibility of walkable neighborhoods by requiring certain zones to be purely residential, without any commercial services. Setbacks and side yards extended the walking distances and exacerbated the cost of

infrastructure. Offices and houses were required to be in separate zones. Restaurants could not be close to houses. Parks were made so large that they became isolated from most residents. Corporate-scale development used large tracts of land for housing and shopping, placing them far apart. Stores could not be close to where people live, so they had to be grouped into separate zones. In the prezoning world, such amenities and conveniences were common rather than in violation of zoning law. For example, when I walk on my errands in my eighteenth-century town, I will pass, on the same short street, houses of minimum living conditions alongside four-million-dollar houses, a small grocery, a shoe repair shop, a blacksmith, and a bakery. You cannot see the different uses from the street because they are all behind doors in the walls of the street. Further on, I will walk through the town square, down a street that contains, in the same block, behind high walls, a church, a shoe shop, a furniture store, houses of both the rich and poor, a fine restaurant, and, of all things, behind simple doors on this same street, an elementary school just before reaching the doors of the bullring. From there it's just a short walk to the park. Compare.

The sixth new concept made the other concepts physically possible. The Interstate Highway Act of 1955, which establised the high-speed freeway system of interstate, intercity, and intracity transportation, was a result of the private car and truck. The facility of the car has already eliminated streetcars and passenger trains, leaving cars, trucks, and buses as the only form of ground transportation. These architecture

A landscape of what is known in the market as *vertical product.*

and planning visions of the future and the other new zoning laws required thousands of new automobiles and freeways for us to drive to and from all the separate uses. The idea seduced everyone and thrilled Detroit. What were lost in these visions of zoning and freeways were neighborhood grocers, small shops, cafes, offices, housing choices, and the critical ingredient of cities: the neighborhood.

These six formative ideas—migration in and out, FHA financing and standards, Corbusier's vision, Wright's vision, zoned separation of functions, and high-speed freeway systems—resulted in spaced-apart buildings, separate home plots, separate stores, restaurants, recreation, and offices and utterly changed our way of life. Our concept of urban form has become so vague that we now need Global Positioning System navigation aids in our cars to find out where we are and where we are going. The seemingly logical separations of zoning ordinances had wide-ranging consequences: they encouraged sprawl and suburbs; they concentrated cars on collector streets and created freeways, making a

geometry that compromised or eliminated the pedestrian and the human dimension. With these separations into large-scale single-purpose developments, the low-income population was left out. Concurrent with these visions were the careful analysis and thoughtful commentary of the planner and social critic Lewis Mumford (1895–1990), who prophesied dire changes in the Modern City, with decentralization resulting in inner-city neglect. Did architects and planners help fulfill his prophecy? Had everyone listened more closely to Mumford, we would not have abandoned trains and streetcars for dependence on freeways and fuels.

Sprawling is spoiling. With sprawl, speed is essential to span the distances that have been so extended by low-density development that they require high-speed freeways and arteries over long distances, requiring driving time and fossil fuels. This condition causes communication to be more cell phone to cell phone than face to face. Getting there became more important than being there. Gertrude Stein's witty description of sprawling Oakland,

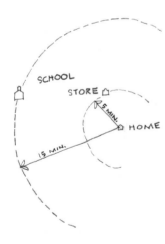

Walking distances from home to stores and schools help define a neighborhood.

"There is no there there," applies to most U.S. cities. Disenfranchised are those without a car: children, elders, and disadvantaged people. Walking is now something we schedule for personal fitness on a treadmill or a running track rather than for getting from place to place. Typical zoning and planning policies work against pedestrian scale and the neighborhood. In particular, zoning does not physically accommodate low-income families, who walk rather than drive cars.

As suburbs replaced neighborhoods, there was a myth that the suburbs were good for families and children. Instead, the child's world simply shrank into the size of a backyard with only other houses to walk to—no stores, parks, or schools because they became big and far away. Zoning as well as mortgage banking had separated land uses too far away from each other for people to walk in between; a car was required because all other transportation systems had been abandoned. About that time, Jane Jacobs, in *The Life and Death of the American City* (New York: Vintage Books, 1961), admonished us, as a basic tenet of community and security, to be aware of our neighborhoods and our neighbors by "keeping eyes on the street," where people met people face to face in their neighborhoods, if only from their front porch. Losing these qualities affected our quality of life, our security, how we use our time, and the quality of our community assets. Think about the attitudes and laws that have to change before heterogeneous pedestrian neighborhoods could exist again. The zoning laws are only sixty years

old; they're not carved in stone. We have stronger traditions to follow than zoning laws. This is another role for the architectural enthusiast—to become an activist and help communities address these issues, not for the sake of nostalgia but for the sake of quality of life.

What would happen if we have a fossil fuel crisis so devastating that we cannot economically drive our cars for miles from home to get a loaf of bread? The suburb might naturally bring in a few stores for their convenience, and that might grow into a neighborhood center, bringing in a walkable scale that would create neighborhoods as they respond to market forces. The new homogeneous residential neighborhoods are less than one hundred years old, and, as history goes, they may be remodeled many times. Creative planning and entrepreneurship could make heterogeneous neighborhoods, if that became our intention.

Now let's look again at those early twentieth-century influences and consider that the reasons that nineteenth-century city planners created some beautiful cities were that they had different models. They worked within a tradition of design. The nineteenth-century civil engineers designed public works with humanity and architectural finesse, often retaining architects to assist them in design. The changes in city-planning objectives over the past century can be followed in four stages. First were the urban concepts described by Camillo Sitte in his book *City Planning According to Artistic Principles* (Vienna, 1889). Then Daniel Burnham solidified the

The design for a suburban micro-neighborhood that allows walking to the center for services and connects to a hierarchy of similar micro-neighborhoods that can provide schools and services for a large, walkable neighborhood. Pratt and Box with Howard Meyer, 1959.

City Beautiful Movement in the United States at the Columbian Exposition of 1893. Within a few decades, Modernism overwhelmed this movement with "City Planning According to Efficient Principles." Then, all was overwhelmed by the concept of "City Planning According to Marketing Principals" (described by Philip Langdon in his book *A Better Place to Live* [New York: Harper, 1994]), wherein the rise of marketing and the decline of planning caused new housing to be considered simply "pods of vertical product" for the marketplace rather than homes and neighborhoods. Shops and services were in a

separate real estate market miles away. What an awkward human condition—what could have made a neighborhood became a homogeneous "pod" of housing product with a separate shopping center reachable only by car. In one century our model for urban life went from artistic principles to marketing principles.

I believe we are victims of some bad stories—myths—that we have come to believe to be our objectives: our twentieth-century tradition based on the six planning concepts described above. Our current communal myths tell us that we must live in a single-family house; we must have yards full of grass all around us; we must not have retail shops near us, only other houses; everyone in the family must drive a car when going beyond the house; and there must be a lot of distance between your home and any place to buy a loaf of bread or a bottle of milk. That set of myths goes back to the individual's "frontier cabin in the woods." This, of course, is not the common myth in other parts of the world. The cities of Europe, the Mediterranean, the Far East, and Latin America have very different myths, many of which are directed toward community rather than individuality. We must examine our old myths and come up with new ones—new story lines and new policies—that support community rather than deny it. We may need a new public policy, one strong enough to affect the marketplace, on planning, zoning, and intracity transportation that would force a way to provide new forms. Because real estate development is undeniably market driven, public policy by governments may be required to make the necessary adjustments that can create the kind of sustainable physical community that is currently missing.

In the face of the real estate development formula provided by zoning and finance, plus the Corbusian ideal of huge voids with skyscrapers, the Wrightian ideal of decentralization into suburbia, and the model of the English New Towns, our chaotic twentieth-century U.S. city was inevitable. City planning became solely a two-dimensional diagram of separated functions and connecting vehicular arteries, drainage, and utilities, rather than a

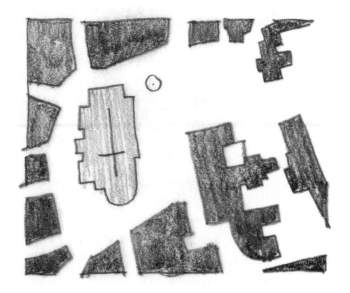

three-dimensional design for a place to live or perhaps a grand design. Design was ignored by the three most recent generations of planners; they were policy planners, not physical planners. The academic training of planners is only just beginning to change.

Just as an architect cannot design a beautiful building without first seeing one, how can a planner design a beautiful city if he or she has never seen one? Today, we only talk about workable cities and their growth. As dean of a school of architecture that included a planning program, I walked down the hall one day and realized, "We're the problem." In trying to change the direction, I said in the introduction to my town-planning course, "Most of what we will study about designing livable cities is currently against the law." I contend that staying within the current laws, ordinances, and planning policies will continue to lessen livability, sense of community, and quality of life, as well as exhaust fossil

The architect Camillo Sitte studied and documented the urban spaces of European towns in the late nineteenth century.

fuel resources, damage the environment, and ignore beauty.

An old axiom of planning said, "Each child should be able to walk safely to school and each adult should be able to walk to basic services within fifteen minutes." That axiom was abandoned after World War II, yet it's still a valuable objective. I like to use the "Five-Minute Popsicle Rule," which says, "A child must be able to walk safely from home to buy a Popsicle within five minutes." This freedom was lost, of course, when zoning separated uses, and freeways were built to serve them.

The Five-Minute Popsicle Rule evolved from a discussion with the planning professor Terry Kahn as we were preparing to teach a class for planning students. It's now an often-heard axiom. I believe this one simple rule can reverse many of the damaging effects of the past generations of planners. The Five-Minute Popsicle Rule, if applied to all new planning decisions, would restore a humane environment to our towns and cities in several ways. Apply the rule to a suburban subdivision, and it would not only give children a place to walk to before they're allowed to drive a car, but would also give adults something to do besides drive their children everywhere and drive themselves between work and home. Apply the rule to a regional shopping center, and housing would have to be part of the development, so that people would have housing and street patterns that would allow them to walk to shops and services as in a traditional neighborhood. Apply it to the center of cities by adding housing, and people would have an option

to live where things are happening and services are convenient. Apply the rule to almost any new large real estate development, and it will be improved by allowing people to walk rather than drive. Only in the areas of polluting industry would one want to keep separation from other human uses—that was the original purpose of zoning before it got out of hand. In all other cases, people should be able to walk.

A device to augment the five-minute walk in a pleasant way is the linear park, a park that is long and narrow and that connects different uses and different neighborhoods with footpaths. The linear park can bring nature within five minutes of each person. The park can be only one hundred feet wide, and, when possible, follow drainage along a creek. These opportunities were often lost when parks were made large, broad areas for recreation facilities and when creeks were covered up and storm sewers put in. Some cities are resuscitating their creeks by pulling out the sewers and reestablishing a natural setting used as a linear park.

Another simple requirement can change the look of the city: require that streets be designed with lines of trees, landscape, and walks as an integrated roadway. Because we sense the city by our travel through the streets, we can affect the appearance greatly by lining almost every street with trees in a variety of street designs. This is design that does more than handle automobile traffic. Yes, it's secondary to the basic function, but we should be civilized enough to do more than just get from place to place with speed. Why not design all aspects of the streets and freeways? Federal and state legislation requiring landscape architects' participation along with that of the engineers could go a long way toward giving our streets and freeways delight.

Changes in transportation and communications in the past fifty years have spawned a different context for community. Herbert Muschamp of the *New York Times* asks, "What is a community at the end of the twentieth century? A focus group, a concentration camp, a chat room on the Internet, an address book, a dance club, all of those afflicted with a particular incurable disease, a gender, an age bracket, a waiting room, owners of silver BMW's, organized crime, everyone who swears by a particular brand of painkiller and a two-block stretch of Manhattan on a weekday at lunch hour." He's right. Each of us has many "communities." The Net, e-mail, iChat community is truly global, yet it's different from a physical community, where one can walk the streets and enjoy the plazas, do errands on foot, meet accidentally, and just look around and enjoy. I think the desire for a physical community with a sense of place is here to stay.

| FINDING POSSIBILITIES

In any evolutionary process,
even in the arts, the search
for novelty becomes corrupting.
KENNETH BOULDING
(1910–1993)

Dear Arquitecta Gutierrez:

My friend, I do respect your grumblings about the current state of design. Architecture would seem to have left the building, wouldn't it? The big questions, for me, are, How do we get it back? and What might it look like at its next stage of evolution?

These are hard questions, but let me start with your own: "Isn't it time for a wholesale change in the direction of design?"

I say yes. The tenets of Modernism that we architects learned in school, and the buildings that express those tenets, have been receiving serious criticism now for forty years, well after Modernism accomplished its chief goal, which was to clean house following the excesses of late nineteenth-century design. While Modernism evolved to produce some great buildings, it also produced a huge number of aloof, unpleasant ones—sometimes whole cities of them. Paul Goldberger of the *New York Times* said it well: "Modern architecture has been too cerebral, too rational, too concerned with appearing beautiful in an intellectual way rather than comfortable in a sensuous or physical way." James Pratt, meanwhile, has noted how Modernism, in promoting the Global Village, has actually promoted a place-destroying sameness: "From a distance, Nairobi looks much like Midland, Texas." But the architect Philip Johnson delivered what may be the most pungent verdict: "Modern architecture is a flop. . . . There is no question that our cities are uglier today than they were fifty years ago."

Inept examples of Modernism have invaded almost every city in every developing country. The examples, with few exceptions, tend to be aggressively brutal, strident, and visually out of place. Take the ancient Sicilian city of Siracusa. It had withstood invasion from at least ten diverse cultures over its twenty-six centuries of history, yet none has been as damaging as Modernism, at least visually. But even with such a rich historic fabric, where Greek architecture was added to by Roman architecture, Moorish architecture, and by Spanish Baroque, I feel confident that the *New* could still be absorbed there, provided a thoughtful, respectful architecture were inserted with great care.

Reconsidering and reshaping Modernism, as we know it in everyday buildings, will involve the discipline of architecture both academically and professionally. Yet most of the issues here are just as relevant for nonarchitects, since everyone is finally involved, one way or another, in buildings, aren't they? So that is why I will speak here not about design theory per se but about four overarching design issues that might inform the possibilities.

The first issue is the presumed moral imperative that architects ascribe to Modernism—that it's the only legitimate way to build, and that aggressive, noncontextual, urban "interventions" are a victory for the imperative.

The second issue is the need for useful vernaculars, or some kind of guide for use in the design of buildings built without architects.

The third issue is the need for architects to offer a better product, so that they might be asked to design more of the world's buildings.

The fourth issue is the millions of ineptly designed private dwellings produced without architectural merit. Even though houses, large and small, are products of good value from home-building corporations, their design is visually so illiterate as to embarrass a knowledgeable owner. Compare the new McMansions with the Newport mansions of the nineteenth century. Or compare the design of the common Prairie School houses and shingled bungalows of a hundred years ago with the builders' houses of today.

To address the first of these four issues, let's examine two hypothetical scenarios. In Scenario A, Modernists continue to ignore previous architecture, as well as today's marketplace, coherent urban form, and ordinary human desires, and continue to create intellectualized innovations in the Modernist dogma. The esoteric poetry of today's Modernism, enjoyed by the indoctrinated, will eventually grow ever more intense and obscure, becoming less and less accessible to the public while becoming still more sublime to insiders. (Some will say, "Yeah, right on!") Meanwhile, the only vernacular guide for ordinary building will continue to be the old International Style, producing the same architecture around the world and placing higher value on being Modern than on the geography and culture of place and people. A few of the buildings in this scenario will be wonderful and make a contribution, but most will ape the current fashion and be less than good. That's a lot of buildings less than good.

In Scenario B, the knowledge and the aesthetic of Modernism get assimilated into the mainstream of architectural history to create a continuum of architectural design that evolves into forms we recognize as a healthy direction to move in. The poetry so painstakingly developed over the past one hundred years is used to promote harmony rather than disharmony, just as modern music advanced beyond its early dissonances to return to sophisticated harmonies.

The goal in this second scenario is to open up the current mind-set and examine ideas outside of and beyond the current Modernist dogmas. Or, to put it another way, the goal is to loosen architects' black-or-white fundamentalist beliefs in the vir-

tues of Modernism enough that they will accept, and even promote, greater experimentation toward a more sensitive, contextually appropriate architecture. The continuum of architectural evolution, including but not limited to Modernism, will then ease the violence to cities, making design better, not just new.

Scenario B would be rather scary to many. Leaving the comforts of dogma to look back, be inclusive, and move forward, all at the same time, will take courage. There would be a period of confusion as different design directions are developed, but this is nothing new. Just a century ago we were actively building in many vernaculars and many different styles: Neoclassical, Beaux Arts Modern, Colonial, Collegiate Gothic, Richardson Romanesque, Arts and Crafts, the new forms of Modernism developing in Europe, and later, the new Modernism in the United States. In that era, an architect might choose the appropriate style for each new building commission. Is there anything really wrong about doing that today—if we only knew how to do it well?

After a whole century of Modernism, with its successes and failures, wouldn't a substantial change be a blessing to ordinary architecture and urban form? The architecture of special buildings would continue developing in ways that genius creates, while everyday architecture would provide harmony, comfort, delight, and a coherent streetscape in a humane city.

How different an attitude this would be from Le Corbusier's proposal to rebuild historic Paris as a Modernist city! Such violence has abated and a peace has been made, so that meritorious "old" architecture is preserved with dignity. Paris was not razed. Yet parts of U.S. cities *were* razed in the mid-twentieth century, as urban renewal legislation destroyed thousands of acres of urban fabric to make way for new buildings, new real estate values, and new social problems. In this era, the Design Award–winning modern high-rise housing of St. Louis's Pruitt-Igoe was imploded, making it a symbol of architectural and social failure. Because most architects, faculty, and students are in the third or fourth generation of Modernist education, the dogmas are now as fixed as in a fundamentalist religion. When you think that the movement started with issues of workers' housing, doesn't it seem that a radical reexamination of Modernism's implacable ideology is in order?

Second, the idea of a useful vernacular or guide for design has intrigued me since my school days. Educated to be aloof to the past, I have to confess that my discovery of the premodern world confounded me when I first saw that it had produced architecture of great significance along with ordinary buildings that were elegantly conceived and executed. Granted, we architects have a responsibility to explore the new ideas, materials, and techniques that have become available to us because, most importantly, we must innovate to design the demanding newer building types where advanced technology is required: tall buildings, airport terminals, hospitals, sports arenas, and other special facilities. To find the appropriate vernacular for smaller buildings, though, there are at least

two directions. Either we find solutions in traditional building materials, techniques, and local forms responding to the specifics of that local climate, history, and technology, or we look beyond our current materials and techniques to find new methods of construction with a new kind of integrity and authenticity. Frank Gehry has said, "Architecture should speak of its time and place, but yearn for timelessness." A building of its time and place would logically have much in common with those that were intelligently built before in that place—recognizable design idioms and similar materials. The time would be shown in noticeable design decisions that reflect the architecture of today.

The third issue is that of architects needing a better product for the public so as to better serve communities and individuals. To be more in demand requires a change. If 95 percent of our buildings are designed without architects, most people must think that architects are not worth the money, time, and effort. The market-driven economy is real and constant for new buildings, so if designers wish to be involved, they must adjust to the marketplace with new attitudes about services and the public's desires. Architecture, the ennobler of buildings, must be of enough value for the client to pay for the architect's effort. Leading architects receive good fees for their services, yet the average architects' fees indicate a low value placed on their product. The fact of those low fees is reason enough for architects and educators to reexamine their current direction. It's not only that the clients are undereducated; it's that architects aren't producing a product that the client wants enough to pay for.

Deterrents to producing a desirable product are, first, the architects' massive time cost in providing their services, which earn unreasonably low financial rewards. The second reason is the proliferation of federal, state, county, and city bureaucracies and regulations that sap the architect's time and resources.

Architects spend an enormous amount of time designing the technical construction details of a building that would not require such effort if they were designing within a traditional vernacular that workmen knew how to build and so would need less direction from the architect. In earlier eras, for example, the much-admired Palladio did very few drawings, yet workmen knew how to build his buildings because the techniques weren't trying to be new each time. A simple Palladian building today would require well over one hundred sheets of drawings. Palladio would have used fewer than ten. Recently, when I designed a traditional load-bearing masonry building in a Mexican village, the only drawings I needed were plans, elevations, and sections of all the interior and exterior surfaces of the building drawn to a large scale; the workmen already knew how to build it. The only thing they needed to know was what I wanted and what all its parts should look like; they knew how to do the rest. Detailed construction drawings would have been confusing for the workmen and expensive for the architect to produce. The manpower involved in producing voluminous construction drawings would be better spent in improving the design of the product. Architects' proclivity

for inventing new ways to build every new building requires making, for each building, a thorough set of instructions on how this particular "new" building is to be built. Is innovation for the sake of innovation worth it? I used to thoroughly enjoy this process, but really, aren't we spending our time in the wrong place?

A building tradition requiring fewer details from the architect could also relieve the architect of some direct responsibility and thus reduce lawsuits where lawyers get into the thick of some very thin things, quickly earning larger fees than the architects' own. Some lawsuits might be avoided if a building tradition were understood as it was in previous eras. We architects enjoy being inventive, of course, and are good at it, but is that the most important objective? True, God is in the details, but we might refine them rather than invent new ones for every building.

As for the growing regulatory controls and permissions, their cost could easily exceed the cost of design and construction administration on a particular project. Some of these services should be outside of the architect's costs. The time spent in following the minute detail of the regulations is burdensome as it is. What a change from fifty years ago, when the city's head building inspector said to me, "Because you are an architect, we don't need to look at your plans. They're approved." In addition to those bureaucracies, the litigious society and the protective liability-insurance costs add another large burden for the architect.

The fourth major issue is that the design of the dominant form of housing, the spec builder's house in which most people live, is ignored in architectural education. On the other hand, the spec house is a product that usually offers the buyer good value. Rarely are these houses designed by architects, not just to save time and a fee, but because the architects' designs are not in demand. Builders' houses, you'll notice, are almost exclusively exercises in nostalgia. That is, they look backward, seeking to evoke some tradition or well-known style rather than what my generation of architects and the one following imagined people would want and should have: a Modern house. It hasn't happened, although the ideology and forms of the 1950s are reappearing as the "Mid-century Modern," or MCM. Look through any twenty popular shelter magazines on the newsstand and you can see what the consumer wants. The houses aren't those designed by architects as architecture but are designed as products that buyers find pleasant and affordable. All that being said, the current level of their design remains extremely low because the designers are trying to design in traditional styles without the knowledge or skills of how to design in that manner, even in their most expensive houses. In sum, what might be called affordable houses are not being taught in architecture schools, even though they dominate the housing market. While accepted in commercial and institutional buildings, Modernism is rarely in demand in a home. And that's a large rejection of today's architecture.

On a more positive note, Modernism continues to innovate, and for all its excesses, it's discovered many fresh, exciting ways to exploit space and light. It has opened up new frontiers. The absence of ornament (the crime) has been partially compensated for by its use of new materials in unexpected ways, such as special glass, enameled metal, copper, titanium, and concrete textures, and sometimes that is enough.

Yet consider the possibilities we have for reshaping architecture by comparing the beginning of this century with the revolutionary beginning of the last century. Do you think everyday Modernism is as tired now as Neoclassicism was a hundred years ago?

Several modifications are in order:

- Redirect attitudes to promote harmony rather than discord in the streets.
- Value composition and proportion, rather than celebrate shock, novelty, and stridency.
- Champion the decorative arts and landscaped gardens rather than override or compete with them—or even scoff at them, as I sometimes hear in school lectures.
- Act locally in a global way—adopt or adapt usable regional traditions and vernaculars, rather than celebrate innovation for its own sake.

While digital globalization of industries and ideas can justify the International Style, it can't satisfy our human dimensions that still require us to have special places and keep the identity of our individual environments. Making it new is, well, getting old.

We might evolve architecture in positive ways by engaging more in the intricacies of its construction. Considering construction systems as form determinants has been a goal for decades, yet it seems to always get tied up in an advanced technology that doesn't exist. One of the excitements of design and construction is to work with new or unusual materials coming either from advancing technology or from extraordinary natural materials found at an affordable price, such as a particular stone, the right type of glass, or new construction techniques such as the new efforts in manufactured prefabricated buildings.

Architects seek to be on the leading edge—that's where, as designers, they can have the most fun. Some are constantly seeking a new revolution; some are seeking an evolution. Both directions are valid if they're not boring; both can be on the leading edge.

There is nothing wrong with being off the leading edge by doing the obvious. You just need to do it better than anyone else! That also is ego-satisfying.

In Mexico, the lineage of vernacular buildings is given finesse by the masters Luis Barragán and Ricardo Legorreta. Both architects are highly respected yet off the mainstream, even though Legorreta is an AIA Gold Medalist and Barragán is a Pritzker Prize Laureate revered by all. I wonder why most schools of architecture in the United States are almost exclusively Eurocentric, with their design values focused there.

Currently, many leading-edgers are at work—Frank Gehry, Zaha Hadid, Renzo Piano, Rick Joy, and Santiago Calatrava, to name a few. Some are finding a wonderful new world in architecture made available by digital design and new high-strength, lightweight materials. Unfortunately, this world is not available to most of those who build.

In an attempt to visualize how modern architecture might evolve into a building tradition strong enough to become an exemplary guide for everyone, I recently made a list of my favorite architects in history, arranged as chronological steps on a stair leading up to Tomorrow. We might all choose a different lineage of architects for a desirable continuum, but the architects I would select for such a lineage would start with the great Classical architects, the Romanesque and Gothic master builders. Then on to Brunelleschi, Michelangelo, and Palladio. Then Bernini and Boromini, Baltazar Neumann, Thomas Jefferson, and Sir John Soane. Then there'd be a big progression—H. H. Richardson, Louis Sullivan, Cass Gilbert, Eliel Saarinen, Eero Saarinen, Charles Eames, Gunar Asplund, Alvar Aalto, Louis Kahn, Luis Barragán, Jørn Utzon, Charles Moore, Ricardo Legorreta, and Renzo Piano. To that list I would add architects significant in their particular regions. For instance, in the Southwest, I would continue with Harwell Hamilton Harris, O'Neil Ford, Frank Welch, David Lake, and Ted Flato. Note that I omitted Wright, Le Corbusier, and Mies, so as to visualize architecture without them, just to see what kind of image would be made. I feel comfortable continuing that lineage of design ideas. Perhaps it would make the appropriate design guide from which anyone could work.

For the aficionado and student, an examination of such a lineage might provide a worthwhile outline for study of these architects and project the lineage into the future. It would be a useful learning experience to study individual architects, evaluate them as models, and decide which architects should be included in this selected history. Examining the design philosophies you choose might help you discover the paradigm to provide the guide we seek. Would 95 percent of the buildings be much different?

The architect William Turnbull gave us wisdom on this subject in a remark he made about two of the architects in my regional list: "Lake/Flato's architecture can serve as a lesson for us all: how a building stands to the sun, how it welcomes the cooling breeze, how it partners with plant materials. Nothing sensational or exotic, no visual fireworks of fashion, just architecture that intrigues the mind, delights the soul, and refreshes the eye with its elegant detail and simplicity. Timeless architecture needn't shout."

Any new paradigm will want to be pluralistic—inclusive and tolerant of all except ineptness. For me, a guiding example, or exemplar, would contain many conflicting attributes: simplicity and complexity, elegance and whimsy, romance and utility, authenticity and irony, timeless and new, gravity-defying form and earthy solidity, natural materials and ersatz materials, old forms and new forms, indigenous materials and forms and international materials and forms. The art made of these ingredients will have benefited from the design studio study of primitive, classic, historic,

and traditional styles, as well as Modernist design methodologies. The architecture we are seeking will come as an evolution of Modernism that brings in historical aesthetic values along with a new edge that gives it excitement. A new paradigm will provide guidance-by-example for nonarchitects eager to improve the design of their many buildings. Perhaps someone will produce plan books as effective architecturally as those used early in the last century.

Success will depend on our attitudes on how each individual building relates to everything else within the complex structures of city planning. If architecture can leave the building to continue out into the street with thoughtful design of the communal open spaces, cities will be more habitable.

Perhaps most important is a new curriculum for architectural education that will not only study architectural history, but also begin design studio instruction in historic styles. This has not happened in several generations of architects; however, many of today's great musicians were classically trained, even the top jazz musicians. Classical training might be considered heresy, but read on. In a conversation with one of my eminent colleagues, Michael Benedikt, I proposed an architecture curriculum that would start with classical training, similar to the Beaux Arts training that early Modernists experienced—one that would provide basic training in proportion, composition, form, ornament, and the rigors of classicism. "I agree, that's essential," Michael said, then added, "but I'd do you one better and start the design studio sequence with studies of the primitive unstylized building methods of prehistory and indigenous examples and hybrid vernaculars." Great idea! I thought. After all, the primal building qualities of the Third World, which still rely on simple materials and basic construction, offer unexpected delights in space and light, openings and roof shapes, textures and forms, as well as expressive ornament.

In addition, I thought, we should carefully fill the void we have in the study of the architectural traditions of Asia. Japanese, Chinese, Indian, Persian, and Turkish architecture have been inadequately studied. The three backgrounds—classical, primitive, and Asian—which are narrowly studied, at best, in architectural education could be a way to begin a reevaluation of our current design direction. This curriculum would help designers work more intelligently and artistically in the historic styles that architects are attempting today with rare success because of their lack of training. It could improve the quality of the everyday buildings filling the streets—and not hamper the design of significant new architecture to dot future history books.

Some architecture schools, acknowledging the need to broaden their approach, address Classicism in addition to Modernism; some even teach Classicism exclusively. The University of Dublin has a full year of classical design in its regular curriculum. The University of Notre Dame primarily teaches traditional and classical architecture in its design studios, with a year at their Rome campus. In the United Kingdom, Prince Phillip formed an architecture program to teach classical architecture because of the dearth of training avail-

able. In the United States, the newly formed Institute for Classical Architecture, with National Endowment for the Arts funding and fifteen hundred members, is offering courses in Classicism as well as Georgian and Greek Revival, Arts and Crafts, Gothic Revival, and Shingle Style. And again, expanding our study of architecture on the other side of the world would enhance our thinking. With university curricula always in flux, more schools might consider broadening their approach to train architects in the historic styles that are ineptly done today because of voids in training.

The study of architecture often isolates the building from it surroundings—that is, it looks at the architecture as an art object independent of its setting and its furnishings. This narrow view is found in schools, boardrooms, and publications. While the architectural object may be the dominant part, the reality, surely, is the landscape, the urban setting, and the functioning interiors that make up the whole. A new curriculum would include integrated studies of these disciplines as a basis for collaboration between them.

The arts and sciences must always advance to be beneficial. To advance is the only way the intellect can acknowledge positive change. If we believe the architecture of other eras is superior to the architecture of today, we might be right, but we couldn't move backward with any kind of integrity. Returning to the past isn't an option. So how will our art advance? A Renaissance, an Enlightenment, or a new Manifesto might work, of course, but while we're waiting, we might rethink our design values.

Michelangelo, Piazza del
Campadoglio, Rome. Begun
1538.

The teacher by example, of many architects, O'Neil Ford once asked, "When will some teacher in some school learn that he must teach the whole of architecture as it has grown, bloomed, and decayed, the results having been sometimes humble and beautiful, sometimes pompous and beautiful, sometimes brilliantly and even laboriously devised—or sometimes, in the indigenous vernacular—just grown?"

Sitting in the library of a house we've just built in San Miguel, I am looking at familiar indigenous forms, Spanish-Moorish-Mexican influences, and Modernist sensibilities everywhere; and it seems almost *just right*.

The right design direction, one that will put architecture in the forefront as a desirable product, will come when someone produces an extraordinarily wonderful and appropriate architecture in a building that many of us fall in love with, one that will become the icon of a new direction.

Thoughtful architects, informed nonarchitects, and well-intentioned clients can cause a wide range of architecture to flourish again. Making architecture a more desirable product will elevate it in the arts and in the marketplace. Success in the marketplace will cause more architecture to be built. The possibilities for a nonarchitect to make architecture will grow as he or she becomes informed. The making of architecture will be greatly improved when those who build *seek to make architecture rather than just buildings*, committing themselves to doing what it takes to make that architecture succeed.

READING LIST

The more that you read, the more things you will know. The more that you learn, the more places you'll go.
DR. THEODORE SEUSS GEISEL
(1904–1991)

BOOKS

Ackerman, James. *Palladio.* New York: Penguin Books, 1966.

Alberti, Leon Battista. *The Ten Books of Architecture.* The 1755 Leoni edition. New York: Dover, 1986.

Alexander, Christopher. *Pattern Language.* New York: Oxford University Press, 1977.

———. *The Timeless Way of Building.* New York: Oxford University Press, 1979.

Alofsin, Anthony. *The Struggle for Modernism.* New York: W. W. Norton, 2002.

———. *Frank Lloyd Wright, Architect.* New York: Museum of Modern Art, 1994.

Andrews, Peter, et al. *The House Book.* New York: Phaidon Press, 2001.

Andrews, Wayne. *Architecture, Ambition*

and Americans. New York: Free Press, 1964.

Arendt, Randall. *Rural by Design.* Chicago: American Planning Association, 1994.

Attoe, Wayne, et al. *The Architecture of Ricardo Legorreta.* Austin: University of Texas Press, 1990.

Bachelard, Gaston. *The Poetics of Space: The Classic Look at How We Experience Intimate Places.* Boston: Beacon Press, 1964.

Bacon, Edmond N. *Design of Cities.* Revised edition. New York: Viking Press, 1967.

Baker, Geoffrey. *Le Corbusier—The Creative Search: The Formative Years of Charles-Edouard Jeanneret.* New York: Van Nostrand Reinhold, 1996.

Benedikt, Michael. *For an Architecture of Reality.* New York: Lumen Books, 1987.

———. *Deconstructing the Kimbell.* New York: Lumen Books, 1991.

Blake, Peter. *The Master Builders.* New York: Norton, 1996.

———. *Form Follows Fiasco: Why Modern Architecture Hasn't Worked.* Boston: Little, Brown, 1974.

Blumenson, John J. G. *Identifying American Architecture: A Pictorial Guide to Styles and Terms, 1600–1945.* Nashville: American Association for State and Local History, 1990.

Box, John Harold, et al. *Prairie's Yield: Forces Shaping Dallas Architecture 1840–1962.* New York: Reinhold, 1962.

Busch, Akiko. *Geography of Home: Writings on Where We Live.* New York: Princeton Architectural Press, 1999.

Brunskill, R. W. *Illustrated Handbook of Vernacular Architecture.* London: Faber and Faber, 1971.

Calthorpe, Peter. *The Next American Metropolis.* New York: Princeton Architectural Press, 1993.

Cambell, Joseph, with Bill Moyers. *The Power of Myth.* Edited by Betty Sue Flowers. New York: Doubleday, 1988.

Caragonne, Alexander. *The Texas Rangers: Notes from an Architectural Education.* Cambridge: MIT Press, 1995.

Carter, Peter. *Mies van der Rohe at Work.* New York: Prager, 1973.

Caudill, William Wayne. *The TIBS of Bill Caudill.* Houston: Cathers Press, 1984.

———, with W. M. Pena and Paul Kennon. *Architecture and You: How to Experience and Enjoy Buildings.* New York: Whitney Library of Design and Watson-Guptill, 1978.

Chuen, Lam Kam. *Feng Shui Handbook.* New York: Henry Holt, 1996.

Collins, George R., and Christiane Collins. *Camillo Sitte: The Birth of Modern City Planning.* New York: Rizzoli, 1986.

Dean, Andrea Oppenheimer. *Rural Studio: Samuel Mockbee and an Architecture of Decency.* New York: Princeton University Press, 2002.

Dillon, David. *O'Neil Ford: Celebrating Place.* Austin: University of Texas Press, 1999.

Drexler, Arthur. *Mies van der Rohe.* New York: G. Braziller, 1960.

Easterling, Keller. *American Town Plans.* New York: Princeton Architectural Press, 1993.

Edwards, Betty. *Drawing on the Right Side of the Brain.* Los Angeles: J. P. Tarcher, 1978.

Fleming, John, Hugh Honour, and Nikolaus Pevsner. *The Penguin Dictionary of Architecture.* London: Penguin Books, 1966.

Fletcher, Sir Banister, with Dan Cruickshank. *A History of Architecture on the Comparative Method.* 20th ed. Oxford: Architecture Press, 1896–2002.

Fluckinger, Dan, ed. *Lake-Flato.* Rockport, Mass: Rockport Publishers, 1996.

Frampton, Kenneth. *Modern Architecture: A Critical History.* New York: Oxford University Press, 1980.

Garreau, Joel. *Edge City: Life on the New Frontier.* New York: Doubleday, 1998.

George, Mary Carolyn Hollers. *O'Neil Ford, Architect.* College Station: Texas A&M University Press, 1992.

Germany, Lisa. *Harwell Hamilton Harris.* Austin: University of Texas Press, 1991.

Gideon, Sigfried. *Space, Time and Architecture.* Cambridge: Harvard University Press, 1941.

Goodman, Robert. *After the Planners.* New York: Simon and Schuster, 1971.

Goodwin, Philip L. *Brazil Builds.* New York: Museum of Modern Art, 1943.

Gropius, Walter. *Scope of Total Architecture.* New York: Harper and Row, 1955.

Hale, Jonathan. *The Old Way of Seeing.* Boston: Houghton Mifflin, 1994.

Hall, Edward T. *The Hidden Dimension.* New York: Doubleday, 1966.

Hall, Edward T., and Michael Hays. *Architecture Theory Since 1968.* Cambridge: MIT Press, 1998.

Halprin, Lawrence. *Cities.* Cambridge: MIT Press, 1963.

Henry, Jay C. *Architecture in Texas.* Austin: University of Texas Press, 1993.

Jackson, John Brinckerhoff. *Discovering the Vernacular Landscape.* New Haven: Yale University Press, 1984.

Jacobs, Jane. *The Death and Life of Great American Cities.* New York: Alfred A. Knopf, 1961.

Joy, Rick. *Rick Joy: Desert Works.* Princeton: Princeton University Press, 2001.

Katz, Peter. *The New Urbanism: Toward an Architecture of Community.* New York: McGraw-Hill, 1994.

Keim, Kevin. *An Architectural Life: Memoirs and Memories of Charles W. Moore.* Boston: Bulfinch Press, 1996.

———. *Placenotes: Guides for Austin, Houston, San Antonio, and Santa Fe.* Austin: University of Texas Press, 2005.

Kidder, Tracy. *House.* Boston: Houghton Mifflin, 1985.

King, Ross. *Brunelleschi's Dome.* New York: Walker and Company, 2000.

Kostof, Spiro. *The City Shaped: Urban Patterns and Meanings through History.* Boston: Bulfinch Press, 1991.

———. *A History of Architecture: Settings and Rituals.* New York: Oxford University Press, 1995.

Krieger, Alex, ed. *Duany, Andres and Elizabeth Plater-Zyberk: Towns and Town-Making Principles.* Cambridge: Harvard GSD, 1991.

Krier, Rob. *Architectural Composition.* New York: Rizzoli, 1988.

Kunstler, James Howard. *Home from Nowhere.* New York: Simon and Schuster, 1996.

Langdon, Philip. *American Houses.* New York: Stewart, Tabori and Ching, 1987.

———. *A Better Place to Live: Reshaping the American Suburb.* New York: Harper-Collins, 1994.

Lawlor, Robert. *Sacred Geometry.* London: Thames and Hudson, 1982.

———. *The Temple in the House.* New York:

G. P. Putnam's Sons, 1994.

Ledoux, De C. N. *L'Architecture*. Paris: Lenoir, 1804. Reprint, Princeton Architectural Press, 1983.

Lewis, Roger K. *Architect? A Candid Guide to the Profession*. Cambridge: MIT Press, 1985.

Lynch, Kevin. *The Image of the City*. Cambridge: MIT Press, 1960.

Lyndon, Donlyn, and Charles W. Moore. *Chambers for a Memory Palace*. Cambridge: MIT Press, 1994.

Marcus, Clare Cooper. *House as a Mirror of Self: Exploring the Deeper Meaning of Home*. Berkeley: Conari Press, 1997.

McAlester, Virginia, and Lee McAlester. *A Field Guide to American Houses*. New York: Alfred A. Knopf, 2003.

McCarthy, Muriel Quest. *David R. Williams: Pioneer Architect*. Dallas: SMU Press, 1984.

McHarg, Ian L. *Design with Nature*. New York: Doubleday, 1969.

Marshall, Alex. *How Cities Work: Suburbs, Sprawl, and the Roads Not Taken*. Austin: University of Texas Press, 2000.

Miles, Mike, et al. *Real Estate Development; Principles and Process*. Washington: Urban Land Institute, 1966.

Mollison, Bill. *Permaculture: A Designer's Manual*. Tyalgum, Australia: Tagari, 1988.

Moore, Charles, with Gerald Allen and Donlyn Lyndon. *Place of Houses*. New York: Holt, Reinhart and Winston, 1974.

———, with Kent C. Bloomer. *Body, Memory, and Architecture*. New Haven: Yale University Press, 1977.

———, with Gerald Allen. *Dimensions*. New York: McGraw Hill, 1976.

Mumford, Lewis. *The Culture of Cities*. New York: Harcourt, Brace, 1938.

Myrvang, June Cotner, and Steve Myrvang. *Home Design Handbook*. New York: Henry Holt, 1992.

Necipoglu, Gulru, et al. *The Age of Sinan: Architectural Culture in the Ottoman Empire*. Princeton University Press, 2005.

Norberg-Schulz, Christian. *Genius Loci: Towards a Phenomenology of Architecture*. New York: Rizzoli, 1984.

———. *Meaning in Western Architecture*, New York: Rizzoli, 1980.

———. *The Concept of Dwelling: On the Way to a Figurative Architecture*. New York: Electra-Rizzoli, 1984.

Oliver, Paul. *Dwellings: The House across the World*. Austin: University of Texas Press, 1987.

Paine, Robert Treat, and Alexander Soper. *The Art and Architecture of Japan*. Baltimore: Penguin Books, 1975.

Pelli, Cesar. *Observations for Young Architects*. New York: Monacelli Press, 1999.

Pevsner, Nikolaus. *Outline of European Architecture*. London: Pelican Books, 1943.

Pollan, Michael. *A Place of My Own: The Education of an Amateur Builder*. New York: Random House, 1997.

Pope, Arthur Upham. *Introducing Persian Architecture*. Shiraz: Asian Institute, Pahlavi University, 1969.

Pratt, James R. *Dallas Visions for Community*. Dallas: Dallas Institute, 1992.

Ramsey, C. G., and Harold Sleeper. *Architectural Graphic Standards*. 3d ed. New York: John Wiley, 1941.

Rasmussen, Steen Eiler. *Experiencing Architecture*. Cambridge: MIT Press, 1959.

Roman, Antonio. *Eero Saarinen, An Architecture of Multiplicity*. New York: Princeton Architectural Press, 2003.

Rowe, Colin; Alexander Caragonne, ed. *As I was Saying: Recollections and Miscellaneous Essays*. Cambridge: MIT Press, 1995.

Rowland, Benjamin. *The Art and Architecture of India: Buddhist, Hindu, Jain*. Baltimore: Penguin Books, 1967.

Rudofsky, Bernard. *Architecture Without Architects, A Short Introduction to Non-Pedigreed Architecture*. Albuquerque: University of New Mexico Press, 1964.

———. *Streets for People*. New York: Doubleday, 1964.

———. *The Prodigious Builders*. New York: Harcourt Brace Jovanovich, 1977.

Ruskin, John. *The Seven Lamps of Architecture*. 1848. Reprint. New York: Dover, 1989.

Rybczynski, Witold. *Home: A Short History of an Idea*. New York: Viking Penguin, 1986.

———. *Most Beautiful House in the World*. New York: Viking, 1986.

———. *The Look of Architecture*. New York: Oxford University Press, 2001.

———. *The Perfect House: A Journey with the Renaissance Master Andrea Palladio*. New York: Scribner, 2002.

Saito, Yutaka. *Luis Barragán*. Mexico, D.F.: Noriega Editores, 1992.

Scully, Vincent J. *The Shingle Style and the Stick Style*. New Haven: Yale University Press, 1971.

Serlio, Sebastiano. *The Five Books of Architecture: An Unabridged Reprint of the English Edition of 1611*. New York: Dover, 1982.

Stern, Robert A. M., and Raymond Gastil. *Modern Classicism*. New York: Rizzoli, 1988.

Sturgis, Russell. *Architectural Sourcebook*. New York: Van Nostrand Reinhold, 1984.

Sullivan, Louis. *The Autobiography of an Idea*. 1924. Reprint. New York: Dover, 1956.

Summerson, John. *The Classical Language of Architecture*. Cambridge: MIT Press, 1963.

Susanka, Sarah, and Kita Obloensky. *The Not So Big House*. Newtown, Conn.: Taunton Press, 1998.

Taut, Bruno. *Houses and People of Japan*. The Sanseido Co., 1938.

Thoreau, Henry David. *Walden*. Boston: Houghton Mifflin, 1995.

Toman, Rolf. *Romanesque Architecture, Sculpture, Painting*. Cologne: Konemann, 1997.

Tunnard, Christopher, and Henry Hope Reed. *American Skyline*. New York: Houghton Mifflin, 1953.

Tzonis, Alexander. *Critical Regionalism: Architecture and Identity in a Globalized World*. Munich: Prestel Verlag, 2003.

Unwin, Raymond. *Town Planning in Practice*. 1905. Revised edition. New York: Princeton Architectural Press, 1994.

Utzon, Jørn, et al. *Jørn Utzon: The Architect's Universe*. Humlebaek, Denmark: Louisiana Museum of Modern Art, 2006.

Van Hensbergen, Gijs. *Gaudí*. London: HarperCollins, 2001.

Venturi, Robert. *Complexity and Contradic-*

tion in Architecture. New York: Museum of Modern Art, 1966.

Vitruvius Pollio, Marcus. *The Ten Books on Architecture*. Translated by Morris Hickey Morgan in 1914 from the ca. 50 BC text. New York: Dover, 1960.

Walker, Theodore. *Site Design and Construction Detailing*. Lafayette, Ind.: PDA Publishers, 1978.

Ware, William R. *The American Vignola: A Guide to the Making of Classical Architecture*. New York: W. W. Norton, 1977.

Williamson, Roxanne. *The Mechanics of Fame*. Austin: University of Texas Press, 1991.

Wolf, Tom. *Bauhaus to Our House*. New York: Farrar, Straus and Giroux, 1981.

Wrede, Stuart. *The Architecture of Erik Gunnar Asplund*. Cambridge: MIT Press, 1980.

VIDEOS

Frozen Music. (The building of I. M. Pei's concert hall in Dallas.) Producer, Director, Photographer: Ginny Martin. Dallas: PBS-KERA, 1990.

The Los Angeles Symphony Inaugurates Walt Disney Concert Hall (Frank Gehry, Architect), PBS Great Performances, 2003.

SEEING LIST

My idea of paradise is a perfect automobile going thirty miles an hour on a smooth road to a twelfth-century cathedral.
HENRY JAMES
(1843–1916)

The architecture and urban settings listed offer experiences for your memory bank. This short list of sites in the United States and Mexico, and the even shorter list for the vast riches of the rest of the world, has hundreds of gaps to fill in as you look for these examples in your travels. Or in the library and on the Web explore these monographs on individual architects, histories of particular eras, regions, and places.

EAST COAST

The CBS Building. Eero Saarinen. 51 West 52d St., New York City, 1965.
Fallingwater. Frank Lloyd Wright. Ohiopyle (Bear Run), Penn., 1934, 1938, 1948.

Grand Central Terminal Concourse. Reed and Stern, Warren and Wetmore. New York City, 1904–1913.

Guggenheim Museum. Frank Lloyd Wright. Fifth Avenue, New York City, 1956–1959.

High Museum of Art. Richard Meier. Atlanta, Ga., 1983.

Johnson House (The Glass House). Philip Johnson. New Caanan, Conn., 1949.

Monticello. Thomas Jefferson. Charlottesville, Va., 1770–1809.

Morgan Library. McKim, Mead and White. 29 East 36th St., New York City, 1910.

Richards Medical Center. Louis Kahn. Philadelphia, Penn., 1961.

Seagrams Building. Ludwig Mies van der Rohe with Philip Johnson. 375 Park Avenue, New York City, 1958.

Trinity Church. Henry Hobson Richardson. Boston, Mass., 1877.

University of Virginia, The "Academical Village," Lawn, and Rotunda. Thomas Jefferson. Charlottesville, Va., 1817–1826.

Woolworth Building. Cass Gilbert. 233 Broadway, New York City, 1913.

Yale Center for British Art. Louis Kahn. New Haven, Conn., 1974.

TEXAS

Battle Hall. Architecture and Planning Library. University of Texas Campus. Cass Gilbert. Austin, 1911.

Chapel in the Woods. O'Neil Ford with Arch Swank. Denton, 1939.

Charles Moore Center for the Study of Place. Charles Moore with Arthur Anderssen. 2102 Quarry Road, Austin, 1985.

Esplanade, State Fair of Texas. Dallas, 1936.

Houston Museum of Art. William Ward Watkins, 1924; Ludwig Mies van der Rohe addition, 1958; Rafael Moneo addition, 2000.

Kimbell Museum. Louis Kahn. 3333 Camp Bowie Blvd., Fort Worth, 1971.

Meyerson Center Symphony Center. Pei, Cobb, Freed and Partners. Dallas, 1989.

Modern Art Museum. Tadao Ando. Fort Worth, 2002.

Nasher Sculpture Center. Renzo Piano and Peter Walker. Dallas, 2003.

Pennzoil Office Building. Philip Johnson with John Burgee. 711 Louisiana, Houston, 1976.

Rachofsky House. Richard Meier. Preston Road, Dallas, 1996.

San Jose Mission. Unknown. San Antonio, 1720–1782.

Temple Emanu-El. Howard Meyer with William Wurster. Dallas, 1957.

Trinity University, Master Plan and Buildings. O'Neil Ford. San Antonio, 1948–1978.

MIDDLE AMERICA

Atmospheric Research Center. I. M. Pei. Boulder, Colo., 1961–1967.

Cranbrook Schools. Eliel Saarinen. Bloomfield Hills, Mich., 1925–1942.

Johnson's Wax Building. Frank Lloyd Wright. Racine, Wis., 1936–1944.

Mesa Verde Cliff Dwellings. Unknown. C. Cortez, Colorado, eleventh to thirteenth centuries.

Monadnock Building. Burnham and Root. Chicago, Ill., 1893.

Price Tower. Frank Lloyd Wright. Bartlesville, Okla., 1937 onward.

Taliesin West. Frank Lloyd Wright. Scottsdale, Ariz., 1937.

Thorncrown Chapel. Jay Jones. Eureka Springs, Ark., 1980.

Unity Temple. Frank Lloyd Wright. Oak Park, Chicago, Ill., 1906.

WEST COAST

Eames House. Charles Eames. Pacific Palisades, Calif., 1945.

Garden Grove Church. Philip Johnson. Los Angeles, Calif., 1978–1980.

Golden Gate Bridge. Joseph B. Strauss. San Francisco, Calif., 1937.

Salk Institute. Louis Kahn. La Jolla, Calif., 1959–1966.

Science Complex, University of Oregon. Charles Moore with Moore Ruble Yudell. Eugene, Ore., 1985.

Sea Ranch Condominium. Moore, Lyndon, Turnbull, Whitaker with Lawrence Halprin, Landscape Architect. Mendocino Coast, Calif., 1965.

MEXICO

Casa Luis Barragán. Tacubaya, D.F., 1947.

Chichén Itzá. Unknown. Near Mérida, Yucatán, AD 200–900.

Hotel Camino Real. Ricardo Legorreta. Cancún, 1975.

Museo Nacional de Antropología de México. Pedro Ramírez Vázquez, Mexico City, 1963.

Santo Domingo. Anonymous. Oaxaca, Oaxaca, ca. 1550.

Town of Guanajuato, sixteenth century onward.

Town of Pátzcuaro, Michoacán, sixteenth century onward.

Town of San Miguel de Allende, Guanajuato, sixteenth century onward.

Tulum and nearby sites. Unknown. Near Cozumel, ca. AD 1200.

Uxmal and nearby Puuc sites. Unknown. Near Mérida, Yucatán, AD 600–900.

EUROPE

Aachen Cathedral. Unknown. Aachen, Germany, 792 to 805.

Alhambra. Unknown. Granada, Spain, 1248–1354 and on.

Altes Museum. Karl Friedrich Schinkel. Berlin, Germany, 1830.

"Barcelona Pavillion" (German Pavillion). Ludwig Mies van der Rohe. Barcelona, Spain, 1928; demolished 1930, rebuilt 1959.

Campidoglio, Capitoline Hill. Michelangelo. Rome, Italy, mid-sixteenth century.

Campo Volantín Footbridge. Santiago Calatrava. Bilbao, Spain, 1997.

Casa Mila. Antonio Gaudí. Barcelona, Spain, 1910.

Centre Pompidou. Richard Rogers and Reno Piano. Paris, France, 1976.

Convent of La Tourette. Le Corbusier. Eveux-sur-Arbresle, near Lyon, France, 1957–1960.

Duomo of Florence. Arnolfo di Cambio. From thirteenth century; dome by Filippo Brunelleschi.

Durham Cathedral. William St. Carileph. Durham, England, 1019.

Eiffel Tower. Gustave Eiffel. Paris, France, 1887.

Einstein Tower. Erich Mendelsohn. Potsdam, Germany, 1921.

Galleria Vittorio Emanuele. Giuseppe Mengoni. Milan, Italy, 1861.

Gothic churches of Chartres, Rheims, Beauvauis, Amiens, Paris. Unknown. Eleventh to fourteenth centuries.

Greek Temples of Paestum. Unknown. Near Naples, Italy, 650 BC–200 BC.

Guggenheim Museum. Frank Gehry. Bilbao, Spain, 1997.

Hermitage. Francesco Bartolomeo Rastrelli. St. Petersburg, Russia, 1762.

Notre Dame du Haut. Le Corbusier. Ronchamp, France, 1955.

Palace and Gardens of Versailles. Andre Le Notre, Louis Le Vau, Jules Hardouin-Mansart, Charles Le Brun, Robert de Cotte, Ange-Janques Bagriel. Near Paris, France, 1661–1774.

Pantheon. Attributed to Marcus Agrippa, later Hadrian. Rome, Italy, 118–126.

Paris Opera House. Charles Garnier. Paris, France, 1857–1874.

Parthenon, Acropolis of Athens. Iktinos and Kallikrates with Phidias, sculptor. Athens, Greece, 447 BC onward.

Pazzi Chapel. Filippo Brunelleschi. Florence, Italy, 1461.

Piazza of St. Peter's. Gian Lorenzo Bernini. Vatican City, Rome, Italy 1656–1667.

Roman Forum. Various. Rome, Italy, 100 BC–AD 300.

Romanesque churches of Caen, Albi, Cluny, Arles. Unknown. Sixth to twelfth centuries.

Sagrada Familia. Antonio Gaudí. Barcelona, Spain, 1882 and continuing.

Sainte Chapelle. Unknown. Paris, France, 1246.

San Carlo a la Quattro Fontane. Francesco Borromini. Rome, Italy, 1638–1641.

San Giorgio Maggiore. Andrea Palladio. Venice, Italy, 1580.

San Miniato al Monte. Unknown. Florence, Italy, eleventh to fourteenth centuries.

Santa Sophia. Justinian I with Isidore of Miletus and Anthemius of Tralles. Istanbul, Turkey, 563.

St. Basil's Cathedral. Unknown. Moscow, Russia, 1560.

Unite d'Habitation. Le Corbusier. Marseilles, France, 1952.

Villa Capra, or Villa Rotunda. Andrea Palladio. Vicenza, Italy, 1571.

Villa Savoye. Le Corbusier. Poissy, France, 1928–1929.

Wies Pilgrimmage Church. Johan and Dominikus Zimmerman. Wies, near Munich, Germany, 1754.

ASIA AND ORIENT

Angkor Wat. Unknown. Cambodia, ca. 800–1200.

Fatehpur Sikri. Unknown. Uttar Pradesh, Agra, India, 1571 to 1585.

Forbidden City Palace and Grounds. Unknown. Beijing, China, 1420.

Imperial Palace. Unknown. Beijing, China, 1279–1420.

Ise Shrine. Unknown. Ise, Japan, 690, reconstructed every 20 years.

Katsura Imperial Villa. Kobori Enshu. Kyoto, Japan, ca. 1650.

Miho Museum. I. M. Pei. Shiga, Japan, 1991.

Naghsh-i Jahan Square. Unkown. Isfahan, Iran, ca. 1500.

Taj Mahal. Emperor Shah Jahan. Agra, India, 1630 to 1653.

PHOTO CREDITS

INDEX

Page numbers in *italics* indicate
   illustrations.

Aalto, Alvar, 33, 34, 37, 184
About the House (Auden), 147
acoustics, 144–147
Acropolis, 27
aesthetics, 30–31, 41, 154; of a building,
   90–91, 118, 137; traditional, 31, 38, 42
agreements, architectural, 60, 62, 89. *See
   also* contracts, architectural
AIA. *See* American Institute of Architects
air conditioning, 86, 127–128
Alexander, Christopher, 117, 131, 149
amateurs, 25, 40, 51, 53; as builders of most
   buildings, 9, 23, 28; definitions of, 9,
   23–24; importance of, 24, 28; roles of,
   24, 103

Amecameca, Mexico, 5–7
American Institute of Architects, 26, 60–
   61, 79; contracts of, 26, 62, 66–67, 121
Ando, Tadao, 157
Archilithics, 78–79
Architecton, 25
architectonics, 125
architects: amateur, 22–24, 28, 51; aspiring, ix, 7, 9, 25; client relationships, 58–
   59, 62, 67, 95; and construction, 65, 181;
   education of, 6–9, 13–19, 29–30, 69–
   77, 152, 154; future of, 179, 181, 183; as
   generalists, 71, 81, 86; Modernism,
   effects on, 31–33, 36–38, 125, 177–180,
   185; passion of, 22, 69–70, 80; professional, 23–24, 52, 57, 94–95, 106;
   regional, 38, 184; responsibilities of, 53,
   77, 84, 180–182; roles of, 18, 23, 52, 58,

63, 77, 89; thinking like, 81–82, 109, 149; working with, 57–61, 94–95, 121. *See also* Modernism; school, architecture

Architectural Registration Exam, 76

Architectural Studies, 70, 72–73

architecture, 77, 182; appropriate, 36, 47, 51, 166, 179–180; as art, spatial, 14, 90–91, 114, 134, 166; as art, unique, 81–82, 109, 125, 186; and buildings, 49, 156, 186; and city planning, 161–162; and culture, 3, 8, 13, 21; and design elements, 138, 143–144; excitement of, 25, 28, 90; experience of, 3, 5, 7, 11–14, 18, 26, 157; form, contemporary, 125, 183; future of, 157, 177, 184–186; and geography, 178–179; historic, 15–16, 22, 130; history of, 15–18, 31; as investment, 21, 83, 181; making, ix, 5–8, 17–18, 57, 66, 81, 151; meaning and, 123–127, 130–131; Modernist changes in, 29–30, 33–37; quality of, 18, 21, 26, 28, 50–52, 95, 154; and the senses, 27, 30–31, 124, 131, 157–158; taste, good, 151–158; types of, 22, 30, 73, 135, 180

ARE. *See* Architectural Registration Exam

art, 26, 90; decorative, 41, 126, 183

Art and Time in Mexico (Weismann), 157

Art Deco, 35, 37

Art Modern, 37

Art Nouveau, 35, 41

Arts and Crafts Movement, 156, 180, 185

As I Was Saying (Rowe), 165

Asplund, Gunnar, 33, 34, 184

Atmospheric Research Center (Boulder, CO), *43*

Auden, W. H., 147

Austin, TX, 154–155, 167

Auto-Cad, 99, 118

axis mundi, 127–128

Aztecs, 5

Bacon, Edmund, 87

Balcones Fault, 110

Barcelona Pavilion (Spain), 39

Barragán, Luis, 4, 183–184

bathrooms, 148

Battle Hall Architecture and Planning Library (Austin, TX), *32*

Bauhaus school, *35*

beauty, 51–52; as forbidden term, 151–152; quest for, 7, 26, 53, 174; seeing, way of, 153

Beaux Arts, 29–30, 31–33, 37, 156, 180; and design charrettes, 74; training in the, 185

bedrooms, 148

Belluschi, Pietro, 37, 61

Benedikt, Michael, 185

Berenson, Bernard, 130–131

Bernini, Gian Lorenzo, 184

Better Living for Middle Income Families Design Competition (1959), 61

Better Place to Live, A (Langdon), 173

Bidding and Negotiating of Construction Contracts Phase, 63–64

bidding process, 64, 89, 121

Bilbao Effect, 43

Blink (Gladwell), 84

Boorstin, Daniel, 9

Borromini, Francesco, 16, 184

Boston, MA, *166*

Box, Eden, 4, 46, 110, 115

Box, Hal: and architectural tour of 1964–1967, 21–22, 27–28; architecture by, 64, 98, 110, 113, 115 (*see also individual building names*); and Austin, TX, 167; and awards, 79; and budgets, 83; career, academic, 27, 72, 100, 174, 185; and city planning, 161; and design competitions, *61*, 77; education, architectural, 7, 29–31, 36, 71–77; and Nob Hill House, 110–122, 124; and O'Neil Ford, 30, 75, 119, 186; as practicing architect, 22, 75, 77; and Pratt, Box and Henderson, 77–80, 98; and San Miguel de Allende, *4, 5, 8, 14,* 166, 169, 186; at the University of Texas at Arlington, 72; at the University of Texas at Austin, 36, 71–72, 157, 174; views, architectural, 45–46, 99, 152, 183–186

Box, Rick, 28

Broadacre City (Wright), 41, 170

Brunelleschi, Filippo, 23, 28, 70, 184

budgets, architectural, 53, 58–59, 199; as constraint, 65–66, 82–84, 90, 118

builders: master, 25–26; nonarchitect, 6–7, 22–23, 95. *See also* nonarchitects

building materials, 6, 137–138; local, 139, 145, 184; types of, 15, 180; unusual, 78–79, 182

buildings: aesthetics of, 27, 30, 86, 90–91; and architecture, 24, 186; character of, 137, 155; codes, 82, 86, 90, 107; and committees, 59; and community, place in, 80; design of, 52, 83–84, 95, 167; experience of, 114, 124, 131, 137; as investments, 52, 80, 83, 97; lifespans, 45, 50, 52; public, 53, 59, 67; purposes of, 23–24, 27, 156; "reading," 92–94; spatial progression in, 130, 143; spiritual content of, 90, 124; types of, 21–22, 52, 130; vernacular, appropriate, 179–181, 183

Bunshaft, Gordon, 61

Burnham, Daniel, 172–173

Bywaters, Jerry, 50

Caine, Michael, 7

Calatrava, Santiago, 15, 43, 154, *183*

Cambridge University, 70

Campbell, Joseph, 116, 129

Caragonne, Alex, 38

Career Discovery Program (Harvard University), 70

Carl Miles Sculpture Garden (St. Louis, MO), 61

carpenters, 17, 78, 89

cars, 163, 166, 170–172, 175

Casa Canal (San Miguel de Allende, Mexico), *14*

Casa Mila (Barcelona, Spain), *32*

Casa Pani house (San Miguel de Allende, Mexico), *4, 5, 14*

Caudill, Bill, 74, 86

ceilings, heights of, 143, 147

Century of Progress (World's Fair, 1934), 169–170

chakras, 130

Chambers for a Memory Palace (Moore and Lyndon), 149–150

charrettes, design, 74. *See also* school, architecture

Chrysler Building (New York, NY), 126

cities, 161–176, 180, 185. *See also* sprawl, urban

City Beautiful Movement, 173

city planning, 73; and architecture, 161–162; changes in, 172–176; as profession, 169

City Planning According to Artistic Principles (Sitte), 172

clients: and architects, 58–59, 95; and decisions, architectural, 65, 67; and design competitions, 60–61; importance of, 24, 181; and programs, architectural, 82–85, 106; roles of, 58–59, 62–63, 186

climate, 135–136

color, 41, 90, 141

Colorado River, 111–112, 127

Columbian Exposition of 1893, 173

columns, 139, 142, 156

community, concepts of, 164–176

composition, 17, 25, 40, 103; as design element, 106, 183; rules of, 139–141, 185

computers, 83–87, 97, 99

concepts, architectural, 84, 85, 94, 111–119, 127

conferences, architectural, 106, 121. *See also* clients

Congrés Internationaux d'Architecture Moderne, 39

conservation, of energy, 113, 135

construction, of buildings, 15, 67; choices in, 94–95, 109; costs of, 52, 64–65, 121, 182; design in, 89; pleasure of, 17, 78, 80, 120; process of, 65–67, 73, 121, 137–138; purposes of, 23

Construction Administration Phase, 63, 65

construction documents, 94–95, 103, 121

Construction Documents Phase, 62–64

construction sites, 89, 100; and architects, 89, 121; culture of, 17–18, 100

consultants, architectural, 59–62, 83; and architects, 118; and construction, 86, 107; and design conferences, 106

contractors, 18, 52; and architects, 65, 95; construction, roles in, 59, 82, 121; general, 64, 66; importance of, 64–65, 121

contracts, architectural, 62, 64–67, 95, 121

Cooper Union for the Advancement of Science and Art, 38

Corbu. *See* Le Corbusier

Corbusian ideal, 169–170, 174. *See also* Le Corbusier

Cornell University, 38

Cortez, Hernando, 5

costs: of construction, 52, 64–65, 121, 182; and decisions, architectural, 24, 51–53, 63. *See also* budgets, architectural

craftsmen, 15, 18, 66; working with, 17, 157

crews, construction, 67. *See also* contractors; craftsmen

critiques, architectural, 104–106

Crow, Trammell, 98

Cuernavaca, Mexico, 4, 8

Cutler, James, 44

Dallas/Fort Worth, TX, 72, 162, 164

Dallas Museum of Fine Arts, 50

Deconstruction, 43, 45, 157

decoration, 41. *See also* ornamentation

Definition of Culture (Berenson), 130–131

degrees, professional, 22, 72–73, 76

Denver, John, 70

Depression, the Great, 75

Derrida, Jacques, 157

design, architectural, 24, 67, 82, 154, 174; architects, without, 52, 179, 181; and city planning, 161–165, 167, 172; complexity in, 88, 94–95, 120; creating, 31, 83–85, 103–107, 145–147; elements of, 13, 17, 25, 89–91, 109, 141; future of, 177, 186; high cost of, 52–53, 182; and myths, 115, 123–134, 126; and place, sense of, 131, 164, 180; of residences, 114–116, 118, 147–150; studies in, 63, 70; style and taste in, 151–158; surroundings, improving, 86, 164, 180; teaching, methods of, 73, 106; trial, 63, 85, 103; values, 89, 186

design awards, 79–80

design-build, 67, 95

design-but-not-build tradition, 26

design competitions, 60–61, 77

design decisions, 24–25, 63, 153; and budgets, architectural, 65; and concepts, architectural, 84–85; guidelines for, 133–139; types of, 88, 94–95, 116, 181. *See also* visualization

Design Development Phase, 63, 94

designers, 67, 84, 103, 114

design idioms, 91–95, 93; and design problems, 95, 181; regional, 127–128

design phases, 62–67, 121

design problems, 38, 90, 94, 149; future, 178–182; resolving, 104–105, 113; solutions, multiple, 84, 154

design process, 24, 26, 67, 121; approaches to, 81–82, 104, 114, 149, 157–158; constraints on, 85, 90, 107; creativity in, 87–88, 102; delight in, 80, 82, 89–91; design idioms in, 94; and myths, 126; tools for, 99–100

design studios, 71, 73, 74–75, 88, 95

de Stijl group, 35

details, architectural, 145–147, 181–182

developers, 53, 82, 95, 163

diagrams, 83–84. *See also* models, architectural

Disney Concert Hall, 42

distances, consideration of, 163–174

domes, 50, 143

doors, 142–146

Doshi, Balkrishna, 157

Downtown St. Louis Urban Design Competition, 61

drawing boards, 99–100, 113–115

drawings, architectural, 12, 18–19; as communication, 89, 103–104, 181; pinning up, 106, 111, 149; as skill, 70–73, 82, 86–87, 97–102, 113, 118; and specifications, 64, 121

Duomo (Florence, Italy), 23, 28

Dvorak, Antonin, 13

Eames, Charles, 184

East Texas State Teacher's College Training School, 81–82

Eclecticism, 37

Ecole des Beaux-Arts. *See* Beaux Arts

education, architectural, 6–9, 13–19, 24, 51; academic, 31–33; curriculum and, 182, 185–186; and Modernism, 30, 36, 40, 180. *See also* Modernism; school, architecture

Eisenberg House (Dallas, TX), 37

elevation drawings, 102–103

Emerson, Ralph Waldo, 88

Empire State Building (New York, NY), 126

engineers, 82, 118–119, 137, 154–155, 172

English New Towns, 170, 174

Enrico Fermi Memorial Plaza (Chicago, IL), 61

entrances, to buildings, 117, 143, 147

environmental: issues, study of, 70; regulations, 107

Euclid, Ohio, 170

façades, 88, 93, 137; design of, 141–143, 166

Fallingwater (Bear Run, PA), 15, 33, 50

Federal Housing Administration, 169

fees, architectural, 59, 62, 181–182

Feng Shui, 130, 148

Fermi, Enrico, 61

FHA. *See* Federal Housing Administration

fire codes, 86, 107

fireplaces. *See* hearths

Five-Minute Popsicle Rule, 175

Flato, Ted, 44, 76, 92, 184

floor plans, 136–137

Florence, Italy, 47

Flowers, Betty Sue, 87, 131

forces, structural, 137–138

Ford, O'Neil, 84; as mentor to Hal Box, 30, 75, 186; as Regional architect, 37, 92, 119, 184; schooling and, 76–77

Ford, Tom, 156

form, architectural, 91, 106, 123–125, 185

foundations, building, 86, 138–139

freeways: cities, impact on, 163–165, 168–169

French Quarter. *See* New Orleans, LA

Fuller, Buckminster, 50, 53, 138

functionality, of buildings, 83–84

funds, 60, 66. *See also* budgets, architectural

furniture, arrangement of, 115, 146–147

Futurama (World's Fair, 1939), 170

Gateway Arch (St. Louis), 61

Gaudí, Antonio, 33, 102, 141

Gehry, Frank, 42, 44, 50, 180, 183

Germany, 22

Gideon, Sigfried, 39, 45

Gilbert, Cass, 32, 74, 126, 184

Gladwell, Malcolm, 84

globalization, 43, 157, 183

Global Village, 178. *See also* Modernism

Goldberger, Paul, 178

Golden Rectangle, 140. *See also* proportions

Goldilocks Principle ("just right"), 30, 90–91, 94; and design, 105, 110, 127; and design process, 149, 153–154, 157, 186

Google, 12

Granger, Charles, 76

gravity, 14, 15, 137, 141

Great Hall of the Dallas Apparel Mart (1964), 98, 144–145

Green, Charles, 72

Griffin Square and Tower, 80

Gropius, Walter, 31, 32, 35–36, 41

Guadalquivir River, 15

Guggenheim Musem (Bilbao, Spain), 42, 44, 50, 145, 156

guidelines, for design decisions, 133–139

guides, architectural, 40, 179–180, 183

Gulf of Mexico, 110, 127

Hadid, Zaha, 183

Hale, Jonathan, 141

Harris, Harwell Hamilton, 37, 38; and regionalism, 92, 184; and schooling, architectural, 76–77

Harvard Graduate Center, 36

Harvard University, 35–36, 72

Haussmann, Baron Georges-Eugéne, 163

hearths, 119, 128, 131, 148

heating, 86

Heidegger, Martin, 157

highways. *See* freeways

Hines, Gerland, 53

Hippocrates, 85

historic preservation, 70

history, architectural, 15–17, 27; and Modernism, 29–47; study of, 70, 157, 185

Hitchcock, Henry Russell, 35

homebuilders, professional, 82

House of Life, 130–131

houses, 179, 182. *See also* residences

How Cities Work (Marshall), 163

Hudnut, Joseph, 35, 41

Hurricane Katrina, 77

iconography, architectural, 124–125, 130–131

icons. *See* design idioms

industrial revolution, 26

inspectors, city building, 101

Institute for Classical Architecture, 185

instruments, surveying, 112

interior design, 73

International Correspondence School, 76

International Design Competition, 61

International Style, 35–38, 42, 179, 183. *See also* Modernism

Interstate Highway Act of 1955, 170

interventions, architectural, 155–156, 179

Jacobs, Jane, 172

Jacobson, Hugh Newell, 44

Jeanneret, Charles-Eduard. *See* Le Corbusier

Jefferson, Thomas, 184

Johnson, Philip, 35, 70, 178

Jones, Fay, 44, 45, 115–116

Joy, Rick, 44, 46, 183

Jung, Carl, 115

Jupiter, Roman Temple of (Baalbek, Lebanon), 22

juries, formal design, 60–61, 106

Kahn, Louis I., 27, 41, 50, 91, 157, 184

Kahn, Terry, 175

Kermacy, Martin, 18

Kimbell Museum (Fort Worth, TX), 27, 41, 50

kitchens, 147

Korean War, 75

Lake, David, 44, 76; regional design idiom of, 92, 184

Lake Austin (TX), 154–155

Langdon, Philip, 173

Le Corbusier, 33, 50, 184; architecture of, 38–39; and La Ville Radieuse Plan, 169; and schooling, architectural, 76–77; theories of, 41, 169–170

Legorreta, Ricardo, 44, 46, 183–184

Leipziger-Pearce, Hugo, 161

L'Enfant, Pierre, 162

Life and Death of the American City, The (Jacobs), 172

light: considerations of, 112–114, 135–136, 143–148; as design element, 90–91, 116, 182

Lincoln Cathedral, 30

living rooms, 147–148

location, importance of, 161–162

Loos, Adolf, 41

Los Angeles, CA, 164, 170

Lyndon, Donlyn, 149

MARCO. *See* Museo de Arte Contemporáneo

Marcus, Stanley, 156

marketplace, value of architecture in, 52, 181

"Marseilles Block" (France), 39

Marseilles Unite d'Habitation, 39

Marshall, Alex, 163

Marsh House (Austin, TX), *14*, 64

Mason, James, 70

Massachusetts Institute of Technology, 61, 72

Matico, Inc., 61

Maya, 125, 129–130

MCM. *See* Midcentury Modern

McMansions, 85, 142, 179

Meier, Richard, 92–93

Metropolitan Museum (New York, NY), 126

Mexico, 4–8, 46, 147, 166, 183

Michaelangelo, 184

Midcentury Modern, 182

Mies van der Rohe, Ludwig, 33, 34, 61; schooling, architectural, 76–77; theories of, 38–40, 41, 145, 184

Minimalism, 43, 45

Mississippi River, 61

MIT. *See* Massachusetts Institute of Technology

models, architectural, 86–87, *88–89*, 97, 102, 104

Modernism, 5–6; aesthetics of, 36, 92, 137, 152, 173, 179; excitement of, 26, 29–30, 33, 38–40; failings of, 22, 44–45, 152, 178; history of, 29–47, 125; ideology of, 31–33, 35, 40, 178–179, 182; as "the International Style," 35–38, 42, 179, 183; reform of, 177–180, 183–184; and Regionalism, 36–38; tenets of, 33, 39–43, 177, 179

Modernismo (Barcelona, Spain), 35, 156. *See also* Modernism

Modernists, 16, 125; education of, 30, 41, 180; figures, major, 33, 40–44; styles, architectural, 156. *See also* Modernism

moldings, as design elements, 142, 145–146

Moneo, Rafael, 44

Moore, Charles, 4, 19, 42, 184; architectural models and, 89; and "the Goldilocks Principle," 90, 157; observations on composition, 149

Most Beautiful Building in the World, The (Rybczynski), 89

Mugerauer, Bob, 157

Mumford, Lewis, 37, 171

Muschamp, Herbert, 176

Museo de Arte Contemporáneo (Monterrey, Mexico), *46*

National Assembly Building (Bangladesh), 157

National Council of Architectural Registration Boards, 76

National Endowment for the Arts, 185

National Museum of Finland, *33*

neighborhoods, 168, 171–174

Neoclassicism, 180, 183

Nervi, Pier Luigi, 61

Neumann, Baltazar, 184

Neutra, Richard, 76

New, the, 31, 40, 45, 183. *See also* Modernism

New Architecture, 41

New Orleans, LA, 77; French Quarter, 164, *165*

New World (Dvorak), 13

New York City, 126, 164

New Yorker, The, 99

New York Public Library, 126

New York Times, The, 80, 176, 178

Nob Hill House (Austin, TX), *110–111, 119*; design concept of, 111, 113, *114,* 115, *116–117,* 127; as example of building, 109–122, 128–131; meaning in, 124, 126–128, 130–131; rooms in, 117, 119, *128–129,* 130

nonarchitects, 6, 8, 36; education, lack of, 9, 52, 95; guides for, 31, 179, 184; and Modernism, 31, 178; tasks of, 9, 186

Notre Dame Cathedral, *12–13*

Notre-Dame-du-Haut (Ronchamps, France), *39,* 50

Oakland, CA, 171–172

Oglethorpe, James, 163

Old Way of Seeing, The (Hale), 141

organization, spatial, 88, 117

orientation, of buildings, 102, 112, 136–137

Orleans Parish Courthouse, 77

"Ornament and Crime" (Loos), 41

ornamentation, 30, 31, 182, 185

Outline of European Architecture, An (Pevsner), 30

Palladio, Andrea, 50, 70, 91–92, 181, 184

Pani, Arturo, 5

Pantheon, 19

paper, tracing, 100–101, 103, 113, 118

"paper architecture," 88

Paris, France, 163

parking facilities, 164–166

parks, 164, 175

Paso de Cortez, 5

Pattern Language, A (Alexander), 117, 131, 149

Pei, I. M., 42

Pena, William, 83

Pevsner, Nikolaus, 30

Philadelphia, PA, 164

Piano, Renzo, 183–184

Piazza del Campadoglio (Rome, Italy), *178*

place, sense of, 3–6; creation of, 36, 125, 134, 176; design as way to enhance, 131; physical and metaphysical, 127

Plan Apparel Mart (Pratt, Box and Henderson), *98*

plans, architectural, 86, 121; drawings, 100, 102, 136, 137; ground, 31; of cities, 162, 167

Posa Chapels, 130

Postmodernism, 43, 45. *See also* Modernism

Prairie's Yield: Forces Shaping Dallas 1842– 1962, The (Box), 79

Pratt, Alex, 19

Pratt, Box and Henderson, 77–80, 98

Pratt, James, 61, 91, 177–178

Pratt, Joanne, 61

Predesign Phase, 62–63

Prince Phillip, 185

Princeton University, 70

problem solving, 82–84, 88, 113

Problem Solving, Program Making (Pena), 83

profit. *See* budgets, architectural

programming, 59, 62–63, 83. *See also* design process; design decisions

programs: architectural, 82–85, 90, 121; iconographic, 125–126, 131

progression, as design element, 90, 130, 137, 143

projects, architectural: control of, 90, 181– 182; public, 60, 64

proportions, 25, 30, 103, 153; classical, 31, 40; as design element, 90–91, 106, 183, 185; rules of, 139–141

Pruitt-Igoe (St. Louis, MO), 180

"Pyramid of the Magician" (Merida, Yuca- tán, Mexico), *124*

pyramids, 118

Quadracci Pavilion (Milwaukee Art Museum), *44*

Quadrangle (Dallas, TX), *14*

Rachofsky House (Dallas, TX), *93*

Radburn, New Jersey, architectural plan of, *170*

ratios, 140, 144. *See also* proportions; light

real estate, 80, 83; for cars, 163–164, 166

Regionalism, 30, 36–38, 43–44, 119, 127. *See also* Modernism

Registry of Midwives and Architects (New Orleans, LA), 77

relationships: architect-client, 58–59, 67; architect-contractor, 65

relocation, 168, 170

Renaissance, 22, 70

Request for Qualifications, 60

Requiem (Verdi), 73

residences: and design, lack of, 52, 179, 182; rooms in, 147–150

RFQ. *See* Request for Qualifications

Rheims Cathedral (Rheims, France), *12–13*, 124

rhythm, as design element, 90, 153

Richards, Ann, 154

Richardson, H. H., 184

Rockefeller Center (New York, NY), 126

Ronchamps Chapel. *See*
    Notre-Dame-du-Haut

roof, as design problem, 104, 137

Room of One's Own, A (Woolf), 116

rooms, 116; design of, 102, 143; and the
    outdoors, 116, 149; in residences,
    147–150

Rowe, Colin, 38, 165. *See also* City, The
    Historic

Ruskin, John, 82

Russian Constructivism, 35

Rybczynski, Wittold, 89

Saarinen, Eero, 76, 92, 93, 184

Saarinen, Eliel, 33, 37, 184

Sacromonte, chapel of, 5

Sainte Marie de La Tourette (Lyon, France),
    39

Salk Institute (La Jolla, California), *42*

Salt Lake City, UT, 164

San Antonio River (San Antonio, TX), 75

San Jose Mission (San Antonio, TX), 75

San Miguel de Allende (Guanajuato, Mex-
    ico), *8, 14*, 46, 166–167, 170

San Miniato al Monte (Florence, Italy), *28*

Santa Maria del Fiore, dome of (Florence,
    Italy). *See* Duomo

Savannah, Georgia, *163*, 164

Saynatsalo Town Hall (Finland), *34*

scale, 25, 30, 85–86, 90

Schele, Linda, 131

schematic design, 63, 94

Schematic Design Phase, 63

school, architecture: and beauty, 51, 152;
    changes in, 29–30, 31–33, 185–186; cri-
    tiques, architectural, 106; curricula in,

38, 70–73, 76, 118, 153, 174, 181–183;
    and design, 26; experience of, 71–77;
    history of, 28, 72–73; intellectualization
    of, 51; success and, 70, 73, 76; at the Uni-
    versity of Texas at Arlington, 72; at the
    University of Texas at Austin, 37

Seagrams Building (New York, NY), 40, 156

Sea Ranch (Moore), *43*

Secessionist (Vienna), 35, 156

seeing, ways of: design elements, 17, 71;
    experiencing architecture, 26–27; as
    skill, 11–13, 15, 19, 153

Señor de Sacromonte, *5–7*

Sert, Jose Luis, 61

Sinan, Mimar Koca, 23

Siracusa (Italy), 178

site planning, 62, 101, 134, 162

sites, architectural, 82–83, 90; designing
    on a specific, 100–102, 112–114, 121;
    physical aspects of, 86, 101, 117

Sitte, Camillo, 172

sketches, architectural. *See* drawings,
    architectural

skyscrapers, 78, 169, 174

Smith, John, 66

Soane, Sir John, 184

sound, importance of, 144, 147

space: as design element, 90, 105, 114,
    134–139, 143–145, 182; exterior, 117,
    134–135; interior, 115, 117, 119, 136; and
    meaning, 124, 144; sense of, 13–14, 91,
    134; sound and, 144, 147

Space, Time, and Architecture (Gideon), 39

Space Is an Illusion (Box and partners), 50

sprawl, urban, 163–164, 171

Stadthaus (Ulm, Germany), 17

stairs, 146

Stein, Clarence, 170

Stein, Gertrude, 171–172

Steinberg, Saul, 99

Stewart, Jimmy, 70

St. Ivo, church of (Rome, Italy), *16*

St. Maclou (Rouen, France), *26*

Stockholm City Hall (Ragnar Ostberg, Sweden), *16*

St. Stephen United Methodist Church (Mesquite, TX), 78–79

styles, architectural, 29, 40, 151–153, 156–158

subcontractors, 17–18, 64, 66, 121. *See also* contractors

suburbs, 163, 167; FHA role in creating, 168–169; neighborhoods, replacement of, 171–172, 175. *See also* cities

Sullivan, Louis, 184

Summer Academy (University of Texas at Austin), 70

Supreme Court Building (Washington, D.C.), 74

surveys, architectural, 62, 101

sustainability, 50–51, 70, 107, 135

Sydney Opera House (Australia), *42*, 50

symmetry, 140–141, 153

Syracuse University, 38

temple, Greek (Paestum, Italy), *124*

Temple, Latané, 152

Texas Department of Transportation, 154

Texas Dog Run House (Austin, TX), 115

"Texas Rangers," 38

Texas state capitol building, 27, 112, 127

Texas Tech University, 70

theories, architectural, 26, 70, 90, 157

Third World, 23, 166, 185

Thoreau, Henry David, 89

three-lamp rule, 144

three-step rule, 147

tools, design, 86–87, 100, 104

transportation, 164, 169, 168–171, 175. *See also* cars; freeways

trees, as design element, 130, 135, 166, 175

Trinity University Campus (San Antonio, TX), *38*

Triumphal Arch, 142

Tucson Mountain House (Arizona), 46

Tulane, architecture building at, 77

Turnbull, William, 184

Twain, Mark, 90

UCLA, 19

Union Station (St. Louis, Missouri), 61

University of Dublin, 185

University of Notre Dame, 185

University of Texas at Arlington, 72

University of Texas at Austin, 19, 36; School of Architecture, 37, 72–73, 157

Usonian House (Wright), 41

Utzon, Jørn, 41–42, 50, 184

Valencia, Fray Martín de, 5

Venturi, Robert, 42

Verdi, Giuseppe, 73

Vietnam War, 75

views, from buildings, 111, 112, 116

Vignola, Giacomo Barozzi da, 33, 142

Villa Rotunda (Venice, Italy), *91*

Villa Savoy (Poissy, France), *35*, 39

Ville Radieuse Plan, La (Le Corbusier), 169

visualization, 12, 71, 118; of buildings, full-size, 97–98, 100, 102; of design concepts, 84–85, 102, 112, 114; importance of, 97; of light, 113, 141, 146; and models, physical, 87–88, 103, 137; tools for, 97–99, 112

Vitruvian triad, 58, 91

Vitruvius, 91, 127, 157

Walden (Thoreau), 89

walk, Via Sacra, 130

walking, 163–169, 171, 175

walls, 30, 103, 138, 141–143, 145, 149

Washington, D.C.: city plan, *162*; urban design of, 164

Weismann, Elizabeth Wilder, 157

Welch, Frank, 92, 184

West Mall (University of Texas at Austin), 55

wheelchair accessibility, 146

White, Lancelot, 61

Widor, Charles-Marie, 13

Williams, David, 37, 76

Willow Way, 75

Wilson House (Dallas, TX), *76*

windows, as design element, 30, 142, 144–145

Woodland Chapel (Stockholm, Sweden), *34*

Woolf, Virginia, 116

Woolworth Building (New York, NY), *126*

workmen, working with, 17, 66, 121. *See also* craftsmen

World War I, 12

World War II, 75

Wright, Frank Lloyd, 4; and Broadacre City, 41, 170; design idiom of, 92, 127; design philosophy of, 92, 156, 170; Fallingwater (Bear Run, PA), *15*, *33*, 50; as Modernist, 33, 37, 41, 184; and schooling, architectural, 76–77

Wright, Henry, 170

Wurster, William, 37

Yale University (CT), 19

Zisman, Sam, 134

zoning: constraints of, 90, 164–165, 169; laws, 82, 86, 90, 107, 164–174; and San Miguel de Allende, 166, 170